THE ENTRANCE

Pacoima's Story

By

Crystal Jackson

BAIT-CAL PUBLISHING

The Entrance: Pacoima's Story

For author bookings and wholesale pricing contact: bcpublishing@baitcal.com
For information about the book, author, and publisher go to: www.BAITCAL.com

ISBN: 978-0-9859619-4-7

Pacoima, California is located in the city of Los Angeles on the northeast side of the San Fernando Valley. The town has a population of just over 100,000 people, however its history dates back nearly 1500 years. This is Pacoima's history and legacy.

Table of Contents

ABOUT THE AUTHOR

Crystal Jackson was born in Pacoima while living on Montford Street. Her family first arrived in the town during the forties. Crystal attended Cal State University Northridge majoring in journalism. During her early years as a journalist, she interviewed some of the most notable entertainers in Hollywood, including Eddie Murphy, Louis Gossett, Jr., Lena Horne, Cicely Tyson, and many others.

Opting for family life, Crystal left the entertainment world to raise her children in Northern California. However, she always maintained an inner desire to pursue her passion. In 2015, that opportunity presented itself when Crystal began working on a film project about the history of her hometown.

Crystal Jackson produced, directed, and wrote the documentary film "PacoimaStories: Land of Dreams." Nominated for "Best Feature Documentary" at the 2018 Pan African Film Festival, this powerful film is also now part of the academic curriculum in universities and high schools throughout the state.

After completing the film, Crystal founded the Pacoima Historical Society. The goal of this 501(c)3 non-profit organization is to preserve the history of Pacoima and surrounding areas. She works tirelessly with PHS, trying to bring awareness to the incredible history Pacoima has to offer. The organization has already received official recognition by the California State Assembly for its work. California Secretary of State Alex Padilla also spoke at their annual Pacoima History Day event in 2018.

Crystal wants to see Pacoima designated as an official Historic Town and a museum opened to display the town's history. She hopes that by releasing this book, it will help bring the attention needed to make her dream a reality.

PREFACE

Overcoming adversity has been a true path to greatness. My hometown of Pacoima has repeatedly followed that trail as it led to many people and stories that reached beyond anyone's wildest imagination.

I was born in Pacoima during a time when we drank out of water hoses, went home when the street lights came on, and our neighbors were like family. It was a time that may never be duplicated.

After my kids became adults, life found me thinking more about my childhood. Having family on every block made everything more enjoyable. My great grandmother would walk me down Filmore Street to Roman's Market, and Gomez, the storeowner, greeted us like we were family. Walking was "our time," and she shared many stories with me.

While growing up in Pacoima, it predominately was African American. After moving to Northern California in 1987, a changed occurred while I was away. It became a Latino town, and most of the Blacks had scattered. Reminiscing and looking at my old Pacoima photos, something came over me. My thoughts drifted to the great people that I knew, my first kiss, and the fun we had.

In 2014, during a trip back to see my mother, who still lives in Pacoima, it stunned me to see the town's evolution. With time on my hands, I decided to do something — tell the story of Pacoima.

My research began with discovering how the demographics had changed throughout Pacoima's history. To my surprise, the area began with Native Americans, who had roamed the land for more than a thousand years. Then came the White settlers, who stole the land and killed most of the Indians. Later, it would change into White and Mexican. Then something unexpected happened; thousands of Blacks began migrating into the town. Eventually, Pacoima's Black population would exceed all others. However, I also discovered that other minority communities had an extensive history in the town, as well.

When deciding to take on the project of telling Pacoima's history, I assumed basic historical facts would be readily available. To my chagrin, nothing could have been farther from the truth. Information was there, but it was misleading or flat out incorrect. It may have been because Pacoima was a minority town, and those writing the stories did not care about the truth. Books showed no people of color in the San Fernando Valley. Rectifying this travesty became a priority.

As a diehard journalist from Cal State Northridge, I was a storyteller at heart. However, having a family and a daughter with Down Syndrome had put my aspirations on hold. However, with the kids now gone, except for my daughter, time was on my hands. That allowed me to tackle a documentary-film about my hometown. It was called "PacoimaStories: Land of Dreams." I interviewed nearly a dozen 90-year-old townspeople, and their stories were compelling. They were so different and contradictory to my early research. It absolutely amazed me.

For example, the name "Pacoima," a Native-American word, is said to mean "rushing waters." Countless references portrayed that as the meaning and not knowing that language, it never was questioned. Tataviam Tribal Captain Rudy Ortega Jr. informed me that the translation of the word is "incorrect." The meaning is "the entrance" or "la entrada" (in Spanish). Finding out this information was just the beginning.

The Indians that San Fernando Mission and Pacoima history say occupied this land was incorrect as well. They claimed the "Tongva" tribe was indigenous to this area, and upon attempting to locate them, I came across the Fernandeño-Tataviam tribe, who still had residents in this area.

I discovered the Gabrieleño-Tongva tribe's territory was in the San Gabriel area of Los Angeles and not the San Fernando Valley. The two tribes served the San Gabriel and San Fernando Missions during the mission era, and how history portrays those stories is most deceiving of all. Nonetheless, it is the Tataviam tribe that is indigenous to Pacoima, not the Tongva tribe.

The town's untold stories and many achievements of Pacoimians take this town from a poverty-stricken Brown & Black barrio to a force on the world stage. For example, Hansen Dam, built in 1940, was the world's largest earth-filled reservoir at that time. Today the Hansen Dam Aquatic Center features the tenth-largest swimming pool in the world and largest in America.

Pacoima has rock legend Richie Valens, actor Danny Trejo, gospel singer Andraé Crouch and many more. The list is massive, especially when you add all the major league baseball players, NFL players, and NBA players. The town also boasts two standing members of Congress and the California Secretary of State. This book will introduce you to all of them.

I want to acknowledge my parents, Frenchy & Tipy, who were always my biggest cheerleaders. Without their input, this story would not be complete. To my brothers Lon and Lance, who put up with me through all my wild ideas, I will always be thankful for your support.

My extended family who listens to me without judgment, especially my sister-cousin Tonice Gilmore Thomas. My other cousins Printes and Jackie Hodges who helped me with our town's history and Ronald "Pookie" Oliver, who has a memory like no other. A special thank you to my sons Wesley and Corbin, who always tell me, "that's what's up, mom." And of course, my daughter queen Tara, who can make your toughest day a breeze with her laughter.

Many people have supported me, and I appreciate you all. I would also like to give a special thanks to the Fernandeño-Tataviam staff for helping me tell their story accurately. Moreover, all the remarkable people who allowed me to interview them and tell their Pacoima story.

Finally, I could never forget to shout out all the history conscious people of Pacoima who have been part of our social media revolution. You have been there with me every step of the way on Facebook, helping to connect and preserve the incredible history of Pacoima. It took a village to tell this story.

So, I will start from the very beginning, during a time before our country began. When Indians roamed this land, and from there, please enjoy this fascinating written and pictorial account of Pacoima's history.

1

Pacoinga
Village

The Tataviam Tribe is indigenous to Pacoima, and their story makes Pacoima unique. Very few towns in America know anything, other than maybe the name, about the people who preceded U.S. colonization. Pacoima has a rich Native American history, although filled with mistruths, that represents this story like no other.

This chapter details how the tribe lived, their values, and why this area was an essential part of their territorial region. It explains how water became the root issue of broken iron-clad treaties that took away Indian land and how stacked the legal system was against them.

The history of Pacoima can be traced back to as early as 450 A.D. when Native Americans held territorial governing reign over the area. Today, these U.S. citizens refer to themselves as the Fernandeño-Tataviam Band of Mission Indians.

The inhabitants knew the village as Pacoinga and referred to themselves as Pacoivitam, which meant "people of Pacoinga" in their Takic language. This language is also responsible for the names of many present-day streets and towns, including Tujunga, Topanga, and Cahuenga, all of which were geographically part of their region.

Before the founding of the Mission San Fernando, Native Americans in the region lived in lineages within villages that were associated with territories. Each lineage was economically, socially, and politically autonomous. Since they were decentralized, there was no collective tribal name above the lineage. Therefore, each held a distinct political entity.

Through exogamy and trade, the linages strengthened ties and maintained a complex social network with other villages and tribal ethnic groups. Today, the coalition of lineages recruited to Mission San Fernando is called the Fernandeño-Tataviam Band of Mission Indians.

Members of tribal villages often spoke more than one language due to sophisticated intermarriage practices with other lineages. Pacoinga consisted of speakers from the Takic branch of the Uto-Aztecan language similar to surrounding villages in the region. "Fernandeño" is a Spanish term representing the people of Simi, Santa Clarita, San Fernando, and Antelope Valleys — enslaved at Mission San Fernando during the Spanish period.

In the early 20th century, a prominent linguist and anthropologist John Peabody Harrington conducted research. He recorded extensive data on the Fernandeño natives, many of which were from Pacoinga village. His notes (Harrington 1916 Reel #106: 106-056:4:1-4) state that the linage at Pacoima was known as Pacuibit. These notes currently reside at the Smithsonian Institute.

His notes, formally called the Fernandeño Reel, describes the word Pacoi as a Takic term meaning "to enter." When added to the suffix –nga (-nga is a locative reference), it becomes "the place of the entrance," which is thought by the present-day community to describe the mouth of a river that once existed.

Harrington's Fernandeño Reel also notes a man of Indian and Spanish descent, named Martin Feliz, who resided not far from the Pacoima Dam. Mr. Feliz also referred to Pacoima as meaning "La Entrada," reconfirming the meaning of the word Pacoima. (Harrington 1916 Reel #106:066:3:3).

Mr. Feliz knew the Native American community. He identified Antonio Maria Ortega as progenitor and leader of the Suitcabit (Encino Lineage) of the Fernandeño Tataviam Tribe. Feliz informed Harrington that Ortega was one of the speakers of the native language.

Today Antonio's great-grandson Rudy Ortega Jr. is the elected Tribal President of the Fernandeño-Tataviam Band of Mission Indians.

With this research in tow, it appears conclusive that the word Pacoima means "the entrance" versus "rushing waters "or "running waters" as presented as the native meaning for decades by the city of Los Angeles and local establishments.

This map shows the geographical locations of the tribes of Los Angeles. The Tongva tribe inhabited the Los Angeles Basin. The Chumash tribe occupied the coastal regions, and the Tataviam tribe had territorial reign over sections of the San Fernando, Simi, Santa Clarita, and Antelope Valleys.

The tribe came to the area approximately 450 AD. They built village huts called "kij" made of willow poles and tule reeds. The flexible poles were placed in an upright position and bent, so they met at the top. (Courtesy of Fernandeño-Tataviam Band of Mission Indians)

The name Tataviam is associated with the people of the northern San Fernando Valley and Santa Clarita lineages and was given to the ancestors by their Kitanemuk neighbors to the north. Tataviam means "people facing the sun."

Traditionally, the ancestors of present-day Tataviam people lived under the sovereignty and autonomy of their lineage. Before the arrival of Spanish missionaries in 1769, they had no concept of brute torture and enslavement.

Villages consisted of dwellings and community spaces. Their homes, called kij, consisted of willow poles to frame the house. Natives placed the flexible poles in an upright position, bent, so they met at the top. Other poles were bound together with a cord and secured across the frame. Bundles of bulrush tule reeds were placed over the poles to make a dome-shaped thatched house. The design of the house kept it warm in the winter and cooler in the summer. A fireplace was in the center of the room with a smoke hole in the roof. The floor was hard-packed earth.

They also needed other structures as part of the village's function. Tataviam ancestors had sweathouses, which was an important ceremonial space within the village. Built similar to the homes, they are much smaller and closer to the ground. These sweathouses utilized mud and kept the smoke contained. It was a way of keeping their bodies clean. Similar structures for socializing, food storage, and other ceremonial gatherings also existed as part of the village.

Tataviam built their homes using bent willow poles and bundles of tule reeds. The design kept them warmer in the winter and cooler in the summer.

Two Tataviam women sit outside Mission de San Fernando during the 1890's.

In 1769, an exposition led by Spanish explorer Gaspar de Portola and Junipero Serra reached the Los Angeles area. At that time, the Spaniards had conquered most of Mexico and were heading towards Alta, California, where the indigenous people had occupied the land for 7,000 years. By 1797, plans to build Mission de San Fernando Reya de España were put in place by the Spanish Conquistadors.

The north-central valley was known as Paséknga, located in the lower foothills of the San Gabriel Mountains, where natural water springs lined the area. Alcalde or mayor of Los Angeles Francisco Reyes (1793–1795), had set up a grazing operation which he called Rancho Encino. Its location was near the village of Achoicominga, in what is now Mission Hills. The name Rancho Encino is not to be confused with present-day Los Encinos State Historic Park, also known as Rancho Encino.

The water supply on Reyes's land and the artesian wells was a desirable location for the next Mission and just a day's walk from the San Gabriel Mission. Reyes was persuaded to cede his land to the Franciscans receiving in exchange a square league (4,460 acres) of land in the southern valley. New Spain renamed the area, San Fernando.

Father Fermin Lasuen officially founded Mission de San Fernando Rey de España on September 8, 1797. That is when the conquest of native lineages in the geographical areas of Simi, Santa Clarita, San Fernando, and Antelope Valleys began. This conquest includes the Pacuibit linage of Pacoinga Village, whom all suffered from this path of colonialism.

The missions were designed to consolidate power, provide forced labor, and teach Christianity to the Native Americans. By 1799, an adobe church at Mission San Fernando was bricked together by the ancestral Fernandeño natives, spearheaded by Father Zalvidea. He was reported to have whipped them so frequently that by 1801, Father Lasuen wrote Spain to defend the abuse. He cited the "Indians were a people without education, without government, without religion, and without shame," none of which were correct.

In 1802, the mission church added another wing, a new partition, and enclosed them with walls, forming the first tract houses in the Valley. All this was much to the dismay of 600 Tataviam, who were kept in fear if they left the Mission.

The Native American population at Mission San Fernando peeked in 1811 as they endured horrific treatment by the Padres and soldiers. Six Spanish soldiers were assigned to each Mission to help keep the natives in tow.

As a form of control and punishment, floggings were prevalent throughout all of the missions in California. This practice reinforced the racial hierarchy, of which the California Indians were at the bottom. Floggings, for any infraction no matter how slight, were brutally inflicted. Scholars and first-hand accounts have characterized California Indian mission labor as "forced labor" or "slavery."

One of the first pictures taken of the Mission de San Fernando in 1875

In 1822 the structure with Roman arches was complete, and although Mexico received its independence from Spain in 1821, the Catholic Church still had control of the missions. Mission San Fernando was the hub of Los Angeles with cattle, vegetation, and superior ironwork. Harrison Rogers noted that the Indians "were kept in great fear; for the least offense, they are corrected." There were floggings that unsettled visitors, and many of the windows had iron bars, which gave it a prison-like appearance.

Once they dismantled Mission San Fernando, the Mexican government set out the Secularization Act of 1834, under which the Fernandeño natives could regain access to their lands under Mexican protection.

Mission de San Fernando and its trademark roman arches was completed in 1822.
This photo was taken in 1897.

In the spring of 1843, forty-one Fernandeño natives representing their lineages petitioned Governor Manuel Micheltorena for land. Among the petitioners were ancestors of the present-day tribe, who gained title to Rancho Sikwanga, Rancho Encino, Rancho Tujunga, Rogerio's Grant, Rancho Cahuenga, Rancho Escorpion, and more.

Their rights to the lands were supposed to be preserved under the 1848 Treaty of Guadalupe Hidalgo in the American period but were ignored and weakly implemented. Had their rights been preserved, it would have supported the placement of their lands, which encompasses a majority of the San Fernando Valley, into a federal trust. Thus, the land would have become the Indian reservation it was legally designated to be.

In 1891, the U.S. government passed the Mission Indian Relief Act, which sent agents to define the land needs of Fernandeños. However, this did not result in land for the Fernandeño natives. Although acknowledged by the federal government, the tribe is still petitioning for official recognition nearly 130 years after the passing of the Act.

Tataviam woman at Mission San Fernando in 1880

Fernandeño -Tataviam woman at Mission San Fernando in 1880; Tataviam tribal members helped build the mission in 1797.

Rogerio Rocha

Rogerio Rocha standing near a cactus patch in 1898. He was a Tataviam tribal leader and among the last Native Americans to live at the Mission de San Fernando.

One of the more fascinating stories of the mission era is that of Rogerio Rocha, who was born in 1801 at the San Fernando Mission and grew up there. He was granted 10 acres of land in San Fernando from the Mexican Government in 1843, just before the Mexican-American War. Rocha built two adobe houses on his land. His wife's name was Manuela (Maria), and they had one daughter, Juaquina that died around the age of one. Rocha was said to have discovered gold in Little Tujunga in 1840, before the gold rush mania of 1849. Three years after his discovery, gold was also found in Placerita Canyon, near Pacoima, on the roots of onions.

Rocha was a Blacksmith by trade and captain or traditional leader, of the Fernandeño tribe. He lived a peaceful life until former senator Charles Maclay and his investors purchased 56,000 acres of land intersecting with Rocha's property. The Treaty of Guadalupe Hidalgo, which was signed when the United States gained possession of California in 1848, ensured the honoring of Indian land rights. In perhaps one of the biggest land frauds against Native Americans, Charles Maclay initiated legal proceedings to evict Rocha. His nephew, Robert Widney, was the presiding judge who issued the documents. He allowed Maclay, George Porter, and Los Angeles County sheriff's deputies to physically remove Rocha from his land on one rainy winter night.

In a two-hour interview with a Los Angeles Herald writer, Rocha told his life story and what he remembered about the land he called Cienega Rancho in San Fernando. After the eviction, he laid his wife to rest in the mission cemetery, and he proceeded to Lopez Canyon, which was government land. Rocha built himself a small two-room cabin with a garden. He had a few effects left from the eviction that he brought with him. The interview required a translator because Rocha spoke Spanish, which he learned, growing up at the mission.

During the interview, Rocha expressed hope he would someday return to his ranch. "He was in good shape for a man of 98," the interviewer said. Rocha explained that two men came on that stormy night. He had acquired the land, which turned out to be the most valuable in the San Fernando Valley, from Governor Micheltoreno, who issued an 1843 land grant to Joaquin Alcalde and 40 others, including Rocha.

Charles Maclay, conspiring with his nephew Robert Widney initially claimed no such grant was in existence, and if there was, they never saw it. However, Rocha was able to produce a document recorded under the name "THE DE CELIS GRANT." The United States Surveyor-general of California report dated 1880 (pages 111, 173, and 233), addressed these Indian land rights.

Photo of Rogerio Rocha

The De Celis Grant designated 4400 acres of land for Indians. As to the subsequent sale of that land, it stated:

"The said purchaser covenanting to maintain the actually existing old Indians on these lands for the remainder of their days, so that they may cultivate, and any other lands they may possess, without previous title from the departmental governor."

After producing the grant, Maclay and Widney submitted a new motion claiming Rocha did not qualify as an "old Indian." They claimed that because he was only 46 years old when the land grant was issued, it was invalid. It was seven years after the first filing with a series of back and forth until ultimately eviction papers were issued by Judge Widney. His ruling on the case was called a "tale of injustice to an

Indian" by the Los Angeles Herald Newspaper. Moreover, an Indian could not sue a white man, so Rocha had no recourse in the end.

The night of the eviction was revisited eleven years later, as the cruelty and heartlessness haunted the San Fernando Valley for a long time. The Los Angeles Herald published another story by a man who wished to stay anonymous but claimed this:

"The day that was selected to evict Rogerio Rocha was such a day as Monday afternoon. The rain was pouring down in perfect sheets. That was the time these philanthropists selected to have the old Indian, and his bedridden wife moved from under their roof. A party of deputy sheriffs proceeded to Rocha's home, where he had lived for over forty years and entering, they carried his poor old wife, over eighty years of age, out into the road in the rain, where they laid her down. She had not the strength to move. She laid there for some time, and finally, as I remember, was carried down to the mission where she died shortly after as a result of the exposure to the rain and wind at the time of the ejectment. Rocha's chickens and personal effects were stowed away in sacks and dumped onto the road. The ejectment was the most outrageous proceeding I have ever witnessed in my life."

The sentiment of the community seemed mixed regarding the Rocha eviction. One reader of the Los Angeles Times was trying to understand what he read about a deputy sheriff's comment regarding the manner Rocha was displaced.

Letters to the Los Angeles Times:

Deputy Sheriff Aguirre wrote: "Will Hammell and I have just got back from San Fernando, where we dispossessed the Mission Indians for Judge Widney and Senator Maclay. They have been there about 80 years, I think; had two good houses - a lot of property. We had to load their stuff on a wagon and cart it off. There were eleven Indians in all, and they all came away peaceably except the old Capitan. We had to grab him and throw him on the wagon to get him away."

"What can it mean?" the reader said after reading this statement.

Los Angeles Herald   11, Mar 1896

ROGERIO ROCHA'S WRONGS

"Justice" Tells More About the Land Grant
A Pathetic Interview- The Roster of the Dead, Alone, and Poor—The Theological
Seminary Idea

EDITORIAL HERALD: In a former communication I stated that I would later ask the Herald to publish an account of an interview with an Indian Rogerio Rocha of which he recited the fate of each of the forty Indians who were interested in the grant of one league of land Juaquin Alcada.

Before proceeding to give an account of said interview I will refer to the grant in question.

This grant was made in 1843. The petition was dated San Fernando April 10, 1843. It was addressed to the most senior, General Micheltoreno, and signed by Joaquin in the name of all.

Now as to the interview with Rocha. It was had about a year ago. It was indeed a melancholy spectacle to see the old Indian, bent with age, answering to the names of his companions, the beneficiaries of the grant in a league somewhere within the limits of San Fernando, and tremulously and tearfully announcing the fate of each. The old Indian must have felt somewhat as a soldier feels who, at the roll call after a battle, answers to the names of his comrades who died on the field. Here is the way his simple but pathetic story ran.

Joaquin? Dead	Jurado? Dead	Jacinto? Dead
Ermterco? Dead	Camilio? Dead	Odon? Dead
Calistro? Dead	Fenislado? Dead	Patricio? Dead
Norberto? Dead	Idon Second? Dead	Manuel? Dead
Herman? Dead		

and so on, and so on…

Poor, old, decrepit Rogerio, alone, being left to tell the tale and be deprived of his possessions, by the cupidity and heartlessness of those who would win a name for benevolence by endowing theological seminaries with land taken from the helpless and defenseless.

Other newspaper articles addressed this story, as well. Another account was from a Senator Del Valle, who claimed to have known Rocha when he was at the mission. He said Rocha sang at the mission church, had a good voice, and read music very well. The senator recollected that Rocha could read and write, which brought into question why an "X" was on all his signed court documents. He said as the years went by, all the Indians died off, mostly from smallpox. However, he said, Rocha escaped because he had the purest, finest kind of mountain spring water on his land.

This spring is what made Rocha's land so valuable, so valuable that others wanted it. They secured the land and water rights and left Rocha's wife to die and Rocha to starve.

The Los Angeles Herald reported this "cruel and inhumane incident" happened in November of 1885. Doctors concluded his wife died from Pneumonia, due to exposure. Rocha retreated to a small cabin in Lopez Canyon until 1904 when he passed away at the age of 103. After the eviction, Maclay built a school of theology on Rocha's land.

Rogerio Rocha home in Lopez Canyon circa 1896

This rendering of Rogerio Rocha's home in Lopez Canyon is from a 1896 newspaper article.

There has been much litigation and conversation about perpetuating this land fraud with no regard for Indian rights. Eventually, the tribe partnered with the City of San Fernando, which officially welcomed the native Fernandeño back into the city in 2009. A park located on a portion of Rogerio's property has been dedicated to his memory and is currently used to host the majority of the tribe's cultural workshops and events.

Named Rudy Ortega Sr. Park, after the great Tataviam leader, the land sits on the corner of Fourth Street and Hubbard in San Fernando.

San Fernando is also the location of the tribe's administration office, which sits near Maclay Avenue, a street whose namesake is responsible for the dispossession of their ancestors.

Rudy Ortega Jr. is a third-generation tribal leader. He tells compelling stories about some of the many challenges his tribe faced throughout the years.

Ortega Jr. says that one little known fact about the struggles of Native Americans in the United States is the challenge of preserving their culture. Rudy's Great Grandfather, Antonio Maria Ortega 1857-1941, was the last fluent speaker of the Takic (Tataviam) language. According to Ortega Jr., he knew two languages, Spanish and their native language.

The dilemma that faced their people was the looming threat of being sent to boarding schools if they exhibited any identification of their cultural heritage. Even when anthropologists such as Peabody Harrington interviewed and photographed community members in the 1900's, they were resistant. There was a fear of being sent to places such as the Sherman Institute Indian Boarding School. According to Ortega Jr., "It was the design of the United States to flush out all the idealism of being Indian completely and just be white." He says the slogan they used was "kill the Indian, save the man."

There were Tataviam forced into boarding schools, so his great grandfather refused to say he was Indian to anyone outside the community. They went into protection mode, fearing if they admitted they were Indian, their children would be taken away and never seen again.

The Federal government still refuses to recognize the tribe, failing to understand they were forced to forget or not acknowledge their cultural identity. Ortega categorizes this as a tragedy. The government asks them, "how come you don't know your history, how come you didn't stay intact as a political government? Why didn't you save your land?"

However, Ortega Jr. says, "it was an act of survival."

This 1919 class photo shows Tataviam and other Native-American children sent to Sherman Indian Boarding School in Riverside to learn how to dress, speak, and imitate the White culture.

Perris Indian School was established in 1892 by the US government to assimilate Indian children into "civilized" society. It was relocated in 1903 and renamed Sherman Institute. Indian children from all over Southern California were sent here. Photo taken in 1939.

Cemetery where boarding school Indian children were buried
(Courtesy Juan Aldana)

Ortega Jr.'s story tells how his tribe struggled for a reservation. An 1845 land grant awarded them property in the southwest valley, which is now called Encino. The village there was known as "Cintunga," which meant "place of the oath." In 1892, the Mayor of Los Angeles took the property for allegedly unpaid taxes. They had hopes that the area would be their reservation.

Another Mexican land grant issued to them was at the Chatsworth reservoir. Three Natives had possession of that property until 1912 when the Department of Water and Power secretly took title to that land. It is unknown how they did it; therefore, in 1971, the tribe sent a letter requesting information on that title transfer but never got a response. The brutal atrocity inflicted on Rogerio Rocha, and the Tataviam tribe was one of the cruelest thefts of Indian land in Los Angeles. Although the tribe engaged in negotiations for a reservation, nothing has ever come from the federal government. However, that has never stopped them from fighting and pursuing that right.

Local Tataviam in 1921 — Juan Jose Fustero (left) and family.
(Fernandeño-Tataviam Band of Mission Indians)

The Tataviam built and were held captive at the Mission San Fernando, yet the Mission fails to acknowledge the correct tribe. They even fail to recognize the difference between Fernandeño and Gabrieleño. Although the Fernandeño and Gabrieleño are linguistically related, they represent two geographical areas that should not be confused. The natives in the Los Angeles Basin were known as the Gabrieleño during the Mission period. Moreover, any natives at the Mission de San Fernando, regardless of tribe, would be Fernandeño. Therefore, in addition to the federal government denying their recognition, they disrespect the tribal citizens by denying them accurate historical records.

Mission San Fernando Rey de Espana
(PacoimaStories archives)

In October 2018, the Pacoima Historical Society recognized the Tataviam Tribe as the original inhabitants of Pacoima. The California State Assembly also honored them with recognition in February 2019.

Rudy Ortega Sr. Park has a tribute to Rogerio Rocha

Rudy Ortega Jr. accepts a Certificate of Recognition from Pacoima Historical Society president Crystal Jackson. The Tataviam tribe was officially recognized as the "Original Inhabitants of Pacoima."

Tataviam Tribal offices are located on Second Street at Maclay Avenue in San Fernando. They seek to change the name of Maclay Avenue to Tataviam Avenue.

Tataviam tribal members return to their ancestral home and celebrate a "Walk for the Ancestors" at the San Fernando Mission in 2015. (Photographer Kimia Fatehi)

Antonio Maria Ortega, born in 1857, worked for Geronimo Lopez in San Fernando. He and his wife Ysidora Garcia had eight children together. He was said to be the last Fernandeño to speak the Tataviam language fluently.

In 1935 the Bureau of Indian Affairs acknowledged him as a tribal leader under the name of Jose Rosario. He opened up a candy store on the corner of Coronel and Mission Blvd in San Fernando.

Antonio Ortega, Rudy Ortega Sr., and Rudy Ortega Jr. were distinguished leaders of the Tataviam tribe in the past century.

Rudy Ortega Sr., known as "Chief Little Bear," Tribal Captain, Fernandeño Band of Mission Indians - 1975. (Courtesy Fernandeño Band of Mission Indians)

2
Charles Maclay

Charles Maclay (1821-1890) was the first U.S. landowner of the area now called Pacoima. There is a middle school named after him in the town and a street in San Fernando, the city he founded. Very few people today know anything about Maclay unless they are involved in the Methodist Church. He was initially a preacher from Pennsylvania who began serving the church as a missionary. Maclay came to Santa Clara, California, and left the ministry to go into politics. He served as California State Senator from 1864 to 1872. After a humiliating election loss and pushback from angry constituents, he left Santa Clara in search of new opportunities. This quest would lead him to Rancho Ex Mission de San Fernando.

Maclay and his nephew Robert Widney had a sizeable stake in early Pacoima. Widney was one of the founders of the University of Southern California, and there were indications of USC owning land in the town. He moved Maclay's school of theology to the USC campus and renamed it Claremont School of Theology after Maclay died.

There is much to understand about how Charles Maclay impacted Pacoima. His road to ownership of San Fernando is a complex but interesting one. Nonetheless, many people forget that Pacoima was once part of San Fernando. The property lines, believe it or not, are still unclear today.

In March of 1874, Charles Maclay was made aware of the availability of the northern San Fernando Valley. Eager to get the property, he rounded up several investors to purchase the 56,000 acres for sale. Maclay formed a partnership with cousins George Porter and Benjamin Porter, along with Thomas McLaren, to acquire the land from the heir of Don Eugelio de Celis' estate.

De Celis had obtained the entire San Fernando Valley in 1845, for $14,000 from California-Mexico Governor Pio Pico, who was raising money for the Mexican American war. De Celis went back to Spain in 1853 where he died in 1869. His son, Eugelio F. de Celis was made the administrator of the estate and managed the rancho.

De Celis (Jr.) was the editor of La Cronica newspaper in Los Angeles and had already sold the Southern half of the Valley to the San Fernando Farm Homestead Association. Their principal backers were Isaac Lankershim and Isaac Newton Van Nuys.

From this point, a series of complicated events occurred. First, upon making the offer for the land, Maclay used attorney Ansen Brunsen, who was also the attorney for de Celis (Jr.), to negotiate the deal that represented a conflict of interest. Maclay had secured $125,000 from investors and conspired with Brunsen to bargain a lesser price, and they would split the difference. Brunsen agreed, making this the first of many questionable legal transactions to be perpetuated by Maclay.

Second, the estate was in foreclosure. De Celis (Jr.) was careless with money and had San Fernando heavily mortgaged with a $37,830 note held by James Patterson, who had filed for foreclosure in 1873. De Celis (Jr.) had six months to redeem the mortgage or lose over half of the ranch. That 6-month period would be up in May 1874.

Third, the sale of the land had to be approved by the probate court before it was final. Maclay was most interested in this land because he knew Leland Stanford's Southern Pacific Railroad would be connecting from Northern to Southern California. The tracks would go directly through San Fernando.

While serving as a state senator, Maclay had worked closely with Stanford, who lobbied him into introducing controversial legislation that benefited the railroads. Maclay engaged in doing Leland Stanford's bidding despite the public's objection to big business and railroads.

Senator Charles Maclay (D) - Santa Clara

In a San Francisco Alta California front-page story dated April 14, 1874, Maclay disclosed his intention to survey 1000 acres in the vicinity of the railroad depot for the town of San Fernando. Maclay was taking advantage of the Los Angeles real estate boom that had begun the year before and acted quickly to put the lots on the market. He posted water notices with the county recorder, which claimed water for irrigation and manufacturing from Pacoima Canyon (referred to as Paycome by some settlers), Canada de Oro, Big Tujunga Canyon, and Little Tujunga Canyon.

56,000 ACRES
OF LAND,

Situated in the San Fernando Valley, Los Angeles Co. Climate and soil unsurpassed by any locality in the State.

FOR SALE OR TO RENT

In quantities to suit parties desiring to purchase or lease. Will rent cheap for

CASH OR PART OF THE CROP.

Railroad from San Fernando to Wilmington. Also, for sale,

TOWN LOTS

In the Town of San Fernando. Title perfect. Rare opportunities offered to parties desiring to rent or purchase. For particulars, apply to

CHARLES MACLAY,
San Fernando, Los Angeles County, Cal.,
Or GEO. K. PORTER,
117 Battery Street, San Francisco.

Despite the pending legal matters, Maclay began organizing an excursion party to San Fernando on a free train ride, compliments of Leland Stanford (founder of Stanford University). With a promise of free barbeque, the excursion gathered 60 people to come and see this new town situated near Pico Station.

However, the trip did not inspire enthusiasm among the prospective buyers, who only saw a small wooden building used as a train station. Mission de San Fernando could be seen in the distance, worn down and practically in ruins. Although frustrated, Maclay remained resolute. It was clear that he had work to do.

While trying to sell the plots, Maclay also needed to deal with De Celis' (Jr.) foreclosure problem. The 6-month redemption time was approaching, and Maclay had already begun parceling off the land. He had ten days to secure payment of the mortgage before it reverted to James Patterson.

Maclay sailed for San Francisco via steamship on May 13 to arrange for financing of the property. A storm delayed the steamer, and Maclay arrived with only two days left. He had hoped to secure the funds from the Porters or McLaren, but neither had the $37,830 needed.

Maclay then went to Leland Stanford, who readily agreed without requiring any form of security.

With a growing sense of urgency, on the last day for redemption and only five minutes before the Bank of California closed, Maclay, Brunsen, and Alfred Cohen arrived to pay Patterson. They telegraphed the Los Angeles sheriff, and the final act of foreclosure was averted.

Maclay returned to San Fernando with a sigh of relief from that experience. He began building the town with saloons and the necessary mercantile needed to make San Fernando a viable place to settle.

He continued with the excursions, which were from Los Angeles to San Fernando, where he highly promoted the abundance of water and oil. Maclay had provided an article to the Los Angeles Herald, which ran in July boasting on the oil and guaranteed wealth for settlers in San Fernando.

The Oil Wells—The Senator's Pumpkins and Sauer-Kraut—The Farmers —Increased Productions of the San Fernando Valley—Tobacco—Change of Railroad Time—Improvements in the Town, etc., etc.

EDITOR HERALD:—There seems to be quite an excitement among people in various parts of the State in regard to the oil wells of San Fernando. Many parties arrive here daily *en route* for this new El Dorado. I, the other day, met with a gentleman who had just returned from a visit to the springs, and he gave me a very glowing description of them, and he spoke whereof he knew, having been a resident of the oil country of Pennsylvania. I was curious to know what kind of a formation the oleaginous fluid was found in. He stated that it was found in the limestone and sandstone formations; that in many places he found better indications than in many places in Pennsylvania that had proved very productive, and had made immense wealth for their fortunate owners. He also informed me that the oil of San Fernando would yield a commercial percentage of seventy-five to ninety per cent.; that they obtained at the new works a first-class illuminating oil of forty to fifty per cent., and besides showing a considerable amount of parafine, naptha and lubricating oil. Now you see, Mr. Editor,

Los Angeles Herald - July 1874

Horses on the outskirts of San Fernando in 1880. The new town can be seen in the background.

In 1875, Maclay and Son-in-law Albert B. Moffit purchased the general retail-merchandising store one-year after it was built. George Porter had a place in town called Porter House on the left.

Deciding the name of the town happened at a town-hall event featuring several speakers and a prominent Los Angeles druggist named Dr. Frederick P. Howard. They praised Maclay for putting forth great effort and advancing the prosperity of Los Angeles while pointing out even London had once been a small village. It was Superintendent Eldridge E. Hewitt of the Southern Pacific Railroad who laid out the discussion for the town's name. The name Pico was put forth referring to Andres Pico, who resided near the mission. However, Dr. John S. Griffin opposed naming the new town after a living celebrity. Maclay or Maclaytown came up, but those failed to win the vote as well. Therefore, the logical name was San Fernando, which was unanimous.

Over twelve thousand lots, twenty-five feet in width, were laid out on a 1,000-acre tract. Major streets were named for prominent local citizens and ran perpendicular to the railroad track. Approval for the sale of the land by the probate court had been filed on April 27, 1874 and took nearly four months to complete.

On August 31, 1874, the court approved Maclay's bid as the highest, best, and deemed the value as appropriate. Now an agreement had to be reached for Maclay and Porter regarding their perspective interests. On September 14, 1874, Charles Maclay and George F. Porter signed an agreement placing the entire property in Porter's name. The deal gave Maclay one-fourth interest and Porter three-fourths interest. There was no mention made of either Thomas McLaren or Benjamin Porter. To meet the down payment of $80,000, Maclay paid $13,580 in cash. Both Maclay and Porter assumed an existing mortgage to Gasper Orena of Santa Barbara for $16,000, and Porter shouldered the remainder.

Maclay executed a one-year personal mortgage with de Celis (Jr.) for $37,500 at ten percent interest. The final agreement between the two was they would first pay off the Orena mortgage with the profits from the initial land sales. Maclay was to be paid $125 per month to manage and sell the San Fernando land while Porter returned to San Francisco.

Real Estate Transactions.

Deeds filed for record for the week ending Sept. 18, 1874, as reported for the HERALD by Judson, Gillette & Adams, searchers of record for Los Angeles county:

Eulogio de Celis et al. to Geo. K. Porter.—Rancho ex-Mission de San Fernando; $1.

Geo. K. Porter to C. Maclay.—Undived ¼ of above; $30,000.

Eulogio de Celis, Administrator, to C. Maclay.—Interest of Eulogio Celis Sr., deceased, in same rancho, less railroad lands; $117,500.

Alfred A. Cohen to Geo. K. Porter.—All of grantor's interest in said rancho, under Sheriff's deed of June 18, 1874; $44,910.

Geo. Treat et al. to Geo. K. Porter.—Grantor's interest in above Rancho; $8,500.

Chas. Maclay to Geo. K. Porter.—Rancho ex-Mission de San Fernando; $120,000.

Geo. K. Porter and C. Maclay.—Agreement as to said rancho lands.

Geo. K. Porter to Chas. Masclay.—Power of Attorney recorded.

Francisco Vejar et al. to Wilson Beach.—184 acres in Rancho los Nogales; $5,481.

Public Notices in the Los Angeles Herald of deeds filed for the week ending September 18, 1874

Maclay had limited success with the conditional land sales, but advertised the lots were selling like "hot cakes" to incite a buying frenzy. The Sunday excursions to San Fernando were further enhanced by Maclay's aggressive print campaign, which highlighted the agricultural potential of the area. He pointed out to prospective buyers the community's assets were a healthful climate, adequate water from nearby springs, fertile soil, and proximity to the Southern Pacific Railroad. He also advertised oil was plentiful, saying a buyer would strike oil by digging for only for two hours. It is unclear if the oil wealth promised ever came to fruition.

Maclay's first known fraud infraction was a lawsuit filed by Josefa Arguello de Celis, the mother, for breach of trust (Celis vs. Brunsen 1876). She alleged Brunsen entered into a "fraudulent combination and conspiracy" with Maclay during the purchase of Rancho San Fernando. The case reached the Supreme Court, where she won a judgment of $7,500 in damages.

The town of San Fernando possessed a host of advantages that encompassed a head start in prosperity and growth. The Southern Pacific and the Cerro Gordo Freighting Company used the town as a service center. De Celis (Jr.) had granted a right of way through the valley and a depot near the mission of nearly thirty acres, which proved beneficial.

From 1873 to 1876, this depot was the terminus of the railway line from Los Angeles to San Francisco. During this time, a 7,000-foot San Fernando Tunnel was under construction, bringing some 1500 workers and nearly $18,000 of supplies each month.

More than a thousand Chinese laborers worked on the tunnel. Construction began on March 22, 1875 and was completed on July 14, 1876.

The final hurdle of connecting San Francisco to Los Angeles via train was the digging of this tunnel through a mountain of fractured rock. The passage was 16 feet wide and over 22 feet high. It was 6,940 feet in length and was adequate size for a single track.

The Cerro Gordo Freighting Company, which transported silver bullion, moved its headquarters from Los Angeles to San Fernando in May 1874. The presence of these companies' activities contributed to the initial prosperity of San Fernando.

In early July, prospective buyers gathered in Los Angeles at Noyes and Durfee Auctioneers to bid on land in San Fernando. They proclaimed, "There will be lots sold at this sale to suit all purses. The capitalist will find a good chance to invest, and the man of small means can here secure a piece of property which must appreciate in value."

The proprietorship of Look and Leonard built a general store in San Fernando. It was purchased shortly after by Maclay and his son-in-law Albert B. Moffit. Two hotels were built to house the needs of the Railroad and Freight company's temporary residents. They included "The Railroad House," which later became known as the "Kittridge House," and the Caledonian Hotel, which became known as the San Fernando Hotel.

In 1875, San Fernando had a population of 125 inhabitants. The town contained thirty buildings, which included two merchandise stores, two blacksmith shops, a saddle shop, a carpenter's shop, bakeshop, and six saloons. Maclay built his sizeable two-story home on the corner of Celis and Workman.

The earliest settlers in the San Fernando Valley were Andres Pico and Geronimo and Catalina Lopez, who purchased 40 acres of land near the Mission San Fernando in 1861. The original adobe became known as Lopez Station. The couple also operated the San Fernando Valley's first general store, English language school, and post office (in 1869) at the site.

The year 1873 had seen real estate prices rise in Los Angeles, and large numbers of settlers came to the area. San Fernando competed with other towns that were emerging. David Berry, the developer of Pasadena, complained that San Fernando was making it difficult for him to sell his Pasadena lots. Other communities were springing up in the Southland as well. Downey, Norwalk, Boyle Heights, Pomona, Santa Monica, and dozens of other settlements began to fill the map.

The railroad connection provided a boost, and Los Angeles grew from a population of 5,600 in 1870 to over 11,000 in 1874. The real estate market peaked in 1875. However, when the Bank of Temple and Workman failed in September and land sales fell abruptly, Maclay's San Fernando felt the sting.

Maclay depended much on the influx of new settlers, and this development was devastating to his ability to pay off his debt. On July 19, 1876, de Celis (Jr.) filed a decree of foreclosure. Maclay became dependent on income derived from the rental of sheep pastures and farmlands. He also received payments from farmers who harvested wheat, hay, barley, and corn. Maclay himself raised wheat, sowing over 1,200 acres in 1875.

Farm income materially decreased after another drought devastated Southern California from 1876 to 1877, the worst since 1864. The vast San Fernando Valley grain fields withered due to lack of water, and forty thousand sheep perished as a result of the drought. This occurrence further exposed San Fernando's vulnerability in agriculture. It ultimately led to Maclay's desperation to gain control of the Indian land that had natural water springs, regardless of the cost. He first filed a petition with the court in 1878 to evict Rogerio Rocha from his property, a process that would not come into play until November 1885. Before submitting the papers, Maclay approached Rocha with an offer of a new home and cash. Rocha rejected this with the words, "I sign nothing."

Faced with foreclosure and the possible loss of his ranch, Maclay's relationship with George Porter became fragile. Porter was already dissatisfied with Maclay's handling of San Fernando and had un-expectantly refused to accept the appointment as the attorney for San Fernando. Porter was going to ask for $2,800 from his cousin Benjamin Porter to avoid foreclosure. However, that amount was insufficient to meet the mortgage. The sheriff sold a three-fourths interest in George Porter's land to Josefa A. de Celis for $14,680.62. Within six months, another Valley farmer, Francis Wright, redeemed the mortgage and sold it back to Porter. These transactions did not include the 1,000 acres of San Fernando.

For nearly two years, the Porters controlled the entire ranch except for the city of San Fernando. It was in 1881 that Maclay and the Porters reached an agreement whereby Maclay received 19,000 acres lying north and east of the railroad track and Pacoima Creek. The Porters equally divided their two-thirds of the ranch. McLaren's settlement was unclear; however, the business relationship was over.

In the 1880s, wheat and sheepherding dominated the San Fernando area. There were approximately 100,000 sheep in the valley, of which 2,000 were estimated to be Maclay's. A significant portion of Maclay's income came from his merchandise store with son-in-law Moffit, rental of sheep pasture, and the raising of sheep. Maclay was now too old for actual farm work and hired a partner named Slaughter to raise the wheat east and south of the city of San Fernando.

Charles Maclay died of cancer in 1890 at the age of 69. His school of theology relocated to the USC campus in 1900.

Senator George Porter

Benjamin Porter

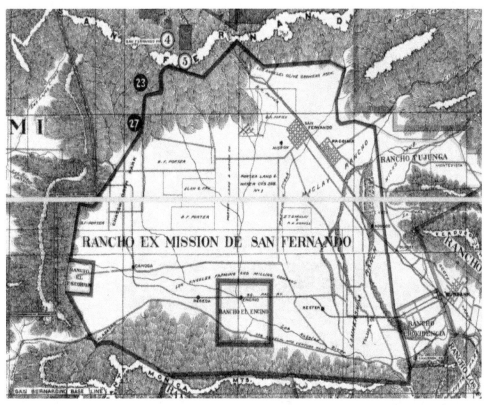

1888 resurvey map of San Fernando Valley

1910 photo of San Fernando Rd near Maclay Ave. Local business people come out.

(Above) Porter Hotel in San Fernando 1890 (below) Billiards and Pool Hall located on Maclay Avenue in the year 1900

1899 photo taken of Lopez Market in San Fernando. Owned by Steven Lopez

North Maclay Avenue facing east in 1911

After evicting Rocha, Maclay founded his school of Theology on that land in 1885. In 1900 it was moved to the USC campus and was there until 1956 when it withdrew from the university and became an independent corporation.

3
Early Pacoima

The early story of Pacoima is fascinating. However, finding information is challenging. For example, the purchaser of Pacoima is said to be Jouett Allen. Searching that name comes up relatively empty. The Los Angeles Herald has stories about Pacoima's purchase but spells the name, Jewett Allin, as does Ancestry. They show investors, along with Allin buying the land, which traces the early beginnings of Pacoima and its development as an American town.

In 1887, Jouett Allen, aka Jewett Allin (1854-1936), purchased 1,000 acres from the Maclay Rancho Water Company (under Robert Widney) that was handling Charles Maclay's holdings. Allin kept 500 acres for himself and surveyed the other 500 to be divided up in lots.

He was a lawyer turned developer from Chattanooga, Tennessee. Much like Maclay, Allin saw the advantage of the railroads to the town's success and bought at a time when there was a fare war between Southern Pacific and Santa Fe Railroads.

Allin wanted to design an elite community with Victorian homes and modern hotels. He sponsored train excursions for land sales, which added excitement to the town.

A BIG LAND DEAL.

A Thousand-acre Buy at San Fernando for a Town.

For a little over thirty days Jewett Allin, a prominent capitalist of Chattanooga, Tenn., has been working up a syndicate to buy a large tract in the San Fernando Valley and put a town there. The company has been organized, and yesterday completed the purchase, from Judge R. M. Widney and his associates, of 1000 acres in the Maclay ranch for $150,000. The tract lies eighteen miles northwest of this city, and just this side of the Pacoima. It is all on the north side of the railroad, and runs clear back to the foothills. All travelers will remember that beautiful slope. It lies in with the 1000 acres of the University of Southern California, the forty-acre tracts belonging, alternately, to the University and to the new company; and the whole 2000 acres will be handled as one tract.

The company has a capital stock of $150,-000, in 1500 shares of $100 each. All are subscribed, as follows: Jewett Allin, 750 shares; R. A. Hoyt, 120 shares; Dr. E. Pinney, 120 shares; G. W. Hoyt, 60 shares; N. O. Allin, 150 shares; J. B. Allin, 150 shares; J. H. Tait, 75 shares; D. L. Lander,

(Big Land Deal article) Los Angeles Times May 17, 1887

46

As the settlers began integrating Native American words and phrases, the area's name evolved from Pacoinga into Pacoima. Newspaper articles referencing the area's name predate Allin's purchase of the land. Because of the linguistic differences, newspapers often misspelled the name when referring to it. After Allin's purchase, a new awareness of Pacoima began to take form.

One of the biggest obstacles to selling the land was water supply because of the area's history of droughts. Due to its need for cultivating agriculture, real estate developers had to convince the public that water availability would be plentiful. Most of their ads claimed water was in abundance and even called Pacoima "a land of running water." For many decades the meaning of the word Pacoima has been erroneously translated as "rushing or running waters." Perhaps this is the reason for its misinterpreted Indian meaning.

Allin purchased the one-thousand acres for $150,000 along with his father, brother, Dr. Elbert Pinney, and Roscoe Hoyt. Allin's vision was for an exclusive community with the highest moral values. He prohibited the sale of alcohol in the town. The land deed contained a clause stating that selling liquor on the property would make it revert to Jewett Allin or his heirs.

He was the first in the San Fernando Valley to install sidewalks and curbs. In 1888, the main road was one hundred feet wide and eight miles long. They named it Taylor Avenue after US President Zachary Taylor and later renamed it Pershing Street. Today the street is named Van Nuys Boulevard. They also built Pacoima School near the railroad.

A subterranean dam was constructed to supply the town with water. Allin had restrictions on the land he sold that were aimed to attract an affluent class of people and required new homes to cost a minimum of $2,000 to $10,000. That would compute to almost $400,000 in 2019.

He began promoting Pacoima very similar to Maclay's strategy with special train excursions. The train stopped through the town, and Allin wanted a Hotel right near the train station.

An early flyer and map of property lots for sale in Pacoima. Documents such as these highlight the strangely inconsistent spelling of Jewett Allin or Jouett Allen's name.

Streets were named after prominent people in the community.

This 1911 photo shows Van Nuys Blvd looking north, which was originally Sherman Way. However, Van Nuys Blvd in Pacoima was originally Taylor Street then Pershing. They later merged with the main boulevard.

In 1886, people gather in Pacoima by Hansen Hill

The land boom of 1887-88 was short-lived and began to collapse as quickly as it started. Buyers would arrive from Los Angeles on a Monday, purchase lots on Tuesday and sell them to trainloads of spectators on Wednesday. It was an unbalanced scheme that was dependent on a constant flow of buyers, and it rapidly collapsed.

Allin had invested a great deal of money in Pacoima with the hotel, houses, school and street improvements and found himself in a considerable amount of debt, much like Maclay. Following the same footsteps, he also was plagued with lawsuits due to unpaid taxes and civil litigation. Allin built himself a beautiful home, but only two years after buying the town, his house mysteriously burned to the ground and was deemed a total loss in 1889.

WAS IT INSURED ?

Jewett Allen's House and Furniture in Ashes.

Jewett Allen is well known up the San Fernando valley as the great Pacoima "promoter." He, in the boom days, got a fine depot built between Dundee and San Fernando and started in to make the town of Pacoima. Mr. Allen showed his faith by his works and built at this point a notably fine residence for his own home. It is said to have been elegantly furnished. But the boom broke its back, speculation came to a standstill and Pacoima did not grow as rapidly as was hoped. Thus Mr. Allen's home looked a little bit lonely where it stood on the mesa.

Newspaper story about Jewett Allen on September 16, 1889

In 1891, there was tremendous flooding that destroyed most of the homes, the school building, hotel, and passenger rail depot. This devastating event led Allin to leave the state for good. However, promotion on the "new" town of Pacoima resumed in 1905 when the San Fernando Land Company, comprised of Robert M. Widney, Randolph Hoyt, George Cochran, Peter Haack, and L.E. Welcome began the sales campaign again.

GET FREE TICKETS NOW FOR

Pacoima

A beautiful townsite, directly in the path of the city's $23,000,000 Owens River Water Conduit, and profiting more by it than any other locality, although we have an independent superb water system of our own.

The extension of the Huntington Electric line goes right through PACOIMA.

The wires of the mighty Kern River Power Line pierce PACOIMA.

The Southern Pacific gives a quick train service to PACOIMA.

If you see the place you yourself will like PACOIMA.

Pasadena, Monrovia, Alhambra nor Hollywood; none of them had the natural advantages there are at PACOIMA.

You did not buy in these towns, but you can make up for lost opportunities by buying NOW in PACOIMA.

You are invited to be our guests and visit PACOIMA on our

FREE EXCURSION
Sunday, December 17

Los Angeles Herald newspaper ad — December 14, 1905

Los Angeles Herald newspaper ad — September 6, 1905

Los Angeles Herald newspaper ad — December 14, 1905

Hoyt House circa 1905. Hannah Hoyt can be seen standing in on the right side of the house. Records show Roscoe Hoyt purchased this home in 1888 from Jewett Allin. It is one of the few homes that survived the flooding of 1891.

(Courtesy of Bill & Sonja Speer archives)

Harvesters at work in Pacoima circa 1900. Hansen Hill can be seen in upper right background of photo

Despite the town's valiant efforts, the real estate boom had bottomed out, and the dream of an exclusive town faded away. Pacoima would have to join the rest of the agricultural community of the San Fernando Valley. Crops such as oranges, lemons, peaches, apricots, olives, alfalfa, and avocado were among the profitable harvests in Pacoima. Water supply became plentiful once the Los Angeles Aqueduct opened in 1913.

Opening ceremonies for opening of Los Angeles Aqueduct in 1913. Automobiles were beginning to overtake horses for the elite. Hansen Hill is the backdrop.

The construction of single-family residences alongside nearby orchards and ranches would begin, and for decades large families of White settlers continued to arrive in Pacoima and were the primary purchasers of land. However, recipients of Mexican land grants had also established residency throughout the area.

Access to the San Fernando Valley from the north became essential in the early 1900s. After construction of the Newhall Tunnel in 1910, the flow of traffic through Pacoima increased tremendously. Moreover, the history of that tunnel is quite interesting.

In the early years, Beal's Cut, called the San Fernando Pass, was the road that connected the Valley to the north toward San Francisco or Bakersfield.

In 1862, the State of California awarded a twenty-year contract to Charles H. Brindley, Andrés Pico, and James R. Vineyard. Their job was to cut a deep slot-like road through the steep pass to make it easier to cross for stagecoaches and travelers. They were to complete and maintain the turnpike, as well as collect tolls. Sometime during that same year, the contract was taken over by Edward F. Beale, appointed by President Abraham Lincoln as a Surveyor-General of California and Nevada, to complete the new San Fernando Road. General Beal, as they called him, had extensive holdings that bordered the nearby Fort Tejon Pass, a new development.

Beal's Cut connected the San Fernando Valley to Northern California

1872 photo of Beal's Cut, also known as San Fernando Pass

Newhall Tunnel circa 1918— The hillside was removed in the 1930's

Despite its steady growth, Pacoima residents in the early 1900's still faced the same challenge as the area's previous settlers, catastrophic flooding. Fortunately for the town, the Pacoima area, because of its geographical location, became essential to the city of Los Angeles. The L.A. County Flood Control District developed a massive project to help solve the problem. In 1928 they constructed Pacoima Dam, the tallest arch dam in the United States, at that time.

1928 photo of Pacoima Dam while under construction

With a height of 371 feet, engineers deemed Pacoima Dam one of the essential flood control projects in Los Angeles County. The dam is a concrete arch that creates the Pacoima Reservoir.

The County of Los Angeles hired Roy W. Carlson, a concrete and soil-testing engineer, when the construction of Pacoima Dam began. Carlson, who had developed the world's first Strainmeter for embedding in concrete, placed these meters in several strategic locations. They register both the vertical and horizontal movements during an earthquake.

During the 1971 Sylmar quake, these meters showed record-high accelerations (1.25g horizontal and 0.70g vertical).

The dam sustained damage in both the 71 and 94 quakes. As a result of these quakes, the County of Los Angeles began continuous monitoring using GPS.

Pacoima Dam is located on Pacoima Creek in the San Gabriel Mountains

4
Early
Schools

The history of schools in Pacoima and the San Fernando Valley accurately represents the real legacy of education in America. In the years before the founding of Pacoima, children in the area attended school at Lopez Station, which was built in the early 1860s by Catalina and Geronimo Lopez. They originally built the facility as a family home after purchasing 40 acres of land west of Mission San Fernando.

Lopez Station would eventually become known as the first English language school in the San Fernando Valley.

First grammar bunkhouse set up for education at Lopez Station. Photo taken 1882.

1890 photo of Lopez Station, owned by Geronimo and Catalina Lopez, who opened the first English language school bunker in the Valley.

Lopez Station served a multitude of purposes. It was a stagecoach line location, US Postal Office, merchandise store, and an overnight stop for Cerro Gordo Freighting Company, which transported food and supplies. It was also where Antonio Maria Ortega from the Tataviam lineage worked.

The school closed in 1884 and had 25 students that final year. The city of Los Angeles demolished this adobe in 1910 after acquiring it to make room for the Los Angeles Reservoir, an essential element of the Los Angeles Aqueduct.

The earliest school to be built in the San Fernando Valley was "Pacoima School," established in 1888. It was a simple but beautiful school building with a bell tower on top and a flag pole in the front. The school, located near the railroad tracks on second and third streets (known today as Sutter and Ralston), was completed the year after Jewett Allin purchased the town. It had four classrooms, a library office, a basement, and bathrooms.

Artist rendering of Pacoima School, built in 1888 (Artwork by Ignacio Gomez)

In a typewritten book entitled "Pacoima in 1976," they chronicled these essential facts and information relevant to this history. The book lists Prudence Harding as the first Principal of Pacoima School (there is also a street named Harding in the city of San Fernando). Survey LA reports that the flooding of 1891 destroyed the schoolhouse. Pacoima endured a host of disastrous floods throughout the 19th and 20th centuries.

In 1905, the town rebuilt Pacoima School on Norris Avenue. It is unclear where the children attended school from 1891 to 1905, but it could have been San Fernando Grammar School, established in 1889. The distance between the two schools was approximately three miles. It was not uncommon for children to walk that distance to school during that era.

Children from the Saugus/Santa Clarita area also attended San Fernando Grammar and had horrible roads and terrain to travel when going to school. Unfortunately, they did not rebuild the new school until 14 years after the flooding. It was built on Norris Ave much farther from the railroad tracks than the first one.

In California, schools had a strict rule of "No Indians," as state law prohibited Indians from attending public schools, carrying a gun, testifying in court against a white man, or intermarrying. Most of the Indians spoke Spanish that they learned during the "mission era" and had Spanish sir names given to them from the Padres. The government set up the Department of Indian Affairs to seek out reservations but never established any in San Fernando or Pacoima. It would be there that the Tataviam ancestors could have held school for their youth.

Pacoima Grammar School was rebuilt in 1905 on Norris Street. It was annexed to Los Angeles City School District in 1915 from the Pacoima Unified School district. This photo was taken 1925.

Arial shot of Pacoima Grammar School 1928. The backside on Herrick Ave became Pacoima Park (later named David Gonzales Park). The Norris side became a part of the San Fernando Gardens Housing projects. (Courtesy LA Unified School District)

The other early schools in the Valley began construction in 1888 and opened in 1889, including Santa Suzanna (Chatsworth) School, Lankershim, San Fernando, and Morningside. Before the school campuses, classes took place in temporary bunkhouses until completion of the facilities.

San Fernando Grammar School ordered their El Camino Bell for their opening in 1889. San Fernando High School opened in 1896. Ten years later, in 1906, it moved its location from Hagar Street to Brand Blvd, the current site of San Fernando Middle School. The campus operated as a facility for grades seven through twelve.

Morningside colony settled in San Fernando in the 1800s, but there is very little information on that settlement. It is unclear how many from that community resided in Pacoima since the school was near the two town's borders. They established an official school in San Fernando around the same time as San Fernando Grammar School. It appears to be an Amish or a Puritan type of community that settled in the area, but again that cannot be substantiated. However, they migrated in the 1800s and established a school.

Morningside High School kids occupied the second floor of San Fernando High on Hagar. It is unclear where they went when the school relocated. Old photos showed the Morningside Grammar children in white clothes, the girls in bonnets, and the boys with Navy style hats. That also leads to the possibility of a Puritan type of colony.

The Los Angeles City School District formed in 1853, covering grades K through 8 (grammar schools and eventually junior high schools). There were feeder elementary school districts throughout the San Fernando Valley in the early days.

In 1915, Pacoima, San Fernando, and Morningside Grammar schools received annexation to the Los Angeles City School District. Oddly, Pacoima Elementary's annexation was not listed on the LAUSD history web site and had to be verified by the Superintendent. Again Pacoima's history remains challenging to uncover, even though it is a significant historical school.

Students at San Fernando Grammar in 1912 — The school is the third oldest in the San Fernando Valley, officially opening in 1889.

San Fernando School aerial shot taken May 1925 – (Courtesy Los Angeles Unified School District)

In 1890, the city of Los Angeles formed the Los Angeles High School District and annexed San Fernando Union High School in 1914. Part of the reason for annexation was the Los Angeles Aqueduct and Owens River water battles. LA had contentious elections and debates concerning the San Fernando Valley's annexation to the city of Los Angeles, and the allocation of Owens River water. Only a few locations were able to remain as cities in the Valley, one of which was San Fernando, incorporating in 1911.

However, allowing Los Angeles to annex their schools provided access to running water on their school campuses. It cost a great deal of money to improve these newly annexed schools with pipes for water distribution.

The city of San Fernando made early attempts to have Pacoima be a part of their city but eventually gave up when the city of Los Angeles fought back firmly.

Los Angeles Unified School District was formed in 1961 and merged elementary schools, junior high, and high schools under the same umbrella. LAUSD became the second-largest school district in the country, trailing only to New York City Department of Education.

Morningside secondary school. Group portrait of students taken in 1890. Morningside Colony settled in San Fernando in the 1880's. (San Fernando Valley Historical Society)

Aerial shot of Morningside School 1925 located 576 N Maclay Ave, San Fernando, CA
(Courtesy LA Unified School District)

San Fernando High in background 1911. School was established in 1896. It was located on Hagar and Fifth street. Man standing by fence outside school yard.

San Fernando High's school photo was used on post cards promoting the city. This photo was taken in the early 1900.

Aerial shot of San Fernando High School taken in 1925
(Courtesy Los Angeles Unified School District)

Haddon Street School house opened in 1926 at 10115 Hadden Ave. The first principal was Louise Seyler. She stayed until 1939. They got a new school building in the 50s. Photo taken November 6, 1939 (Courtesy Los Angeles Unified School District)

5
Mexican Migration

It was in the early 1900s that Mexican immigrants began to flee both the Revolutionary War (1910) and the Cristero War (1924) to seek safety in the United States. Many families came on horse and carriage (some on foot) taking as long as a month to travel from Mexico to Los Angeles and, ultimately, Pacoima.

The Mexican Revolution came about because Mexico was beginning to modernize. The rich were prospering and living well, while workers lived a life condemned to hard labor.

Some revolutionary leaders fought to change the class divide. Leaders such as Francisco Madera and Pancho Villa demonstrated in 1910 that ordinary people could revolt and resist their oppression. While this resulted in many Mexicans fleeing, it also allowed some to receive farmland and gave them the ability to profit from their hard work.

The 1917 Constitution supposedly resolved some of the class issues, but the Catholic Church was very wealthy and known to favor the rich at the expense of the poor. It was one of the core issues with the Revolutionary War. The constitution had placed some restrictions on the church resulting in their resistance.

When a power struggle ensued, the Mexican government began persecuting citizens and church clergy, forcing families to leave. This persecution led to the Cristero War, a battle between the influential Catholic Church and the Mexican government. This war was in full effect by 1927 and in the end, claimed 90,000 lives.

Traveling from Mexico and crossing the border was not an easy feat for the immigrants. Most were on foot, trying not to be detected. While researching when Mexicans first began immigrating to Pacoima, our team uncovered one family that arrived in the early 1900s. They were the Lozano family, and their history tells a compelling story of fleeing Mexico in 1918 and arriving in Pacoima.

The Lozano family was one that traveled the dangerous roads from Jalisco, Mexico, across the plains on a covered wagon with a priest by their side. After a month of travel, they arrived in Los Angeles and heard about Pacoima. That is where these families decided to settle down.

Photo taken in 1927 of families who migrated from Jalisco, Mexico fleeing the violence. Jesus and Valeria Lozano and their children are in this photo along with the priest who traveled with them. (Courtesy of Manual and Lupe Hernandez collection)

There was not much in the town when they arrived. Pacoima consisted of dirt roads, rocks, fruit trees, and houses that were shacks. Jesus and Valeria Lozano had nine children while living on Judd Street. There were no hospitals close. Some of their kids were born in a garage by Gomez Market across the street from their home.

Jesus Lozano was initially a baker but became employed for the City of Los Angeles, laying slab foundations for sidewalks and structures. As avowed Catholics, the Lozano family also helped build Guardian Angel Church in 1929.

Valeria Villanueva Lozano, Jesus Lozano and Angelica Lozano late 1920's on Judd Street in Pacoima. (Courtesy Manuel & Lupe Hernandez collection)

Guardian Angel Church was built in 1929. It was the first Catholic Church in Pacoima. The Lozano's were a part of building and the opening of the church. Their family stories tell of how mass was delivered in the open field until the church was complete.

(Courtesy of Manuel & Lupe Hernandez collection)

Aerial view of agricultural land in Pacoima taken in 1924

Paula "Lupe" Lozano Hernandez is one of the children of Jesus and Valeria Lozano. She was born in a garage located on the property of one of the earliest markets in Pacoima. She tells how Pacoima was nothing but empty land during her childhood.

"You could see all the way to San Fernando," she said.

Paula also described Pacoima as being divided by race. The east side of the railroad tracks was mostly Mexican, while Whites inhabited the west side. The same division was true in San Fernando, except the Whites were on the east side of the tracks and Mexicans on the west.

Lupe and Carmen Lozano with brother in door on Judd Street during the 40's. (Courtesy Manuel & Lupe Hernandez collection)

The early settlements in both Pacoima and San Fernando clearly showed racial division. Whites in both towns did not want Mexicans moving into their neighborhoods. However, Pacoima and San Fernando were among the few places in the valley where minorities could live at all.

The Los Angeles County Deed Book recorded property on December 31, 1924, sold by San Fernando Mission Land Company, which Leslie C. Brand formed in 1895. The property encompassed today's Mission Hills area, Granada Hills, and some of their surrounding parcels. One of the infamous conditions of the sale was:

"The said premises shall not be sold nor leased to any person other than one of the white or Caucasian race."

These standard real estate stipulations were predominant in the San Fernando Valley and remained in place until January 1, 1935. However, racial covenants remained well into the 1980s, despite the passing of fair housing laws in 1966. Real estate agents were notorious for refusing to sell or lease to people of color for decades and likely still practice this is some areas today.

Victoria and Connie Hernandez pose with young boys. Mike Hernandez is working on the car. Photo taken on Filmore Street in the 1930's.

(Courtesy of Manual and Lupe Hernandez Collection)

Another challenge that Mexicans faced was burial after death. There were no cemeteries in Pacoima. San Fernando Pioneer Memorial Cemetery, once known as Morningside Cemetery, was an early location. It was established in 1874 when Charles Maclay first purchased the town. However, they ended funerals in the 1930s. Allegedly only Caucasians were allowed to be buried there. The Valley's oldest graveyard is the San Fernando Mission Cemetery. Initially established in 1800, that cemetery had a separate location for the Native Americans, and there are claims they denied burials to people of Mexican heritage.

Some Pacoima families shared stories of having to bury their loved ones in Los Angeles due to their heritage. The same scenario was true for hospitals, who would not treat people of color and forced them to get treatment or give birth at Los Angeles County Hospital.

Mariquita Negri (1886-1942)
(Photo courtesy of Libertad Ayala)

The San Fernando Mission Cemetery denied burial to Mariquita Negri due to her heritage. Her lineage was Spanish Moor, but her family assimilated to the Mexican culture and changed her name from Negri to Negrete to further blend in. She now rests at Calvary Cemetery on Whittier Blvd in East Los Angeles.

Unfortunately, there are many who suffered the experience of burial discrimination throughout in the San Fernando Valley. Juliana Canchola Ayala, Negri's daughter, was also denied services in San Fernando as well.

Daniel Lozano was born in Pacoima in 1933. He attended Pacoima Grammar School and told a compelling story about the treatment of Mexican Americans in school. His experience describes how the White kids and the kids of color were often separated, and made to feel inferior.

One stringent rule in school was no speaking Spanish. It was this rule that led many Mexican families to avoid teaching their children the Spanish language. The Lozano family spoke their native tongue in their home, but the rule was to refrain speaking it in school. Lozano once forgot and spoke Spanish to his friend. Overheard by a teacher, he was pulled aside to have his mouth vigorously washed out with soap. Lozano spoke about the incident and what is was like at Pacoima Grammar School.

"There used to be colored people, about three of them, I don't remember their names, but I remember they used to seat us all in one group. Mexicans and Colored people on one side and the white in front. If they catch you speaking Spanish, you get punished. Put some soap around your mouth.

"It happened to me once," he added. "I was talking Spanish to my friend, and they caught me and took me to the front office, and I got punished. They got some soap and put it around my mouth."

When asked how he felt when that happened, Lozano replied, "Well, you feel kind of humiliated, you know, in those days. After that happened to me, I don't feel like going to school no more. I wasn't interested in school because of that."

There were also challenges in the work environment. Lozano, who began working the fields at an early age, shared his experience.

"I started working in the fields to help out. They didn't pay much at that time, but they used to pay a dollar fifty way back for working in the fields. Not per hour, per day. It was the most we could get. With a dollar fifty a day, we would get about six to seven dollars a week. That's why I didn't do too much education because most of the time, I would help my Dad working. Then I keep on working...I started working in the fields since I was 13 or 14 years old."

When Lozano turned 19, he was one of the first Mexicans to work at General Motors. In 1953, when he first started working there, he described the atmosphere as rough.

"Well, they used to give you the worst jobs in the plant. You know, physical work. I used to get home, and I used to lay down, and that was it, but I would say I'm not gonna give up. I gotta fight 'em back. It was me, my brother and one of my friends. At that time, we were the only Mexicans working there at General Motors. We showed them it wasn't true what they believed about Mexicans. That we were lazy. They used to tell us you're not gonna be here Monday cause your gonna be tired. You're gonna be drunk. I said ok, that's what you think, that's fine. But we fight them. Not by fist, but physically. Show them we can do the job. We can do it. It wasn't easy, but we proved to ourselves we can do it."

Lozano says that after showing they were good workers, General Motors began hiring more Mexicans.

"In 1955, they hired more Mexicans than anyone else," he said.

He also described what Pacoima was like.

"We used to have only one market. We used to call it Tien Tien La Blanca. There used to be some Jewish people, and they used to help families, especially the families that needed it. They used to give credit or whatever they needed. They used to sell everything, old tools, whatever you need. Before, it was easier here in Pacoima to raise your own, like a little farm. Have your own chickens, cows, and goats. We used to feed ourselves a meal with the eggs, chickens, you know. All that. It was fun. I used to have fun."

Lozano remembers hearing stories from his parents about coming to America and settling in Pacoima.

"They came from a little town named San Julian Jalisco. It's a little town, but now it's different. I can remember stories about traveling from Mexico from my Dad and my mother. They came in through El Paso on one of those, what you call them a wagon or buggy? But they took a long time, about a month to get from El Paso over here to Pacoima. There wasn't only my father, there was about 5 or 6 families together that came all the way from Mexico. They traveled all the way and settled here in Pacoima."

Daniel Lozano and brother Jesus Lozano, Jr. in the 1950's
(Courtesy of Manual and Lupe Hernandez Collection)

The **Dramatic Club of** was a group of Mexican residents that performed plays and music for the community in the 40's. They had costumes and instruments for their performances.

(Courtesy of Manual and Lupe Hernandez Collection)

Irene Diaz is another longtime Pacoima native. Born in 1941 to a Mexican mother and Filipino father, she provides an early glimpse into the town's multi-ethnic history. During her interview for the "PacoimaStories" documentary, Diaz told a captivating account of how her family arrived in Pacoima and what life was like during those early years.

"My father and my mother wanted to open a business, and they started a ranch, a flower business, ten acres on Foothill and Pierce Street before anything was there. My mother, at the time, was living in San Fernando, and they decided to buy a house here in Pacoima on Mercer Street, and that's where all of us were born. My father started putting in new foundation for each one of us because there was seven of us, but it never got completed. That's where I was born years ago, back when you couldn't have kids here in the valley. You had to go all the way to the county. That's where I was born in LA County (hospital). Most families would have to travel over there because there were no hospitals.

"My mother Mary Guerrero was born in Clovis (California), next door to Fresno, a little town up north, but she was raised in Corona, in San Bernardino County. During the time my mother and my father met, they were working in the ranches. Years back, the only jobs available were on ranches, especially for Mexican Americans. My father was Filipino. At that time, when he migrated from the Philippines, he started working on the ranch. And that's how they got together. Working on ranches. Most families, Mexican American families used to go out of here, the town, and go up north to work on ranches cause that's the only job that was available then. And that's how a lot of people met in ranches."

Irene also tells of her unique experience with Filipino and Mexican culture.

"My mother and my father had a lot of parties. We used to kill pigs and chickens. We raised chickens, pigeons, and roosters. Then you could have fighting roosters. So, my father had a fighting rooster, and we used to go to Saugus and get together and have rooster fights. They still have them in the Philippines. Even here, my cousins in Corona have roosters. We used to have Filipino parties here in Pacoima. People brought crates and crates of peaches, plums, fruits, onions, and tomatoes. My father used to have stacks and stacks of crates. They used to bring them. I guess it's something Filipinos did. It was beautiful because everything was dirt. I remember when I used to go to Rinaldi, where Kmart is. It used to be dirt. When it got wet, I used to like driving my car so you could slide. I used to slide."

In the forties and fifties, when Diaz was in school, she explained the demographics of Pacoima.

"During the time when I was going to Pacoima Elementary, it was integrated. Let's put it like this, that school was integrated with all the races you could possibly think of. And that's the way I grew up. And that's where I met Ritchie Valens in elementary school. We went to elementary all the way through junior high and San Fernando High School."

Irene Diaz' mother, Mary Guerrero (L), brother Randy Guerrero (C), and sister Patsy Guerrero picking grapes on Filmore St. in 1960

Irene Diaz' sister Mary Guerrero Jr. (L), mother Mary Guerrero Sr. (C), and sister Irma Guerrero (R) on Filmore St in 1960's

Irene Diaz father Pedro Guerrero with mom Mary and sister Belinda Guerrero during the 1960s (Courtesy Eileen Becerra)

The early Mexican migration into Pacoima laid the foundation for Latino growth in the town. Many of these migrants raised highly successful children, defying every stereotype imaginable.

The Camacho family arrived in Pacoima in the late 1930s from Santa Fe, New Mexico. They stayed with family members at different places (like many other Mexican migrants) until finally settling in Pacoima. Diane Corinne Velarde Hernandez explained the living conditions when her grandparents, the Camachos', arrived in the town.

"My grandpa was finally able to scrape up enough money to buy a lot on Mercer Street in Pacoima. That became the family's home on 13122 Mercer Street. The main streets like Van Nuys Blvd, were not paved, and many of the side streets were not paved either. People built their own homes first or lived in tents until they could get a better home. It wasn't just a house you lived in — it was a neighborhood, a community. You knew everybody in the neighborhood. And in our community, you became Comadres. You baptized each other's children. You were their Godparents for first communions or confirmation. It was a big extended family for the most part."

1952 — Diane Corinne Velarde Hernandez on Mercer Street where her grandparents purchased their property lot. They bought a tract home a few years after this photo. (Courtesy Velarde archives)

Late 1950's on Pinney Street. Velarde's maternal grandparents Genaro and Aurelia Camacho (left) with Mr. & Mrs. Martinez. (Courtesy Velarde archives)

"The lot that my grandparents bought was 50 ft by 150 ft. It was a deep lot, but narrow. The first house we lived in, my grandfather poured a slab of cement concrete and then built a wood structure," added Hernandez.

"We had a curtain in the middle to make it a two-bedroom. We also had an outhouse. Then we had a kitchen that was apart from that building. All of that was in the back part of the lot. It was in 1954-55 that they bought a home from model homes that were being built in our community."

Genevieve Camacho married Ignacio Velarde, and they had three children Diane, Michael, and Jimmy. Diane went on to become an educator at San Fernando High School, and Michael is a biomedical engineer. Jimmy Velarde is a television and film industry veteran who has won multiple Emmy Awards.

It was from families like these that Pacoima's Mexican American community grew. They endured the challenges of migration and marginalization to become successful, productive Americans. This community has faced housing discrimination, job, and career limitations while still forging forward to overcome social disparity. As Daniel Lozano said, "we fight back, not with our fist, but hard work."

While other Latin American countries have immigrated to Pacoima, it was those from Mexico that have defined the town's history. It is the Mexican community that later got involved in civil rights for Chicano's and rebelled against the injustices of society while forging ahead with education. Pacoima salutes those proud Mexican Americans and their legacy in this town.

Ida Granados Moreno & Genevieve Camacho Velarde on Pinney St. and Lehigh Ave. in 1951 (Courtesy Velarde archives)

6
Japanese Migration

The Japanese history of Pacoima is one that has been typically ignored, much like the Native American history. Most of the town's residents know little or nothing about it.

The story of how the Japanese community migrated and the challenges they faced before and after World War II is compelling. Because of their success in farming and agriculture, the state passed laws that made it difficult to forge ahead. In 1913, California enacted the "Alien Land Act," which put limits on agricultural land ownership and leases.

The apparent reason for this and subsequent laws was that Japanese and other minority cultures were skilled and hugely successful in agriculture. These laws provided ways to tip the scale against successful people of color.

What is impressive, however, is how they outsmarted the government by finding ways around these racist land ownership laws and flourished despite the obstacles.

It was in the 1880s the Japanese began to migrate to Hawaii and slowly found their way to San Francisco. After experiencing negative racial sentiment there, they ended up in Los Angeles by the 1890s. With the vast farming opportunities in the San Fernando Valley, a significant number began to purchase land and settle. The farms were highly successful, outperforming the White landowners and creating an uproar from local farmers. These landowners lobbied state officials who enacted The California Alien Land Law of 1913 (also known as the Webb-Haney Act). This law prohibited "aliens ineligible for citizenship" from owning agricultural land or possessing long-term leases over it. Although Chinese, Indian, and Korean immigrant farmers in California were affected, the law primarily targeted the Japanese.

The Japanese were somewhat limited to where they lived in the Valley due to extreme racism and ultimately settled in North Hollywood and Pacoima. They began to find creative ways to own land by putting property titles in the names of their American born children. However, complaints from White farmers continued, who forced the passing of another law. The California Alien Land Law of 1920 continued the 1913 law while filling many of its loopholes. Among the loopholes filled were short term leases, which were no longer allowed. Owning of stock in companies that acquired agricultural land was also forbidden, and guardians or agents of ineligible aliens were required to submit an annual report on their activities. The 1920 Alien Land Law was a reaction to the intensification of anti-Japanese sentiment, and to the fact that the 1913 Alien Land Law was doing little to stem Japanese immigration to California.

The Japanese farmers, despite the harsh rules, continued to farm in the San Fernando Valley effectively. They were particularly successful with green onions, carrots, and seasonal vegetables.

It was on December 7, 1941, that Japan bombed Pearl Harbor, and a reign of terror began that engulfed their living landscape. Ten months later, President Theodore Roosevelt ordered all persons of Japanese descent to report to train stations with one bag. Trains delivered them to internment camps where they endured prison-like living conditions and poor treatment by military guards. Interrogations determined if they were loyal to the emperor of Japan or the United States of America. The government seized their land and assets. Moreover, the already built-in racism was further exasperated and raged throughout the West Coast.

The government forced Japanese-American families to surrender themselves. Trains and busses transported them to internment camps where they were processed. One bag was all they could bring.

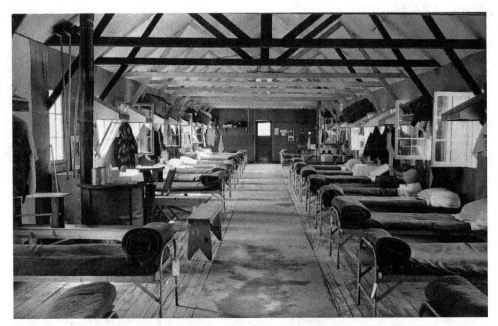

Housing barracks at Manzanar Internment Camp

Among the many thousands of Japanese Americans forced into the internment camps is James Higashida, who went to Manzanar. Located 230 miles north of Los Angeles, Manzanar is the most notorious of these prison facilities.

"It was very difficult. Apparently, the houses were ready, and we came in busloads. In May, Manzanar, it was cold and windy, the wind was just horrendous. We were given a mattress cover, and we had to go to pile of hay and stuffed it in, and that was our mattress for about six months. And the bad part of that was there were ticks, and we used to get bites, and it was very difficult."

Many Japanese delayed returning home from internment camps because they knew the degree of prejudice would be substantial. Re-establishing life after the experience of internment camps proved to be challenging for the Japanese-American community. Pre-war wealth, although modest, had all but disappeared, and coupled with the city of Los Angeles's housing shortage, they were forced to find alternative locations. Empty army barracks and trailer camps would serve as housing.

Trailer Park Camp in Sun Valley in the1950s.
(Courtesy SFVJACC)

Open displays of prejudice gripped the nation as fears were stoked.

The Los Angeles Times reported approximately five-thousand Japanese Americans with prewar roots in the Valley, lived in government trailer camps in the surrounding area from 1946 to 1956. Some community members recalled how frightening it was without money and no place to go.

Those living in trailer camps reported residing in poor living conditions coupled with backlash from nearby white homeowners. When the camps began to close, the residents were able to purchase or rent homes in the east S.F. Valley. Pacoima continued its legacy of being the unofficial minority section of the San Fernando Valley. The last trailer park site closed eleven years after the war ended, which demonstrates the struggles endured during those hard times.

2,364 Japanese-Americans populated Pacoima by 1960 and had fully integrated into the fabric of the town. With a Gardeners Association, fish markets, appliance repair shops, landscapers, and hardware stores, the town flourished with the character of a thriving working-class community. A few barriers broke down when the San Fernando High Class of 1958 saw a Japanese-American Student Body President named Harry Muranaka and vice president Nancy Fuluda. Officers of the Kiwanis Club of Pacoima included Dr. H.E. Hashioka, which is a small example of a town fighting for inclusion despite a well-defined history of exclusion.

In 1959 several men, together with a residuum of charter members of the Pre-World War II Farmers Association, decided to pull their money together to build a living memorial. They built the San Fernando Valley Japanese American Community Center (JACC), a remembrance of the hard struggles and sacrifices endured by their parents. Located on Branford Street in Pacoima, the center still serves the community today.

A core concern of its programs is reverence for the various aspects of Japanese American history, including preserving their culture. The JACC projects include courses for all ages, food programs, and cultural dancing, among many other things. Most importantly, they preserve American history while giving recognition to World War II veterans, physicians, and prominent community members.

The San Fernando Valley Japanese American Community Center is located of Branford Street in Pacoima. It was built in 1959

Founders of the Japanese American Cultural Center from left: Berry Tamura, Mitsuo Usui, and Tom Ikuda (Artwork by Ignacio Gomez)

One of the most prominent Japanese trailblazers was Dr. Mary Sakaguchi Oda founder of Serra Memorial Hospital in Sun Valley. Her family suffered through a horrific experience at the Manzanar concentration camp. However, her resilience and life philosophy were inspiring. After having her education at medical school interrupted and forced to endure inhumane circumstances, she became a pillar of the Pacoima community.

Dr. Sakaguchi Oda was born in 1920, one of 7 children to Shiichiro and Hisoji Sakaguchi. She was born in Fresno, where her father owned 150 acres of farmland. It was one of the biggest farms in Fresno, and they grew peaches and grapes. Even during the depression, the agriculture business flourished. The Sakaguchi family made enough money that by 1940, they were able to pay cash for their home on 2 ½ acres in North Hollywood where they continued farming. North Hollywood and Pacoima were the only areas that allowed non-Caucasians to lease or own.

The Japanese were not as trusting of banks and gave money to what they called the Kama Mushi, who also set up the Japanese language school. That was how they were able to expand their businesses or start new ones. They put money in every month, and when they needed it, it was there.

Mary's father was treasurer for the Farmers Association, and before the mandate by President Roosevelt was issued, they knew, through the underground, something was about to go down. So, they changed the names of the officers, making it harder to target them.

On the day Pearl Harbor was bombed, the FBI came into their home without knocking and said, "We're FBI agents, and we're looking for contraband; radios, shortwave radios, and guns." After searching, they found nothing. However, signs were posted shortly after with instructions to vacate and report to the train station. It was a terrifying experience for them.

Before the war, the Sakaguchi family was doing well financially. The kids helped farm the land, and all of them went to college. Mary was in medical school when this all happened. She had to leave in the middle of the semester.

She explained that one of her friends, an Italian boy, was studying with her when an air raid alarm went off. They turned off the lights and were heading out. The boy squeezed her hand and said, "when they come over, you'll protect me, won't you?" Suddenly the fear was real, and she said, "Don't worry, they're not coming over."

Dr. Mary Sakaguchi Oda spent three and a half long years at Manzanar.

Before they left for the internment camp, the family locked up all their belongings in a small house in the back. When they returned, everything was gone. Fortunately, they owned their home. For many Japanese families who had a mortgage, their houses no longer belonged to them.

Dr. Mary Sakaguchi Oda (artwork by Ignacio Gomez)

There are many noteworthy Pacoima families of Japanese descent. One of them was the Takayama family, who arrived in the San Fernando Valley around 1916. Originally farmers located in North Hollywood, the family migrated to Pacoima in 1952 following their release from Manzanar.

Nancy and Patricia Takayama both attended Haddon Elementary, Pacoima Junior High, and San Fernando High School. They have also stayed active with the San Fernando Valley Japanese Community Center, which was a gathering place for first and second generations. Their father, Toshio Takayama, was a farmer who grew up in North Hollywood and worked as a young boy on his father's farm. His father was able to take the test to become a citizen.

Toshio Takayama

"My first recollection of Pacoima was before the community center was built," said Nancy Takayama during her PacoimaStories interview.

"It was even before the Golden State Freeway was built. Directly across the street from the community center, which was Branford, there was Roger Jessup Dairy, and there were cows and where you go to get your milk. Just down the street, there was a Manfull Dairy, which was also a place where you bring your glass bottles and get your milk. It was the dairy that our family went to. But in between those two dairies there this strawberry farm and it was operated by the Oda family. The reason why I know that is because of the girls. There were two girls the same age as I was. We would go across the street, and they would have this fruit stand, and you could buy your strawberries; you could buy your green onions. We would also pick up my grandmother because she sometimes worked out there to help out the family. That was Pacoima back in the fifties.

My father was a farmer, pre-war, who grew up in the North Hollywood area. He and his father had a farm, and that's what most of the Japanese did when they came to the San Fernando Valley because they were able to cultivate the land when no other families could. For some reason, they said the Japanese were able to come in cultivate the land and produce things like green onions, basically seasonal foods that produced yearly."

When asked why they choose this town, Nancy responded.

"It's not like they were given any choices. After World War II, most of the people could not come back or chose not to come back to the area that they lived in. Because it was the west coast, there was still a lot of racial prejudice. My parents chose to first go to Chicago, and other relatives went to Detroit, and my grandparents went to New Jersey. This was kind of away from the basic war zone. A lot of prejudice was held for the Japanese on the west coast. So, when they came back, of course, they wanted to come back to the San Fernando Valley cause that's where they were raised. Except they could only lease the land that they chose to live on, and even leasing the land was temporary.

"Some of the people, pre-war were smart and took the advice of Se Fu Ji, who was a Japanese immigrant who went to USC to become an attorney but couldn't take the bar because he was an immigrant. He suggested to members of the Japanese community to purchase land in the name of their American born children. So, some of the property that exists here in Pacoima was still owned by the Japanese. When World War II was breaking out, the government froze the assets of all Japanese Americans. After the war, when the funds were unfrozen, the land was still in the name of America born children.

"This land (JACC) was sold at a lower cost from another Japanese American family. With the funds that were frozen from the Hollywood Burbank Farmers Association, they were able to construct this facility here. When the Japanese came back to live here in the San Fernando Valley, no one would sell them land outside of Pacoima. So, the block that my family ended up purchasing a house on in 1952 had maybe about five or six Japanese American families. Then you go down the next block and another five or six Japanese American families. Anything from west of San Fernando Road had this enormous amount of Japanese American families. I don't even think it went very far past Laurel Canyon because when I went to Pacoima Junior High, there was a lot. I noticed there was a lot of Japanese American kids, but Pacoima Junior High seemed to be mainly white.

"But I remember Pacoima in the early fifties when we moved into the house my parents bought. There were no fences. This was wonderful because, with no fences, your back yard was up against the neighbors back yard. I could cut through everybody's backyard to go to school. So, in elementary we could walk to school, whereas now, that's a thing of the past. People even left their doors unlocked. That was wonderful. My house and the house across the street were the first to have sidewalks. No streets, but we had a sidewalk, which was kind of interesting. You can see what it has become now. Light post, speed bumps, and things like that."

Patricia Takayama, Nancy's sister, is an author who has written about the impact of the Japanese internment. During her interview, she spoke about this period of American history.

"This whole history of what happened to the Japanese, really not only impacted what happened in Pacoima, it affects all of US history and how minorities were treated. We always think the worst thing that happened in the US was how people were slaves. Afro American were made into slaves. But the internment of Japanese was such a significant impact on how things changed in the United States, and it isn't even discussed in any of our schoolbooks. In some places, even in law school, one woman said when they study constitutional law, the case is never even discussed. She said none of the Japanese cases were brought up in constitutional law class. We have a history that doesn't include us. That's what the story is. If we don't write it, it doesn't get done."

Patricia also provided some key details about what happened when the concentration camps were closed, and the Japanese went back home.

"A lot of people didn't go back home right away. Everybody that could moved to the Midwest or some other locations to get jobs. Because no one was anxious to move back to the west coast because they knew that the degree of prejudice was still really strong. So, I guess people trickled back and resettled. There were places where they could stay, maybe in Buddhist churches and maybe some boarding houses. But for the most part, there was a tremendous influx to the Southern California area because there was a war industry, and a lot of people moved to the San Fernando Valley.

"Here, the Chevy plant popped up, Lockheed, and a lot of industry that supported the war. People moved here from the south and all over the place. And that's when the largest influx of Afro-American came to the valley. There was this infusion of multi-cultural values that came to the valley during the war. So, when people wanted to come back to the valley, there wasn't any place for them to stay because a lot of the farmland that they had been working had been eaten up by tract housing and the industry. What ended up happening was there were areas of trailer camps where the Japanese moved in, and there were still barracks that Caucasians rented (to Japanese) on a temporary basis until they could get jobs or find farmland. So, part of what happened is people weren't settling in the same locations they lived in before because they weren't available. One of the areas very open to the Japanese and other minorities was this area of the east valley called Pacoima."

Patricia Takayama also spoke about growing up in Pacoima and the racism she experienced.

"I'm 68, and I was in elementary school in the 50s. It was still close enough after the war where, on the way home from school, people would call me Jap. In the fifties, there were a lot of Japanese in Pacoima because it was a place they could buy homes and not suffer a lot of discrimination. I went to Haddon Avenue Elementary, which is two blocks away from Pacoima Junior High School. I was there when they were still doing take cover drills during the cold war period. I remember the day of the plane crash (at Pacoima Junior High), well that plane crash was two blocks away and I remember how the building shook. I thought aww this is what they were talking about, something horrible is happening, a building was bombed or an earthquake or something. It becomes a horrible memory that you don't forget about because you witnessed it.

"There were so many families. For the most part, all of the Afro Americans were only allowed to live on the east side of San Fernando Road. On our side, there wasn't any Afro-Americans at least not in elementary, maybe one in my junior high. But for the most part, they lived in the projects that were south of Van Nuys Blvd., the middle-class lived north of Van Nuys Blvd. and there were really nice homes. But they couldn't live outside this area until much later."

The Japanese community contributed a great deal to the Pacoima community, and although housing restrictions have changed, some still live there.

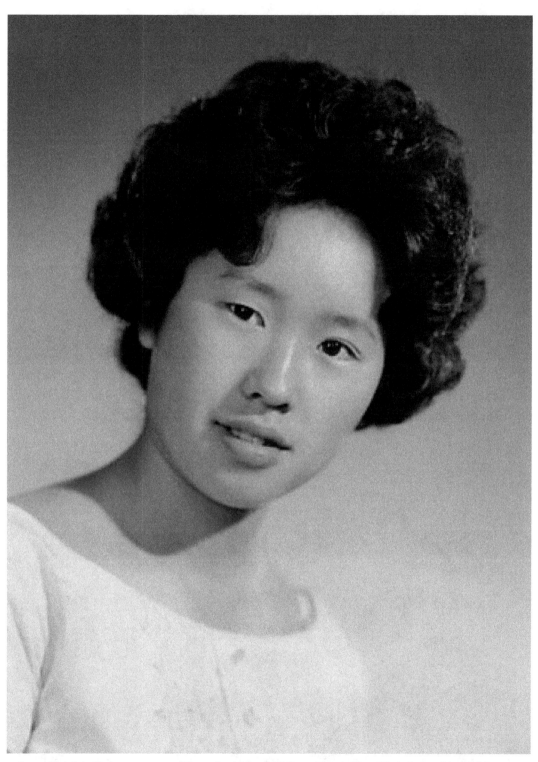

Patricia Takayama was Class President of Pacoima Junior High School in 1961

San Fernando Valley Japanese American Community Center's Obon Dancers celebrate Pacoima History Day in 2018. Nancy Takayama (right) is a Pacoima Historical Society Executive Board Member.

L-R Alina Grandison, Patricia Takayama, Alexis Grandison at the 2017 Pacoima Holiday Parade.

7

Hansen Dam

The building of Hansen Dam brought world significance to the Pacoima area. After devastating floods drenched Pacoima in 1938, the US Army Corp of Engineers built the largest earth-filled reservoir in the world. For decades San Fernando Valley residents flocked to enjoy the recreation facilities created by the city of Los Angeles who later leased land.

However, the story of Hansen Dam also has a seldom told beginning. To build the dam, the Army Corp of Engineers seized land via eminent domain from Homer and Marie Hansen, who were very prominent landowners in the area. Their story is a forgotten part of Pacoima's history.

Homer Alfred Hansen was born on November 8, 1872, in Logan, Ohio. He was a doctor who invested in land development. Hansen first came to California in 1891 and spent time with the Tataviam tribe elder Sespe, who joined him scouting out Big Tujunga. He returned to Ohio to become a doctor, attending Rush Medical School in Chicago. However, after his doctor told him only to expect a few more years to live, Hansen went back to California in 1903. Once regaining his health, he built his rock house and a two-story lodge in Big Tujunga. The Hansen Lodge became a fashionable resort that attracted a high class of society for many years.

Hansen Lodge was the talk of the elite in the 1920s. They came to relax and enjoy the many stories of Dr. Hansen. A flood wiped out the lodge in 1926, and they sold the upper section of the area for the construction of Big Tujunga Dam.   Hansen rebuilt the lodge in 1931. He also purchased land in Los Angeles, Kern, and San Diego Counties.

Hansen was the founder and general manager of Tujunga Water and Power. He was also the organizer and President of Searchlight Bank & Trust and Searchlight Railroad of Nevada.

He married Marie Huber in 1920. The two owned a horse ranch at the current location of Hansen Dam, which was called Hansen Heights. Years after the land seizure, the entire area became known as Lake View Terrace.

The Hansens also owned Hansen Lodge in Big Tujunga, had a home in South Pasadena and were also responsible for developing the small community of Cache Creek, five miles north of Mojave. Homer Hansen was 88 when he passed away in 1960. They had two sons, Homer and Albert, along with two daughters Anna and Mary.

Dr. Homer A. Hansen, California, 1904
Courtesy of Little Landers Historical Society/Bolton Hall Museum, Tujunga, CA

Dr. Homer A. Hansen and his dog

Photo courtesy of Little Landers Historical Society/Bolton Hall Museum, Tujunga, CA

Hansen Lodge
ca 1931

Hansen Lodge was a hub for elite, wealthy visitors. Photo taken in 1931.

In February and March 1938, a pair of Pacific storms drenched the Valley. The storms killed an estimated 115 people in what became at that time, one of the worst natural disasters in Southern California history. Roads washed away, and people became stranded as floodwaters engulfed the Valley, forcing evacuations.

After the first storm hit, it left 4.4 inches of rain and minor flooding. It was the second storm on March 1 that had gale-force winds and 10 inches of rainfall that ended March 3, resulting in massive damage. The Tujunga wash reached its peak flow after the Big Tujunga Dam began emergency spillway releases. The floodwaters swept through the area after escaping the normal channels of Tujunga Creek.

The Hansen Lodge was lost as the stormwater surged 5 feet over the dam spillway, whose crest height was 200 feet. The building was beyond repair with only a chimney left standing.

Flooding in 1938 in Big Tujunga after the third day of torrential rain and a broken levee

This disaster ignited the US Army Corp of Engineers to seize the ranch land owned by the Hansens. Hansen Dam's construction began in 1939 and was a two-mile long, 97-foot-high dam built to control the runoff and floodwaters. Construction took eight months less than expected. Unlike most dams, the design was to distribute water versus conserve it. The total cost to build Hansen Dam was thirteen million dollars.

1939 Construction of Hansen Dam
(Creative Commons Public Domain)

1939 Construction of Hansen Dam
(Creative Commons Public Domain)

IN ELEVEN PARTS — 130 PAGES

Part II — LOCAL NEWS — 16 Pages

TIMES OFFICE
202 West First Street

CC   SUNDAY MORNING, AUGUST 18, 1940.   CITY NEWS—EDITORIAL

WORLD'S LARGEST EARTH-FILLED STRUCTURE

Hansen Dam Dedicated

Largest Earth-Fill
Reservoir in World
Cost $13,000,000

Oratory flowed over the new Hansen Dam in San Fernando Valley yesterday when the largest earth-fill dam in the world was dedicated with a marching band and flying colors.

Designed to control the turbulent floodwaters of the Big and Little Tujunga rivers, the 10,500-foot-long structure was built by the Guy F. Atkinson Co. under direction of United States Engineers of the War Department under Lieut. Col. Edwin C. Kelton in cooperation with the Los Angeles County flood control office. It was started Sept. 1, 1938.

AHEAD OF SCHEDULE

More than a year ahead of schedule and well ahead of the winter rains, the dam with its gigantic concrete spillways is ready.

Before the dedicatory exercises, which were attended by more than 2500 persons, a luncheon atop the spillway bridge was given by Contractor Guy F. Atkinson honoring all responsible for the success of the $13,000,000 project. Army engineers, Los Angeles County flood control officers, construction superintendents, night foremen, Councilmen, Mayors and Chamber of Commerce officials from all parts of the country were introduced.

ENGINEERING MIRACLE

"This great dam is just one more addition to a long list of engineering miracles," declared

AT CEREMONY—Luncheon scene yesterday above spillway of Hansen Dam, showing dam in background. The structure was built at $13,000,000 cost.

Following the construction and dedication of Hansen Dam, the US Army Corp of Engineers leased 1550 acres to the City of Los Angeles for a new recreational facility. Initially called Holiday Lake, it quickly became a popular location for boating, picnicking, horseback riding, hiking and fishing. Hollywood celebrities and Southern California elites frequently visited the lake and purchased property in the surrounding area.

Boating, swimming, and fishing were in high demand on this warm summer day at Hansen Dam in 1962.

The name Holiday Lake eventually evolved into Hansen Dam Park, becoming the San Fernando Valley's biggest attraction. Events of great interest were held there, such as the Los Angeles Sports Car Road Race, hosted by the California Sports Car Club in the fifties. The legendary actor Clark Gable served as an honorary chairman for the event in 1955.

Hansen Dam Park attracted thousands of visitors every year for a variety of activities operated by the City of Los Angeles. The recreational area was well known for featuring a series of horse stables, which had been operating along Foothill Blvd since shortly after completion of the dam. It was one of the few remaining areas in Los Angeles zoned for horses.

The park also featured children's pony rides, a miniature train ride, a full-size merry-go-round, and a beautiful 18-hole golf course where many celebrities played.

However, the lakes biggest attraction was fishing. Anglers would come from all over Southern California to catch catfish, trout, bass, bluegill, and carp, which were all in abundance. Many Pacoima residents would camp at night by the lake to take advantage of the evening and morning catches.

Visiting Hansen Dam Park and enjoying its amenities became a tradition for generations of Pacoimians.

Tim Morris at one of the Hansen Dam horse stables in 1970's. Morris owned a horse stable on Filmore Street and participated in parades and horse shows.

(Courtesy of Pansie Gayton)

David Aguilar Hansen Dam merry-go-round 1958
(Courtesy David Aguilar photography)

Mario, Ismael Aguilar Jr. and David Aguilar at Hansen Dam 1958 at the entrance to Hanson Dam on Osborne St.
(Courtesy David Aguilar photography)

1961 Michael & Chas Cochrane and Gary Wilson at Hansen Dam
(courtesy Ida Cochran collection)

Carl Rucker and Michael Cable show off their catch in 1970
(Courtesy Michael Cable & Ronald Oliver)

George Skipper, Mildred, Clyde Thomkins, and James Bates. Smaller kids include
Ruthie Ralph and Camille Skipper Going for a fun day at Hansen Dam early 60's
(Courtesy Camille Watkins collections)

Hansen Dam Pony Rides in the 80's. Shown is Justin Ector.
(Courtesy Tonice Gilmore Thomas)

Over the years, 30 million tons of silt, gravel, and sand built up from heavy rainstorms as it flowed down from the mountains. By 1980, the city wholly banned boating and swimming at the lake. During that decade, the debris-filled lake all but dried up, and was abandoned. The once-popular pony rides, merry-go-round, and train ride disappeared as well. However, families could still enjoy barbeque and picnic at the park. Moreover, Hansen Dam Park was the official hangout spot for local teens and adults who still loved to gather there.

Floods and debris caused swimming and boating banned from Hansen Dam in the 70's.
(Courtesy of Ronald Love)

R&B singer Howard Huntsberry grew-up in Pacoima and shared his fond memories of Hansen Dam.

"On the weekends, we hung out at Hansen Dam. All the low riders would hang out and show off their cars. It was a really big thing. Hansen Dam was the ticket if you wanted a girl and you wanted to look at good cars. It was the place to go. Saturdays and Sundays, that was a real good time. You could swim, barbeque, look at cars, and chase the girls. Back in those days — violence, we had our problems, but it wasn't a bunch of guys shooting up everything. You could actually go somewhere, have a good time, sit down with your friends, and make it home that night."

Comedian Gilbert Esquivel, another Pacoima native, added, "I remember everybody would go to Hansen Dam and cruise Hansen Dam Park. Everybody would blast their music from their trunk. It was a hangout."

Gilbert joked, "I remember I caught a big ole giant frog, it was a huge bullfrog. He had tattoos on him and everything. He was from Pacoima."

Low Rider cars were the cool vehicles to cruise in at the dam.
James Tolliver III owned this beauty in 1978.

(Crystal Jackson collection)

With the arrival of the new millennium, Hansen Dam Park received a long-awaited renovation. The City of Los Angeles Department of Parks and Recreation built the Hansen Dam Aquatic Center, which features a 9-acre recreation lake for fishing and public boating. Also located at the site is the largest swimming pool in the country and the tenth-largest in the world. It has a capacity of 2800 swimmers.

Hansen Dam Aquatic Center
(Crystal Jackson collection)

8
Whiteman Airport

For more than 70 years, Whiteman Airport, or Air Park, as originally called, has been a fixture of Pacoima. This private airport, which now sits across the street from a housing project in a low-income area, seems bizarre, but most Pacoima residents have never given it a second thought. Some of the town's old-timers tell stories of the airport's eccentric owner, who owned a house on the hill above the airport. They say how he would chase kids away who ventured onto the property, and some even said he would fire gunshots.

Marvin E. Whiteman was born March 7, 1909, in Texas and married Hazel Thornton. They had two children Marvin Jr. and Lynn, and owned the property today known as Hansen Hill.

In 1946, Marvin Whiteman Sr. founded Whiteman Air Park on Osborne Street and San Fernando Road. The airport sat on thirty two-acres of property that he purchased from Roger Jessup of Jessup Dairies. The land where Whiteman built the small airport was carrot and corn farmland. He initially used it to store his fleet of retired civilian pilot training planes, interstate cadets, PT-19s Stinsons and Beeches. Whiteman thought the northeast portion of the San Fernando Valley needed aviation badly after World War II, so he decided to open a private airport.

Around the same time, actors Andy Devine and Dick Probert, who were flying buddies before and after the war, were looking to open a flying school. The two had made movies and wanted to utilize their flying skills. They needed a good location, and after dealing mostly with the Van Nuys Metropolitan Airport, they chose Pacoima. In the middle of 1946, they purchased the school and equipment, including the fleet of Interstates (airplanes) from Marvin Whiteman, calling it Probert-Devine Aviation Corporation. Devine, who was known for his raspy voice, was a character actor in films such as Stagecoach with John Wayne (1939), A Star is Born (1937), and How the West was won (1962). Dick Probert was known for his flying stunts in "Forced Landing" (1941) and Sea Hunt (1958-60). Devine sold his half of the flying school back to Probert in 1949.

The airpark was also a regular location for Hollywood productions, ranking 19th in the world for the number of TV and film airport scenes. Television shows shot there included Perry Mason and The Andy Griffith Show. One of the films include the Jane Russell movie "Fate is the Hunter" by 20th Century-Fox. Whiteman was good friends with Senator Barry Goldwater, President Richard Nixon, and numerous celebrities, including Jimmy Stewart and John Wayne.

There was a pool on the south side of the flying field built-in 1947 by Whiteman for entertainment. His many famous friends would land at the airpark to enjoy partying with the stars.

Dick Probert opened the flying school at Whiteman Air Park

Actor Andy Devine partnered with Probert in 1946

Marvin Whiteman opened the Whiteman Air Park in 1946
(Courtesy Whiteman Airport)

1960 Landing at Whiteman Air Park

Whiteman Air Park planes 1963

1964 Actress Jane Russell on the set at Whiteman Air Park

Glenn Ford and Director Ralph Nelson on the set at Whiteman Air Park in Pacoima. March 9, 1964

Pool on south side of flying field at Whiteman Air Park in 1948

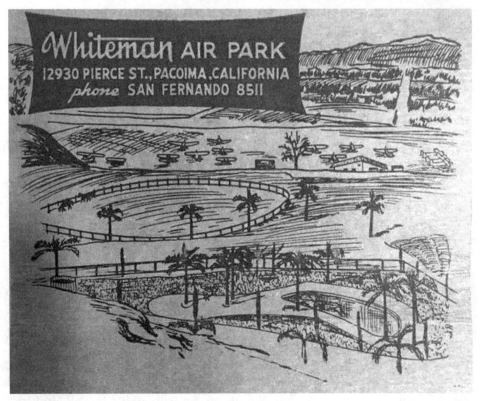

Matchbook cover

In 1955 the San Fernando Gardens Housing Projects were built directly across the street from the airport. During that same year, Glenoaks Blvd was extended through Hansen Hill to reach Sun Valley. In the years to follow, this created an exciting dynamic as the airpark began hosting sports events, including drag races and roller derby.

Dude Criswell, a motorcycle racer/promoter, took out a lease at Whiteman Air Park in 1968 and built a quarter-mile asphalt oval stadium in the corner of the property. He was attempting to revive the sport of speedway racing. Later, Criswell added an eighth-mile speedway track inside the oval. Mike Bast, a top American speedway racer, categorized racing at Whiteman in 1968 as actually being in the middle of the rebirth of speedway racing in America. He went on to be a champion during the seventies.

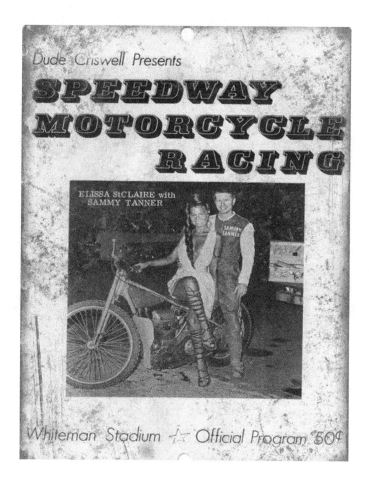

In 1970, the County of Los Angeles took over Whiteman Air Park and later renamed it Whiteman Airport. Marvin Whiteman Jr. took over Whiteman Industries in 1976 when his father passed away and moved the manufacturing company to Boise, Idaho.

In 1988, Whiteman Airport received an FAA-approved and funded air tower, which is home to over 600 aircraft. It has a flying school, restaurant, and other aviation-related businesses that contribute to the Pacoima economy. The airport provides twenty-four hours a day, seven days a week availability to small and medium-sized aircraft. It is still referred to as Whiteman Air Park by the old-time local pilots.

Elizabeth Ford and Sheila Ford ready for a flight with pilot Daryl Ford. Samuel Ford, their father and father-in-law respectively, was a Tuskegee Airman in the 40's.

(Courtesy Daryl Ford)

9
Military Veterans

Pacoima is undoubtedly a military veteran town. Housing tracts built with veterans in mind arose in the fifties due to a severe housing shortage in Los Angeles. Pacoima became home to some very notable vets, including World War II Medal of Honor recipients, Tuskegee Airmen, and more.

There were veterans from many nationalities that encompassed Pacoima. Japanese, Native American, Mexican, African American, White, and Filipino all enlisted and served. The hunt is still on to complete the veteran registry of these celebrated Pacoimians and pay homage to their service. The town is very proud of the military soldiers that rose up the ranks, fought, and came home to a country that did not respect people of color.

Although most military veterans from the forties and fifties were migrants to Pacoima, some were native. One of these was David M Gonzales, who was a private first-class United States Army soldier. Born in Pacoima on June 9, 1923, he entered the military at the age of 20 as a skilled machine shop worker.

A year after Gonzales joined the army, he found himself at Valle Verde Trail in the Philippines engaged in heavy combat against the Japanese. The Army Air Corps was fusing bombs for delayed detonation, a tactic called "skip bombing," in an attempt to destroy the Japanese caves and tunnels in that area. The bombs were buried deep in the ground before detonation.

However, five American soldiers were trapped in their standing foxholes when this tactic occurred. Gonzales was pinned down with his company when enemy fire swept the area. Any movement was life-threatening.

Suddenly a 500-pound bomb smashed into the perimeter burying the five men. Without hesitation, PFC Gonzales seized a tool and under a hail of bullets crawled 15 yards to his trapped comrades where he and his commanding officer began digging them out. After nearly reaching his troops, he saw the commanding officer get struck and killed by machinegun fire. Despite that, PFC Gonzales continued digging out troops with imminent danger surrounding him and successfully saved four men before he was struck and killed.

PFC David Gonzales' heroic and intrepid conduct exemplified the highest tradition of military service. His sacrifice earned him the Medal of Honor, which was awarded by President Harry S. Truman.

This image of PFC David M. Gonzalez, part of the Pacoima mural mile, is located behind Pacoima City Hall.

Pacoima Park was renamed David M. Gonzales Pacoima Recreational Park and the interchange between Interstate 5 and Hwy 118 was renamed David M. Gonzales Memorial Interchange.

Another noteworthy Pacoima veteran is Lt. Colonel Mike Alba, who was a decorated WWII military captain fighter pilot in the 339-fighter group. Born in 1917, he attended air tactical school at Air University of Tyndall Air Force Base Panama City.

Lt. Alba went on to become successful in numerous missions against the war enemies. The first enemy plane that he reportedly destroyed happened while he was returning from an escort mission to Germany. Alba spotted two German planes on the ground, swooped down, and set them on fire.

The next day he was escorting bombers again to another target in Germany when his crew encountered some ME 109 fighter planes. He chose one and engaged with it until he saw the pilot bail out of the aircraft.

His awards include the Air Force Distinguished Flying Cross, 9 Air Medals, WWII Victory Medal, and Presidential Unit Citation. Lt. Col. Alba also received many formal recognitions from foreign military organizations. He served as President of the 55th Fighter Group and 442 Air Service Group Association, where he was instrumental in the dedication of the P-38 and P-51 memorials at the USAF Academy.

Lt. Colonel Mike Alba on the Pacoima City Hall Mural
(Artwork by Ignacio Gomez)

Pacoima was also home to members of what might be World War II's most famous military unit. Walter Hightower Thomas and Samuel William Ford Jr. were proud members of the Tuskegee Airman, the first Black military aviators to serve in the US Armed forces. They proved to be an elite group of men that flew with distinction and honor during the war.

The Tuskegee Airman consisted of 996 soldiers and 15,000 ground personnel. These all Black units are credited with 15,500 combat raids and maneuvers and earned over 150 Distinguished Flying Crosses for their achievements. Although they faced racial discrimination at home and abroad, these soldiers paved the way for the integration of US Armed forces under President Harry S. Truman.

Walter Hightower Thomas was born in San Bernardino, Calif, and entered the service during WWII. He met his wife Doris Wall, who was from Atlanta, Georgia, and they married three months later. Upon returning home after tremendous aviation and combat success, they moved to the Basilone Homes in Pacoima and had their first child in 1950.

They purchased a brand-new home with his GI bill in the Joe Louis Housing Tract on Montford Street. There were only two places in Los Angeles that accepted GI loans from "colored" people, Watts and Pacoima. His dream was to be a commercial pilot as he raised his five children Walter III, Ronnie, Renee, Malcolm, and Patricia. However, he was repeatedly denied employment by the airlines due to his race. This policy of not hiring "coloreds" as pilots, even though they put their lives on the line for their country, was incomprehensible. It was not until a 1963 Supreme Court ruling that this policy changed.

Samuel William Ford Jr. trained as a pilot at the Tuskegee Army Air Core. He met his wife, Helen Roberts, at a dance in Jackson, Mississippi. After the war, he married her and came to Pacoima, where they purchased a Joe Louis Housing Tract home in 1952.

The Ford's raised three children, Daryl, Patricia, and Elizabeth, while living on Weidner Street. Airman Ford worked at Lockheed Aircraft, where he retired working for the Skunks Work Air Force Plant. His only son, Daryl, followed in his footsteps as a pilot and is the owner of a Cessna 172. His wife, Helen, became a registered nurse and worked for Sun Valley Medical and Serra Memorial Hospital. The family also attended Parks Chapel AME Church.

Tuskegee Airman served America proudly during World War II – Photo circa 1942

Walter Hightower Thomas   Walter and Doris Thomas

Samuel Ford was a Tuskegee Airman originally from the Phoenix Arizona. He and his wife Helen purchased their Pacoima home in 1952.
(Courtesy Daryl Ford Collection)

Pacoima's Japanese American community has also proudly served in the US Military despite their mistreatment by the American government. Kiyoshi K. Muranaga was a purple heart and medal of honor recipient, the United States' highest honor, for his actions during World War II.

Muranaga was raised one of nine siblings and joined the US Army in 1943. He volunteered to be a part of the 442nd all Nisei (2nd generation Japanese) Regimental Combat Team made up mostly of Japanese Americans.

While in Italy, on his first day of action, Muranaga displayed extraordinary heroism in harsh terrain and severe conditions. On June 26, 1944, while battling a strong enemy that had superior firepower, he single-handedly manned his squad's mortar weapon in an attempt to destroy an enemy artillery weapon. Muranaga had the foresight to move his men away from the gun to positions of safety. He then operated the mortar weapon alone and managed to get off three rounds, the third landing directly in front of the enemy.

However, they were then able to identify the source of the mortar fire and turned their 88mm weapon on Private First Class Muranaga, killing him instantly. Because of the accuracy of his previous fire, the enemy retreated and abandoned their position. This act of heroism earned Private First Class Muranaga the highest military honors.

Kiyoshi K Muranaga (1922-1944)

Pacoima is incredibly proud of our veterans and gives thanks to them for their commitment to this country. Many great military people comprise Pacoima, and the following incredible pictures contain captions that allow a glimpse into some of their lives. All are members of the Pacoima Historical Society Military Registry.

Michael Negrete served as a US Marine during WWII in the Pacific Islands. He earned Distinguished Service medals and survived the infamous Battle of Iwo Jima. This photo was taken in 1942 on Pinney Street with his wife Frances and baby daughter Kathy. (Courtesy Suzanne Llamas)

Rudy Ortega Sr., former Tribal Captain for the Tataviam Indians, served in the US Army during World War II from 1943 until the end of the war. He fought on the Pacific front as well as the Philippines campaign. Ortega Sr. was the father of ten children and had two stepchildren.

Rudy Ortega Sr. with son Danny before leaving for Korea

Pete Prieto was born on June 29, 1924, and served in the United States Marine Corp from 1942-46. He joined the 2nd Marine division in New Zealand and then the 2nd Motor Transport Battalion. Prieto landed in Saipan in the Marianas and then Okinawa, Japan, where the US dropped the atomic bomb. Upon returning to civilian life, Prieto joined the Los Angeles Police Department, where he was a detective at the Foothill Division for 29 years before retiring. Pete and his wife Carmen have four children Todd, Marsha, Bobbie, and Debbie.

Pete Prieto (Courtesy Marcia Prieto)

Garfield C. Coleman II (aka) Pop's (far left) was a professional Boxer before entering the military. He oversaw this battalion-sized US Army Calvary unit of segregated Black soldiers. (Courtesy Betty Coleman)

JB Hodges and his sister Emma Alexander in 1947. JB purchased one of the first homes in the Joe Louis Housing Tracts on Herrick Avenue. Pacoima was one of the only areas in the Valley that would accept GI bills from veterans of color.

David Johnson serving in Vietnam with troops in action.
(Courtesy David Johnson)

Xenaro Ayala 1948 during World War II.
(Courtesy Xenaro Ayala archives)

Arturo Ramos US Army 1975 Jungles of Panama

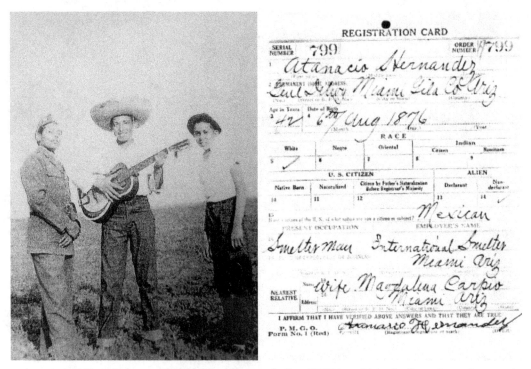

Atanacio Miguel Hernandez (left) on leave during WW I and his draft registration card
(Courtesy Lupe & Manuel Hernandez collection)

Sargent James Tolliver Jr. receives military Certificate of Achievement honor
(Courtesy James Tolliver III)

ANGEL VELARDE
KOREAN WAR
ARMY
2ND INF. DIV.

TONY VELARDE
KOREAN WAR
ARMY
K MAG

IGNACIO VELARDE
KOREAN WAR
ARMY
40TH INF. DIV.

MIKE VELARDE
KOREAN WAR
ARMY
1ST CAV. DIV. 7TH CAV. REG. CO. K

The Velarde brothers all served in the Korean War together.

OATH OF ALLEGIANCE

TO THE UNITED STATES OF AMERICA

I, James William HERNDON do solemnly swear (or affirm) that I will bear true faith and allegiance to the United States of America, and that I will serve them honestly and faithfully against all their enemies whomsoever, and that I will obey the orders of the President of the United States and the orders of the officers appointed over me, according to the rules and articles for the government of the Navy.

James William Herndon
James William HERNDON

Subscribed and sworn before me this 27th day of March, A. D. 1940, and contract perfected.

W. B. Cranston, Lieutenant, U. S. N

JOE C MENDIBLES

Rank=CPL Serial Number=RA19390217
MOS=04745 Year of Birth= March 21, 1932
State of Residence= Pacoima, CA
Unit=21st Inf. Regt., 24th Inf. Div.
Date of Casualty =1951 10 27
Type of Casualty=Killed in Action

Here are some additional veterans from the PHS Military Registry:

Leo Neal US Navy	**Alfredo Mendoza** US Army	**Russ Gonzales** US Army	**James Chandler** US Army
Printes Hodges US Army	**Victor Lyons** US Air Force	**Thomas Williams** US Army	**George Stewart** US Army
Matthew L Harville Sr. US Army	**Arvel Jackson Sr.** US Air Force	**Lacy Clifford Wright** US Army	**Edmond Oliver** US Army
George James US Army	**Kenneth Haywood** US Army	**Howard Sorrell** US Army	**Curtis Verge** US Army

Fred Burley US Navy	**James Wesley Smith** US Army	**Charles Perkins** US Army	**Hoover Lavender** US Army
Willie Leopold Sr. US Air Force	**Ralph Guerrero Jr.** US Marines	**Printes Hodges Jr.** US Army	**Lt. Col. Gerald Grass** US Air Force
Kenneth Neal US Army	**Glenn Marshall** US Marines	**Carmen D Elizondo** US Army	**Andrew Riley** US Air Force
Leo Neal Jr US Army	**Tony Green** US Navy	**Dennis H Ware Sr.** US Air Force	**Wilfort Foster Sr.** US Army

James Kenion	Louis David Johnwell	Wendell Beasley	David Johnson
US Navy	US Army	US Army	US Army

While building Hansen Dam, the engineers had temporary housing bungalows where they resided. After its completion, this housing became available for military veterans returning from the war. This facility became known as the Basilone Homes, named after Marine Congressional Medal of Honor Hero Platoon Sergeant John Basilone.

Platoon Sergeant John Basilone

The Basilone Homes were developed and managed by the Housing Authority of the City of Los Angeles. Military veterans and their families of all nationalities were able to live in this housing project comprised of 1500 units. This migration of military members would eventually usher in an unprecedented new era for the town of Pacoima.

Panoramic view of Basilone Homes located on the eastside of Glenoaks Blvd

1948 photo of Basilone Homes with Hansen Dam in the distant background

10
Black Migration

In the 1930s, only a few Blacks lived in Pacoima. By the late thirties, North Hollywood had a couple of streets that accepted Blacks. Some settled in Van Nuys and found extreme racism, comparable to the South, if not worse, they said.

With built-in mechanisms in the land title deeds prohibiting non-Whites from buying land, the reality of dealing with race in the Valley became real. After all, this was the suburbs of Los Angeles. The fight to maintain colonial culture was real. In the early1940's, there was an increase in Blacks coming to the Valley. However, where did this all begin? What enticed Blacks from the South to come to Los Angeles? It appears this may have been a plan since the late 1800s.

On December 6, 1885, Charles Maclay wrote the LA Times regarding his dislike of Chinese laborers and a preference for the "colored" laborer.

To the Editor of the Times--Sir,

"There is considerable said about the going of Chinamen, but where is the laborer to fill his place? The vast machinery of work must have a power behind it to make it move. Labor must not come and go at haphazard, like one having fits and spasms. What is wanted is the steady laborer, who loves his place and home, with a desire to drive his stakes and build in the waste places. There is a laborer of that kind at hand--this is to speak a good word for him. Surely, he ought not to be neglected, for he is already a citizen, with the power of the ballot. His morals are above those of the Chinaman. It is scarcely necessary to say that I mean the colored laborer who is now being crowded in the Southern States. The writer of this saw 300 colored immigrants passing out of South Carolina and on their way to Arkansas. Why not bring a few thousand to Southern California? They are industrious laborers; they love home and schools and churches. They would fit admirably to take the place of Chinamen in all departments of labor; besides, they are a cheery people. Who has not heard and been pleased with the old-fashioned plantation songs and quaint negro philosophies? Such human beings have natures to rise above low levels and become among the most useful citizens. Somebody should get up a 'Negro Immigration Society.' Bring them out here and prove their quality to benefit this section."

By the turn of the century, Maclay's thoughts came to fruition. Blacks began to migrate to Southern California for a multitude of reasons. Two thousand one hundred thirty-one were recorded in Los Angeles by the 1900 census. Most landed directly in Los Angeles, and Watts. Racially restrictive covenants prevented Blacks from living in certain areas. The Central Avenue District and Watts were the only neighborhoods that allowed Blacks. By 1940, Watts became predominately Black, and after WWII, tens of thousands of Blacks from the segregated South piled into the town.

Next door to Watts is Compton, which was a predominately White farm community. Blacks migrating from the South were able to find work in the agriculture arena. In the late forties, middle-class Blacks began moving to the west side of Compton. However, there was still a shortage of housing for returning military veterans from WWII. Around 1950, Compton saw a significant amount of Blacks moving in, but they still needed more homes. It was this that is said to have triggered land developers to build in Pacoima in 1950.

Therdgill G. Pledger came to Los Angeles in 1938 from Alabama and was one of the earlier Blacks to arrive in Pacoima in 1942. Several Black families resided in both Van Nuys and North Hollywood before Pledger's arrival, and most relocated to Pacoima when the new housing tracts became available.

Pledger came to Pacoima after living in Watts and founded the Greater Community Baptist Church. Reverend Pledger was married to Annie White, whose father was also a minister. Every year Pledger went to his hometown in Alabama and brought back more fellow Blacks from the South.

Pledger, a plasterer by trade, became one of the most prominent Black pioneers in the history of Los Angeles. His church was the earliest Baptist church in the San Fernando Valley. Every Baptist church in Pacoima originated from GCBC, and Reverend Pledger ordained all the ministers in Pacoima and many others in California.

Rev. Therdgill G. Pledger

At the time he arrived in Pacoima, Herrick Ave was the only paved street besides Van Nuys Blvd with no streetlights or sanitation. They had outhouses with cesspools, and it was extremely dark at night. He first began preaching in a Pacoima dance hall building that he rented for five dollars a week. He knew he needed to do something when he met another Black man who said they had to drive all the way to Pasadena for church. The long drive seemed endless since there were no freeways at that time, and San Fernando Road was the only path to their destination.

It was a small crowd at first, but the enthusiasm encouraged him to go through the channels to establish his church. After several locations, he was able to purchase the land and construct a building. By 1946, Basilone Homes had hundreds of military veteran families living there and had standing room only services.

This sign sits in front of Greater Community Baptist Church on Norris Avenue in Pacoima

It was around this time that Hillery T. Broadous came to Pacoima. Broadous was originally from Arkansas and lived in Oregon before arriving in Los Angeles in 1946 after being discharged from the US Army. He and his wife Rosa had five children at that time, but the housing crisis prevented him from finding an adequate home for his family.

Due to his military service, he was able to get into Basilone Homes in 1948. He met Reverend Pledger while there and eventually became a deacon in his church.

He worked at the Red Barn Restaurant on Van Nuys Blvd (in today's Panorama City) while getting licensed as a barber. He then opened a barbershop with Freddy Carter next to Tresierras Market on Van Nuys Blvd in Pacoima.

Broadous purchased land on DeGarmo St, where he built his house. He said there were approximately 100 Blacks in Pacoima when he arrived in 1946. He and his wife ultimately had eleven children and founded their church, called "Calvary Baptist" in 1958.

Reverend Hillery T. Broadous

His daughter Pamela Broadous explains what Pacoima was like in the early days.

"We moved into that house in 1953, and there were several vacant lots on the street, and the street was a dirt road. My brother Hillery (now named Abdullah) says that when we first came here, the only paved street was Van Nuys Boulevard. I remember going to school one morning and coming home, and the street was paved. That's the memory I have. We grew up on DeGarmo between Van Nuys Blvd and Pierce. It was like a little United Nations on that block. It was a long block, but it was African American, Filipino, Hispanic, White, Asian I mean literally every nationality you want to find was on that block. And that was the beauty of the community. As the years progressed, Pacoima became 75% African American. We had a really, really great upbringing. The neighbors taught my mother to cook Mexican food. It was just a nice, nice neighborhood, nice area, great people. It was wonderful."

Broadous Family (L-R) back row: Furaha (Rosita), Alicia Broadous Duncan, Hillery Broadous holding baby Francine, Rosa Broadous holding Cecelia, Marie. (L-R) front row: William T, Pamela, Zedar Thompson (maternal grandfather), Arthur, Alice Thompson (maternal grandmother), Zadar, Abdullah (Hillery Jr.)

(Courtesy Pamela Broadous Silver stream collection)

For many years Reverend Hillery Broadous was the link in Pacoima that represented the spiritual, political, and humanitarian power of this bold new community. There is no way to deny his influence and sculpturing of Pacoima.

He was the thirteenth of nineteen children born to Reverend Z and Mrs. Mattie Thomas in Texarkana, Arkansas, on January 16, 1912. Broadous grew up on a farm, plowing fields, milking cows, and all the elements raising animals required.

His father, too, was a Baptist preacher, which helped expose him to a family of preachers at the district, state, and national levels. With this background, he attended formal education institutions that earned him an honorary "Doctorate of Divinity." He attended Reeds Bible College of Religion of Los Angeles, where he majored in psychology and religion.

Broadous was an influential community activist and helped anyone he could. After opening Calvary in the late fifties, he got involved with numerous community organizations, including the Board of Fair Housing Council of the San Fernando Valley and the NAACP.

Recognizing the youth needed a park in east Pacoima, Reverend Broadous led the charge in 1960 to get the city to purchase a corner of land on Filmore St and Dronfield. It was named Filmore Park, now known as Hubert Humphrey Park.

1977 Reverend Hillery T. Broadous at microphone with Mayor Tom Bradley, Mrs. Bradley and Dr. Elliot Mason (Courtesy Broadous family)

He worked with Mayor Tom Bradley's office on many councils and committees, including the Mayors Council for International Visitors, the mayor's advisory committee on the San Fernando Valley, and numerous faith-based organizations.

In 1983, Filmore Elementary School, across the street from the Humphrey park, was renamed Broadous Elementary after him, a reminder of all the tireless work he did to improve Pacoima.

As a trailblazer and pioneer, his image, along with his wife Rosa, is on the Pacoima City Hall Mural.

Pacoima City Hall Mural includes this beautiful art rendering of Mother Rosa and Hillery T. Broadous who will be remembered in Pacoima history.

Irene Diaz is a long-time Pacoima resident who remembers when the first Blacks moved into her neighborhood.

"Before the Joe Louis tract homes, it used to be nothing but fields here, nothing but dirt roads. In Sylmar, they use to raise olives and have olive groves. We used to have Japanese, and they had a really big field, and they used to raise vegetables. They used to have some Italians too.

"The first Blacks that moved in here, I know them. They were the Macons from Alabama. I remember they used to live a block away from me. It was the Macons, and they had cousins, the Carters, and they all went into construction. They lived here near Pacoima Elementary School.

"Julia Carter, the Carters and the Macons they were cousins. They were the first Black family that came into Pacoima then. My sisters were not used to having Black people because they were the first Black family to come in. I remember my sister used to say things they didn't have any business saying. And it's amazing because they used to throw rocks then. We had a Mexican family like the hillbillies right. When we said nasty things as kids, we used to throw rocks at each other. They hit me in the head, and they would clap right.

"When the blacks came in, my sisters and my family started (saying) derogatory, you know the traditional (names) that they used to say. It's amazing cause they all married Black, all of them.

"I have one sister that she's fortunate. He's got a son that is a minister she's got a son that's a fireman. They all really did something of their lives. But it's amazing because people would discriminate. And it's really bad because we were bought up that it doesn't make any difference as long as they are good to you. That was my mother's philosophy — even though you get mad at people, don't be revengeful."

Here are the names of some early African American families and residents in the San Fernando Valley prior to 1950.

- Thergill & Annie Pledger
- Hillary & Rosa Broadous
- Mr. & Mrs. Thomas Patton
- Mr. & Mrs. Tracy Leggett
- James & Ellie Mae Purdue
- Mrs. White
- Bessie White Houston
- Ida Benyon (San Fernando)
- George & Phyllis Parker
- Jessie "Blonde" Mitchell (shoe shine)
- Emil Norwood & Lucille Bridges
- George & Rosa Henry
- Ted & Dorothy McClellan
- Thomas & Minnie Williams
- Clarence & Mary Lee Lane
- Ora Hutchinson
- Rosa Lee
- Bob & Emma Alexander
- Irvin Walker
- Trudy Simms (Chicken Shack)
- Henry Gilkey Sr
- Charles & Fannie Macon
- James Robinson (real estate)
- Pearl Levy
- Raymond & Julia Carter
- Curtis & Madell Steiner
- Ernest Polk
- Leroy Fontenot
- Washington family
- Gill family
- Burney family
- Martin family
- Cantloe family
- Gandy family
- Johnson family

Ora Hutchinson came to North Hollywood in 1941, then sent for her entire family from New Orleans, LA. They moved from North Hollywood to Filmore St in Pacoima.

(Courtesy Ora Hutchinson Collection)

Ora Hutchinson, Rosa Lee, Bernice Hodges arrived in Pacoima during the 1940's. Rosa Lee lived on Hoyt Street by Tresierras Market. The name of the lady on the far left is unknown. (Ora Hutchinson collection)

Raymond and Julia Carter in the 1940's

Many Pacoimians have heard of the Joe Louis Housing Tract, but not many understood what it was. As military veterans began coming home, they needed housing. The city of Los Angeles faced a severe dilemma trying to balance the racial climate and the need for homes. There needed to be a solution, and Pacoima was the answer.

By creating an affordable housing tract named after a famous Black boxer, developers lured African Americans into the town. Most Caucasians and many Mexicans were not happy with the Black migration to Pacoima. Ultimately, it would change the dynamics of Pacoima for years to come.

In the late forties, a lawyer named Macbeth presented himself to Reverend Pledger and invited him to a groundbreaking of the land where he was going to build new homes. Pledger and a few others went and blessed the proposed land. It was not until several years later when a different man carried out building the homes. Advertisements suggested that Joe Louis petitioned the Los Angeles planning commission for permits to build on a 53-acre tract in Pacoima, and the promotion began.

Joe Louis was the World Heavyweight boxing champion from 1937 until 1949 and held that title longer than anyone in history. He was one of the greatest boxers in sports and became known as the "Brown Bomber." His family, however, claims he had no real estate ventures and is uncertain if he licensed his name for this project. Nonetheless, the name "Joe Louis" gave the green light to African Americans to buy these homes and build a new community.

The Joe Louis homes were three-bedroom, one bath, 700 to 900 square foot homes designed by Joseph Eichler. There was very little detail put into the boxy design, and the price ranged from $7,000 to $9.000. Word spread quickly, and the list of veterans filled up fast. Most of the GIs were already living in the Basilone Homes or Roger Young Village, waiting for the houses to be complete. GI loans were available to the veterans, and there was a significant number returning from World War II, which is why the waiting list filled up relatively fast.

The Evening Independent - Sep 27, 1949

Joe Louis To Construct Several Hundred Homes

LOS ANGELES — (AP) — Joe Louis Homes, Inc.

Under this firm name, the former world's heavyweight champion seeks to build several hundred non-restricted homes on a 53-acre tract in the San Fernando Valley.

Louis petitioned the Los Angeles planning commission Monday for a zoning change to permit consruction of the low cost housing project at Pacoima. The ex-champ said the houses, containing 700 to 900 square feet, will sell for $7,000.

New Coaches

TULSA — Five new assistant football coaches have been hired

Joe Louis was very popular with the Black community. This 1949 newspaper article falsely reported that Joe Louis was a partner in the project.

Mazie McGee sits in front of a brand-new Joe Louis Home on Herrick Avenue.
A model home can be seen across the street (Hodges collection)

In 1948, the United States Supreme Court Shelley vs. Kraemer case struck down racially restricted covenants. Despite this, the San Fernando Valley remained engaged in racial segregation. Lenders would only approve loans for people of color in certain areas, and real estate brokers had guidelines on where those areas were. Pacoima was on that list. The topic was so hot there was also occasional violence and intimidation when minorities attempted to leave the confines of a town like Pacoima.

The popularity of the Joe Louis homes prompted developers to add another 87 units that they called San Fern Manor. It was no longer necessary to use Joe Louis's name because the word was out to Blacks down south and in Los Angeles.

It was around this time that Black realtors got involved in home sales. James Robinson, Johnny Jordan, and James Carter all sold houses in San Fern Manor. The tract extended from Weidner to Filmore Street and included Herrick Avenue. Those houses began at $9,999. They were the same boxy three-bedroom 700-900 square foot structures.

These sold just as fast as the Joe Louis homes, with military veterans being the primary purchasers. The next housing tract was Glen Manor on Glenoaks Blvd and De Haven Ave, whereas the price once again was increased, this time to $11,999.

Michael, Ida, and Zenola Cocharane in their front yard on Louvre St. with other neighborhood children in 1956 (Courtesy Ida Cochrane collection)

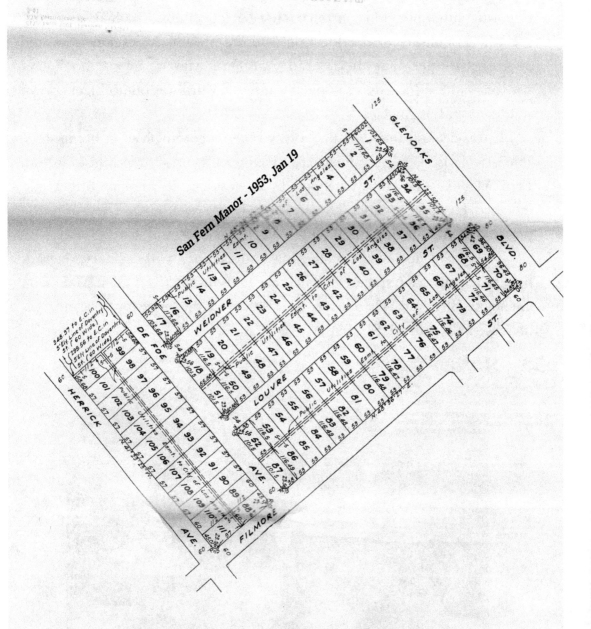

San Fern Manor - 1953, Jan 19

TRACT № 17691

M.B. 427, PGS. 38 & 39

 This is not a survey of the land but is compiled for information by the Title Insurance and Trust Company from data shown by the official records.

168

This 1953 photo was taken on Louvre Street (San Fern Manor) before fences with new homeowner William Charles Cochrane (Courtesy Ida Cochrane collection)

This 1955 photo was taken on Louvre Street (San Fern Manor). The Smith Family (left to right) Jerry, Jethree Smith Sr., Alexia, Dollie J. Smith, Patricia, Kathy.
(Courtesy Patricia Flowers collection)

1957 Stephan Chandler on Paxton Street before fences.
(Courtesy Stephan Chandler collection)

Faye (Gayles) Hodges in backyard on Desmond St before fences in the fifties

Jackie Hodges (L), Essie May Hodges holding baby Iris Hodges (C), Printes Hodges Jr. (R) on Cochran Street in 1958. (Courtesy Hodges collection)

Alithra "Tipy" James on Louvre Street in 1957
(Veda James collection)

1954 Birthday Party on Paxton St. — Wilson family, Connie O'Neal, Barry and Anita Toler

(Courtesy of Stephan Chandler)

It was almost immediately after Blacks moved into Pacoima that they organized social clubs, groups, and organizations. Pacoima was a bonified suburb that defied the image of how Black communities were perceived.

Within a few years, an NAACP branch was in operation. Churches, Boy and Girl Scouts, equestrian clubs, socialite clubs, and Eastern Star, all formed in the fifties. Although other organizations were already in Pacoima, all of them did not welcome Blacks. However, Pacoima was changing rapidly, and a new day was dawning in the town.

Emma Alexander on Filmore Street 1954 in her hat representing the Order of the Eastern Star. (Courtesy Hodges collection)

This photo taken in 1955 shows Pacoima chapter members of the Order of the Eastern Star, which was formed by the town's early African American community. The Order of the Eastern Star is a Masonic appendant body open to both men and women. The Freemasons established it in 1850. Based on teachings from the Bible, the order is open to people of all religious beliefs.

Mary Neal, another long-time Pacoima resident, was 90 years old when she shared her story about coming to Pacoima in the fifties.

"I originally came from Texas and lived on the west side for about a year then moved to Watts for three years. My husband's cousin told him about Basilone Homes. So, we moved to Basilone Homes in 1950. Then they decided to close it. We started looking for a place. I didn't want to move back to Los Angeles. We heard about this building tract, so we investigated and moved here in 1952."

Mrs. Neal's husband, Leo, served in the Navy during World War II. Her outlook on this new community was very positive.

"It was really nice. I really liked it. Because regardless of your financial status, people were still very community-oriented. We had teachers that lived here; we had doctors that lived in the community. We had professional people that worked at Lockheed. But everybody just wanted to pull together and make it a good community. They always like to keep their property up nice. We didn't have fences in the front yard. We had them in the back, but no fences in the front. The kids could roam from one end of the block to another, and the parents knew each others children because they played together. It was like a village, it really was."

The community, according to Mrs. Neal, was interested in their children, the schools, PTA, boy scouting, and girl scouting. She remembers the days when she knew everyone on the block and nearby streets. However, it was how everyone got along that she treasured.

"People communicating with each other, and I think most of them had the same interest and wanted their children to be successful. On the corner was the Baileys, and next to them, Dr. Wilson, he was a chiropractor. Then the Reece's and the Solis', which was a Mexican family that I still keep in touch with. After the Solis', the Williams, the Mances, the Finches, the Gilleries, the Duplechans, the Browns, and Freda Carter, a teacher at Vaughn Street. We had an attorney too, Mr. Bryce and Dr. Moreland.

"The real estate agent sold the property to these tract homes out of that room (in her home). There was another real estate guy that was very prominent... Johnny Jordan. He lived in the corner house in this tract. Sold real estate, but Mr. James Carter was the one who sold these tract homes. Prominent real estate guy. His wife went on to sing opera in New York. For the life of me can't think of her name right now."

However, things began to change after the demographics evolved. Children grew up and moved away, people died, and new neighbors meant a new, different community. The shared values and experiences no longer existed. At 90 years of age, she still lived in the same home on Filmore Street.

"It's not a community like it was. I don't even know my neighbors name, neither one of them. This neighbor doesn't communicate that with that neighbor. That neighbor doesn't communicate with the neighbor across the street. I don't know if that's because they are from different countries or South America, one is from Guatemala, from Mexico or what.

Even though we came here from different sections of the country in America, we were able to communicate because we had goals for our kids."

Mary and Leo Neal, along with their neighbors socialize on Filmore Street in 1956.
(Mary Neal collection)

Thomas and Jeanette Love moved on Glenoaks Blvd in the fifties. The construction of their home came after the Joe Louis and San Fern Manor tracts. Ron Love talked about his family's experience moving to Pacoima.

"When they built Pacoima, and they named it the Joe Louis homes — Joe Louis didn't have nothing to do with it. But it was the suburbs...it was the first black suburbs that they made — I'd say in the country. All Blacks lived in the city; they didn't live in the suburbs. Only whites lived in the suburbs when they moved from the city. So, not saying that they made one for Blacks, but by giving it the name Joe Louis homes, now who else gonna buy a Joe Louis Home? That's who mostly bought the Joe Louis homes, all black. But they started building other homes after that."

The Love family originally came from Knoxville, Tennessee. They moved to Los Angeles until their new home was ready.

"I think they were called Green View, that was after the Joe Louis homes. We used to come from LA about once a month, sometimes twice a month. Me, my brothers and sister watched our home being built. We'd say this is my room...this is going to be your room. Every month we'd see the progress, the color, and everything. I think at that time it was gray and burgundy."

Thomas and Jeanette Love bought this property on Glenoaks Blvd. in the 1950s

By the seventies, Pacoima's population became seventy-five percent, Black. African American owned businesses permeated the area, and the small town became known across the nation. The decade saw the pinnacle of growth for Black residents, with an estimated ten thousand living in the seven square mile area.

However, by the eighties, housing discrimination advocates began to ease redlining in other areas of the valley. Blacks slowly began moving out, and into nearby towns such as Panorama City and Granada Hills. The eighties were a pivotal time when drugs began to consume the landscape, and crime increased drastically. Moreover, General Motors, Price Pfister, and Lockheed all began having mass layoffs.

By the nineties, Latino immigrants began to outnumber the African American and Mexican American communities. For both of them, the migration was no longer entering Pacoima but exiting. Many Blacks and Mexicans moved to Palmdale or Lancaster, which had very affordable real estate as did Nevada. Some Blacks also moved back to the South, where their roots originated.

The 1994 North American Free Trade Agreement (NAFTA) slammed the door on Pacoima by causing the closing of General Motors and Price Pfister. The combination of drugs, crime, and lack of jobs was the recipe for the demise of an upwardly mobile community of color.

By the mid-nineties, Pacoima acquired the label of most impoverished in the San Fernando Valley. The African American population dropped from seventy-five percent at its height to ten percent. The job market changed from high paying blue-collar fields to lower-paying factory jobs. The Census report of 1990 showed Pacoima with a 14% unemployment rate versus the 8.4 rates of the entire city of Los Angeles.

However, the legacy of African Americans in Pacoima still has an impact today. The labors of this Black community started the Boys and Girls Club, Pacoima Skills Center, Northeast Valley Health Corporation, Pledgerville, and others, and still serve the town today. One thing is sure, despite moving away, many Black families still consider Pacoima "home," particularly those who endured the joy and struggles of those pioneering years.

(Left to Right) Apostle William Broadous, Alicia Broadous-Duncan, Mayor Tom Bradley, Rev. Lact. The city of Los Angeles built the Alicia Broadous-Duncan Senior Center on Glenoaks Boulevard named in honor of this Pacoima matriarch.

11
San Fernando Gardens

Pacoima's San Fernando Gardens is the last public housing development constructed in Los Angeles and the only one in the San Fernando Valley. Built after a strategic request for affordable housing by Reverend T.G. Pledger, along with a few other Pacoima residents, the LA Department of Housing Authority completed this housing project in 1955.

Pledger first made this request in the late forties knowing that veterans at Basilone Homes were looking for housing. At the time, there were only single-family homes in Pacoima. San Fernando Gardens represented the first multi-family dwellings, and for those unable to afford homes, it was a welcome invitation to the town.

Some residents, including many Whites in Pacoima, were not happy with the decision to build the projects. However, with the Joe Louis Homes already targeting African Americans, it was an easy decision for the city to build the units.

The San Fernando Gardens Projects contained 448 units built with a townhouse style design. Located on Lehigh Ave, between Van Nuys Blvd and Pierce Street, the Projects sit near Pacoima Elementary. The southern side of the Projects is across the street from Whiteman Airport.

The fate of Guardian Angel Church was in question after the decision to build the Projects. The church was fenced up for years and remained closed. Building the Projects affected others as well. Eminent domain laws forced many property owners to sell their land. At least one store, Lozano's Market, was demolished to make room. Land in Pacoima was very cheap at the time. Some property owners were happy to take market value for their homes, while others protested.

The property where the projects were built was small shacks and houses until the county of Los Angeles when they seized the land to build low cost public housing.

Carmen Galindo, an 80-year-old resident who has lived her entire life in Pacoima, recalled the town's initial sentiment about the San Fernando Gardens.

"Some people were very happy they were gonna get paid to move out, and some didn't like it at all. There was a lot of houses left empty there, and somebody went and turned them on fire. There were fires going on. Then they tore all the houses down.

"There was a store right across the street from the church … a grocery store, Lozano's Market. In Pacoima, there was only two families named Lozano — my father and that man from the grocery store. And people used to go buy whatever they needed in there."

Residents protest being forced to leave their homes in 1953 for the San Fernando Gardens housing projects. They ultimately lost their homes via eminent domain laws.

Additional public housing projects built in 1955, under the umbrella of providing low-income housing in Los Angeles, were Jordan Downs and Nickerson Gardens, the largest housing project in the nation. Watts is the location of both facilities. However, neither of these were the first. Hacienda Village (1942) and Imperial Gardens (1944) were both built earlier.

Despite these multiple housing projects, housing for Blacks in Los Angeles was still a problem. With Watts and Compton running out of space, the city accepted Reverend Pledger's request to build in Pacoima.

The projects were the only apartment-style housing in Pacoima until the Van Nuys-Pierce Apartments came in the sixties.

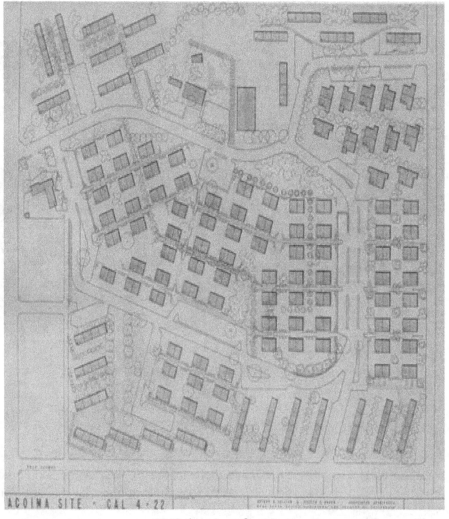

1949 drawing of projects

San Fernando Gardens Housing Projects built in 1955

Father Mattick at Guardian Angel located in the San Fernando Gardens Projects 1964 (Courtesy Lupe and Manuel Hernandez collection)

James Tolliver III and friends in the projects 1961
(Courtesy James Tolliver III collection)

Although the projects had military veterans in mind when built, most of the veterans purchased homes in the new housing tracts. However, a very diverse demographic of low-income families from throughout Los Angeles did move in.

During those early years in the projects, Whites, Mexicans, and Blacks were equal in numbers. In the sixties, it was a family-friendly environment that greatly benefited the Pacoima community. However, during the seventies and eighties, social changes began to occur. Crime, drugs, and gangs began to filter in and ultimately consumed the San Fernando Gardens Housing Projects. It earned nicknames such as "Sherm Alley" and forced its residents to confront a new social reality that would last decades.

12
Pacoima
Businesses

Pacoima was an agricultural town in the early 1900s. By 1913, a US Post Office opened, and in 1916 the Pacoima Chamber of Farmers began. As construction grew in the town, Anawalt Lumber Company, which opened in 1921, became one of the first successful Pacoima businesses. Their location was alongside the railroad tracks where modern-day San Fernando Road intersects with Van Nuys Boulevard.

Photo 1954 - Hal Anawalt opened Anawalt Lumber Company in 1921.

Lopez Market in San Fernando was also among the first businesses in the area, but as Pacoima grew, small markets, dairies, produce stands, and restaurants emerged.

Banking institutions arrived when Empire Savings and Loan was opened by Glen Raddatz, who formed a group of investors in 1955. A year later, the San Fernando Valley Commercial and Savings Bank opened and later changed the name to Trans World Bank.

During the 1929 Great Depression, Victor Ayala opened The Hub Liquor on the corner of Van Nuys Boulevard and San Fernando Road. Ayala also owned another store on Van Nuys and Haddon Avenue.

The HUB LIQUOR STORE
10801 San Fernando Road
Pacoima 91331
Telephone: 897-1908

Early oral stories speak of the Red Barn Restaurant located in today's Panorama City, which was once was considered Pacoima. Nothing surrounded the restaurant, but the dirt road to get there. Furthermore, when it rained, the road produced massive mud puddles. However, it was one of the only restaurants in the area.

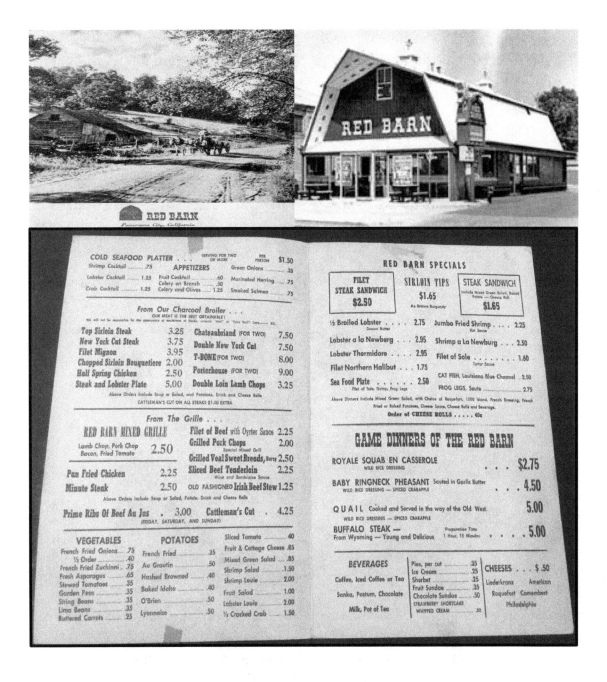

Roman's Market first opened as Gomez Grocery on Judd Street in 1926. The owner, Prudencio M. Gomez, worked as a fruit picker from a young age and later decided he wanted to be his own boss. He took the gamble while having a wife, five daughters, and a niece to support and began his grocery business.

During the Great Depression, Gomez took the unusual path of extending credit to his patrons during these hard times and giving food to those in need. Known for his kindness and helping the community, he later moved his store to Filmore Street and renamed it Gomez Groceries & Meats.

The store passed on to his daughter and son-in-law, Rosalie & Ralph Roman, who changed the name to Roman's Market after Gomez retired. However, they maintained the Gomez customer service tradition. Pacoima Historical Society honored Roman's Market in 2017 as one of Pacoima's oldest businesses.

Prudencio Gomez opened Gomez Groceries in 1926 on Judd Street.
(Courtesy of Mercedes Salazar collection)

PM Gomez moved the store to 13319 Filmore Street. Shown here is Mercedes Gomez
(Courtesy Mercedes Salazar collection)

Gomez Groceries became Roman's Market on Filmore Street
(Pacoima Historical Society Archives)

In 1944, Pacoima's iconic market, Tresierras, opened on Kalisher Street in San Fernando. Founded by Francisco "Frank" Tresierras Sr. and his wife, Pilar, it was first known as "Frank's Market." At that time, they had a 12-year-old son, Richard, and two older sons Frank and Daniel, who fought during WWII in the Philippines and Saipan, respectively. The Tresierras family also had three daughters: Isabel, Virginia, and Delfina. The girls helped with the market too.

The Tresierras Family worked hard to establish the business. In two short years, they outgrew the store in San Fernando. Frank then bought a piece of land on Van Nuys Boulevard and built a new market in Pacoima. He renamed it "Tresierras Market."

Unfortunately, Frank Tresierras Jr. died during WWII, fighting in Luzon, Philippines. However, his wife Belen worked with the family at the store. Daniel Tresierras Sr. returned from battle to help his parents and Richard run the business. Frank and Pilar eventually had a third son, James.

By 1958, Richard, Daniel, and James took over the day-to-day operations and were successful in growing the business. In 1997, the name changed once again to "Tresierras Supermarkets" when they opened larger-format stores.

The company has also opened locations in Oxnard and Santa Paula while celebrating its 75th year of business in 2019. They have helped pioneer the "Latino Supermarket" concept in the Western United States.

Richard's three sons, Art, Mark, and Chris Tresierras, now run the Supermarkets as they continue the family's grocery legacy. Tresierras is one of Pacoima's oldest and most loved businesses.

In 2018, the Pacoima Historical Society honored and declared Tresierras an official "Historic Business" in Pacoima.

Store founder Frank Tresierras with sons, Richard and Daniel in 1945
(Courtesy Art Tresierras)

Richard Tresierras with older brother Daniel in 1947
(Courtesy Art Tresierras)

Richard Tresierras 1948
(Courtesy Art Tresierras)

Pacoima Tresierras Supermarket on Van Nuys Blvd is still a popular neighborhood store.

(Photographer Lorenzo Grandison)

During the fifties and sixties, drive-up dairies were as popular as today's 7-Elevens. Milk delivery was commonplace up to the mid-sixties, and Roger Jessup Dairies, located on Glenoaks Blvd, was one of the most popular businesses in Pacoima.

Roger Jessup Dairies began farming cows in 1919 in Glendale and had several dairies in Pacoima and many throughout the Valley. Roger W. Jessup was born November 5, 1889, in Salt Lake City, Utah. After starting his business with Jessup Certified Farms with only forty cows, his company became the largest individually owned dairies in the world. He and his wife Marguerite had over 1200 cows by 1960. They also had Jessup Breeders, which for years was the largest western-based artificial insemination company. He and his wife moved to Pacoima where they lived until his passing in 1971. Named in honor of this business pioneer is Roger Jessup Park, located on Osborne Street.

Milk delivery was commonplace in Pacoima up until the mid-sixties. Roger Jessup Dairies was located on Glenoaks Blvd in Pacoima.

Roger Jessup Dairy - 1960

Roger W. Jessup (1889 – 1971)   Most Dairies used glass bottles with their trademark names on them.

Another Dairy in Pacoima was Manfull Dairy Farm, opened in the 1930s by Cyrus and Lucille Manfull. It was located at 13152 Wentworth Street and was said to be one of the first drive-up Dairies. According to the granddaughter Natalya Livingston, the dairy not only had cows, but they milked them, processed the milk, and delivered as well. There were heartwarming stories about Cy Manfull and his neighborly generosity. These included giving free milk service to a widow and paying for broken windows after kids hit baseballs through them. Operations ceased in 1971.

Lee's Restaurant opened in 1947 on Van Nuys Blvd right next to Tresierras Market. It was the only place where Blacks could eat out and dance at that time. Rosa Lee opened the restaurant after wanting a place where Black people could eat, and she could utilize her Southern cooking skills. She was born in Mississippi but moved to Louisiana before her family packed up and headed west. She lived on Hoyt Street when she decided to begin her new venture. She served hamburgers, French fries, fried chicken, beer, and wine. Her daughter, Emma Middleton, helped her run the restaurant, as did other family members. The restaurant eventually became too much for Rosa, and she closed it after a few short years. However, the door to Lee's Restaurant remains a part of Tresierras Supermarket, at its original address on 13160 Van Nuys Boulevard.

Lees Restaurant on 13160 Van Nuys Blvd in 1949. People of color could eat a meal and dance after hours. Pictured is Emma Middleton, Rosa's daughter. (Ora Hutchinson Collection)

Rosa Lee opened Lee's Restaurant on Van Nuys Blvd in the late 40's.
(Ora Hutchinson Collection)

Printes Hodges is Rosa Lee's great-grandson. Raised in Pacoima, he has many memories of the restaurant. Hodges explained that during the day, regular people would come in and have lunch; hamburgers, chicken, and French-fries. However, things were different at night.

"In the evening party, people came in. For example, I remember my cousin Dennis and I was there having a hamburger during the summer. It was about 6 o'clock but wasn't dark. It was still light outside. This guy came into the restaurant, and I remember him dancing and hollering, talking about having a good time. Yeah, he was having a good time in the restaurant all by himself. He was having such a good time that grandma and great-grandma had us go into the kitchen and finish our hamburgers. Then they took us home."

He added, "At that time, Van Nuys Blvd was full of black-owned bars on both sides of the street. Dew Drop Inn was the name of one of them. I can't remember the names of all the others, but there were about 10 bars on both sides of the street. So, Van Nuys Blvd, during the early fifties, was not a safe place to be at night. Yeah, I remember we weren't allowed to go on Van Nuys Boulevard when it got dark because it got crazy."

This 1950 photo was taken in front of Lees Restaurant on Van Nuys Blvd. Shown are Ora Hutchinson and Percy Somprac getting ready to enter the eatery.

halls where they could go socialize and pass the time away. The restaurant was a very interesting time. The whole family worked in there. But all they could sell was beer. It was kind of rough. They had to charge high prices to make money on food. Liquor was the easiest way to make money. They never got a liquor license."

Rosa Lee's daughter Minnie Williams and Printes Hodges in 1946,

Frenchy and his grandfather Tom Williams during a Boy Scouts photo shoot in 1952.

While the earlier businesses were essential to Pacoima's growth and development, there were still only a few before 1950. Major shopping typically was done in San Fernando, which had Sears, JC Penny, and a popular Levi's store.

When Reverend Broadous opened his barbershop in 1950, it was the only one in the area at that time. In 1947, Louis J. Mendoza and Jimmy Servilla had opened Pacoima Food Market on Van Nuys Blvd.

Trudy Sims Chicken Shack was on San Fernando Road in the forties. She freshly killed her farm-raised chickens for diners.

However, once Joe Louis Homes began to fill up in 1952, and the San Fernando Gardens opened in 1955, old businesses began to thrive and new businesses started to emerge.

There was a malt store on Herrick Avenue called Herb's Market, which later became known as "Grandpa's." Shop Easy Grocery Market on Glenoaks and Paxton Ave is another. The market was in a mall that had a Hudson Shoe store, fish market, and liquor store. When the 118 freeway began construction in 1970, eminent domain eliminated some of those businesses.

However, Mexicans and Blacks were not the only small business owners that flourished during this population boom. Pacoima was a very diverse community, and business success came in all colors and nationalities.

Sal and Esther Del Gaudio arrived in Pacoima in 1949 and opened Del Gaudio's Market on San Fernando Road in 1950. Their families had immigrated from Italy. The Del Gaudios came from Philadelphia to Pacoima and became part of the town's Italian community, which Esther claims was substantial.

Sal and Esther Del Gaudio in 1956 on San Fernando Rd. in front of Del Gaudio's Market. Whiteman Air Park is across the street.
(Courtesy Esther Del Gaudio collection)

Their son, Salvatore, describes the early days. "My mom, she had myself, my older sister Bee, when she started. She just found this open front market, and she would sell orange juice. She went to the packing house across the street. I think it was Southland Packing. She got a case of oranges and squeezed the oranges for the truckers. Because in 1950, that was before the 5-freeway existed, and 99 (route), San Fernando Road, was the main thoroughfare to LA. So, she had customers all day long. It was a really busy highway. She stayed open until midnight taking care of the customers."

Del Gaudio's Market - Jules, Sal, Sal Jr. and Uncle Tony in 1974
(Courtesy Esther Del Gaudio collection)

The store became known for its Italian submarine sandwiches. Esther expressed her experience running the store while raising five children.

"I always loved my work…I didn't consider it work. It was something I enjoyed doing. It was a very friendly area, and it was surprising to me because it was in an area we weren't used to. We got along really well and didn't have any problems."

Del Gaudio's Market is one of Pacoima's historic businesses. It remains a family-run establishment known for its excellent customer service and great food.

Del Gaudio's Market is located at 10567 San Fernando Road in Pacoima

Stylesville Barbershop and Beauty Salon opened in 1957. Owners Freddie Carter and his wife Ollie arrived in Pacoima in 1955. They were both raised in Los Angeles and attended Jefferson High School.

Freddie Carter first began sharing a spot with Hillery Broadous, called Quality Barbershop, located by Tresierras Market. At that time, regulations prohibited men and women's hair from being styled in the same room, so Freddie had a room in the front and Ollie in the rear.

Then in 1977, the opportunity came to purchase the Dew Drop Inn property, which was right across the street. They had long outgrown the small shop they rented from Tresierras. They purchased the building, renovated it, and the legend of Stylesville began.

Freddie Carter operated with class and style as the founder of Stylesville. Even after many left Pacoima they still came back to get their hair styled.
(Courtesy Greg Faucet Stylesville collection)

Freddie and Ollie Carter (above) were staples of the Pacoima community for decades. During the 60s and 70s they attracted patrons from around the country.
(Courtesy Stylesville collection)

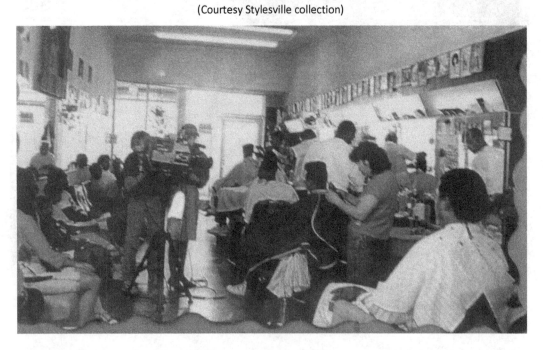

Stylesville employed some of the city's most talented hair stylist. During the weekend, patrons spent hours at shop socializing and having a great time, while waiting to get a shave and cut. (Courtesy Stylesville collection)

Aerial view of Stylesville on Van Nuys Blvd
(Courtesy Greg Faucet Stylesville collection)

The legendary Freddie Carter and Stylesville attracted high-profile Black celebrities such as Redd Foxx, Billie Eckstein, Jackson 5, New Edition, and numerous NFL, MLB, and NBA sports stars. It was one of the most popular shops in all of Los Angeles. Ollie Carter maintained a separate woman's area even after the removal of gender regulations.

Stylesville is the oldest Black-owned business in the San Fernando Valley, still operating in 2019.

"My grandmother and grandfather wanted to have their own business," says Gregory Faucett, Freddie's grandson. "It's a Black man's dream to have their own business. The opportunity came, and they ran with it, and I'm kind of glad they did. When you have a business like this as long as it's been here, it kind of makes you look at things from a different perspective."

Faucett and his mother, Artinella Carter, took over for Freddie and Ollie Carter and assumed business operations.

Greg Faucett operates Stylesville, but the town's demographics have changed.

Stylesville Barber & Beauty Salon located on Van Nuys Blvd is the oldest barbershop in Pacoima.

Here are some of the many other iconic Pacoima businesses from over the years.

73'S FROM N. WINTER - 10107 LEV AVE. - PACOIMA, CALIF.

KGIL radio opened in 1947 in Pacoima and later moved to Mission Hills. It was initially a Big Band radio Station that switched to talk show format in 1985. It closed its frequency in 1993.

Dales Market opened in 1949 on Laurel Canyon Blvd. This photo dated 1950

The Pacific Theatres opened the Laurel Drive-In on May 11, 1955 with Glenn Ford in "Blackboard Jungle". It was closed on May 11, 1969. Demolished in the early-1970's

1958 Ralphs Markets receives citation from Pacoima Community Coordinating Council in recognition of their fair employment policies.

1959 Opening Thom McAn Shoes 8915 Woodman Ave Pacoima Councilman Earl Earnie, Darlene Tomkins and Warren Van Denplas cut the nylon ribbon.

Groundbreaking ceremony for the new Blue-Chip Stamp Redemption Center on 9040 Woodman Ave in Pacoima on March 31, 1960. Blue Chip Stamps were issued by participating vendors and were pasted in booklets. The booklets were turned in at the store for merchandise.

Shoestring was a fast food spot that opened in 1961 at 13045 Van Nuys Blvd. It was one of the favorite places on the boulevard.

El Indio Restaurant opened in 1975 and is a popular Mexican eatery Located at 13403 Van Nuys Blvd. (Lorenzo Grandison photographer)

Baby Beef was located on the corner of Osborne and Foothill. It was known as a popular place due to its proximity to Hansen Dam. Residents used to call them fly burgers. The horseback riders from Hansen Stables used to tie the horses to the hitching rail, and the manure attracted a lot of flies.

James Wynn was the founder and owner of Jim's Wholesale Meats and also opened Jim's Happy Chicken.

Fantastic Fair on Van Nuys Blvd held its grand opening in 1962, It was the first major department store in Pacoima.

Helms Bakery and Mr. Stamps drove through the streets of the valley selling donuts and snacks.

1964 grand opening of the new, nine-hole Hansen Dam Golf Course on Glenoaks. It later expanded to 18 holes and was frequented by numerous celebrities. OJ Simpson was a noted frequent visitor. The Tavern on the Green clubhouse and restaurant was opened later.

Early days at Hansen Dam Golf Course, where golfers are forced to use portable facilities. This photo was taken in 1965.

Tavern on the Green at Hansen Dam Golf Course was the venue for weddings and special events. It was also a nightclub in the 70's and 80's with a DJ that Pacoima folks enjoyed.

1959 Neil's Sporting Goods and Boat Sales, 13354 Van Nuys Blvd

Rex's Western Ware in 1962 gained notoriety after fighting the removal of this Indian statue by the city's Board of Public Works. It was removed after a month-long fight despite a petition signed by some Pacoima residents.

White Front stores began in 1929 and opened a store in Pacoima on the corner of Van Nuys Blvd and Laurel Canyon in 1968.

Boys Market was located on the corner of Van Nuys Blvd and Glenoaks.

Keys Burgers opened in 1979 across the street from Maclay Junior High on Glenoaks Blvd.

1965 photo of Virgil Walkers AAA Drapery Service and Travel Agency located at 13460 Van Nuys Blvd. Developed first modern drapery cleaning equipment.

Gemco opened up on Van Nuys Blvd. It was a membership department store that was very popular in the 70's until closing in 1986 when its chain of stores was sold to Target.

Gemco introduced one of the first department store membership cards

Some additional noteworthy Pacoima businesses include:

Pacoima Hardware	Country Fair Market
Joe's Swing Shop	Robinson Realty
Pacoima Food Market	Rucker's Mortuary
Rib Rack	Shop Easy
Mohawk Gas Station	Wong's Kitchen
Esquire Barber Shop	Key's Burgers
CB Auto Parts	Video Agenda
Crest Loan & Jewelry	Elias Brake and Tires
Bayshore Fish Market	Alpha Beta (Foothill)
Leon's Jr. Market	Pearl's Fish Market
Safeway	Lion's Den
Zody's	Shone's Drug Store
77 Club	Golden Lion Barber Shop
BB's	Ott's
Tastee Freeze	Dr. Marshall (Dentist)
Bonanza Liquor Store	Garcia's
Dr. Harvey	Dr. Downs (Veterinarian)
Dr. Moreland	BJ's Glenoaks Room
Paxton Liquor Store	The Green Jug
Go Carts Foothill/Arroyo	Williams Furniture
Elsies Beauty Shop	Annie's Beauty shop
Ada's Beauty Salon	Ramon's Market
Eden Roc Jr. Market	Doohinky's Night Club
Black & White Towing	Tony's Union 76
Family Affair Record Shop	Thrifty'

13
Community Growth

The services of local government and community organizations in Pacoima have benefited the town tremendously over the years. While some have fought the injustices of racial discrimination and civil rights, others have fulfilled a vast number of needs. These have included jobs, healthcare, youth programs, senior care, and a variety of community services. Typically, non-profit or public service, some of them are highlighted here.

Pledgerville

Pledgerville Senior Citizens Villa was a vision that began in 1972 by Reverend T. G. Pledger , founder of Greater Community Baptist Church. However, the first resident would not move-in until 12 years later. Pledger, along with Paul T. Lewis and a host of other community members, navigated the complex bureaucracy and red tape needed to make this vision a reality. In 1979, an architectural proposal and funding request submitted to Housing and Urban Development got rejected. However, with determination and dedicated support, it was later approved. After groundbreaking ceremonies on February 19, 1983, its first occupancy happened in March of 1984.

The first Board of Directors were Joe Phillips (Chief Executive Officer), Earline Stepney (First Vice President), Frank Divens (Second Vice President), Jane McGlory (Executive Financial Officer), and Eula C. Rose (Executive Secretary).

Ted Minor was Pledgerville's Social Services Director and was also a teacher at Kennedy High School. He said it was years of hard work, but the villa gave the community a much-needed lift and was a big step in revitalizing the look and depth of Pacoima. As of 2019, the facility operates at 90 percent occupancy and is among the tallest structures in the town.

Pledgerville is located at 11060 Norris Avenue.
(Photographer Lorenzo Grandison)

Pacoima Skills Center

The Pacoima Skills Center was started in 1964 by residents John Mance, and Carl McCraven, who recognized the youth in Pacoima needed marketable job skills to succeed. Mance worked in human resources at Lockheed and knew the hiring process. He had two sons that were in their twenties by this time and saw how important this was.

They opened the center in an industrial area on Louvre Street at a small facility. In the early years, it mostly served Pacoima's Black community. Funded through the Manpower Development and Training Act of 1962, PSC opened in 1966 with Harian Barbane as Principal.

It quickly turned into the top skills center in the country in terms of students completing programs and job placements. Later, PSC became part of the Los Angeles Unified School District's Division of Adult and Career Education branch. As the clientele grew, it moved to Van Nuys Blvd in 1995, to become more accessible for transportation. The new location allowed them to offer more services.

As the demographics in Pacoima changed, PSC added Spanish-speaking instructors, and today's students are predominately Latino. In 2012, the center relocated to Arleta Ave in Sun Valley and changed its name to East Valley Skills Center.

John Mance

Carl McCraven

Skills Center Given Credit for Job Gain

Success of the Pacoima Skills Center in upgrading unemployed persons for places in today's market and heavy emphasis on development of positions for veterans, the physically handicapped and the lesser-skilled were among the factors contributing to an increase in job placements in the Valley during October.

Three offices of the California State Employment Service reported 4001 persons found jobs during the month. This compares with a 3563 placed in the Valley during September.

This 1967 news article discussed the success of Pacoima Skills Center. Pictured is Al Landeros taught auto mechanics at Pacoima Skill Center for 20 years.
(David Aguilar Photography collection)

Northeast Valley Health Corporation

Northeast Valley Health Corporation (NEVHC) was a shared vision of Pacoima civic leaders Luis Garcia, Ed Kussman, Carl McCraven, and Thomas Montgomery. These men saw a need for health services in Pacoima, envisioning a healthcare system that catered to uninsured individuals in need of services. Being active in the community, they utilized their influence and experience to incorporate in 1971. Two years later, in 1973, the San Fernando Health Center was opened and officially dedicated by Senator Ted Kennedy.

Today NEVHC is the lead agency for managing one of the nation's largest healthcare grants for the homeless. It has 14 health centers in the San Fernando and Santa Clarita Valleys and continues to serve uninsured and medically underserved individuals in the area.

They help nearly 70,000 patients annually by providing medical, dental, and behavioral healthcare every year. NEVHC is a nonprofit joint commission accredited Federally Qualified Health Center and one of the nation's largest community health centers.

Louis Garcia, Carl McCraven, Senator Ted Kennedy and Ed Kussman were responsible for opening the Northeast Valley Health Corp in 1971.

Northeast Valley Health Corporation on Van Nuys & Glenoaks
(Photographer Lorenzo Grandison)

Boys and Girls Club of San Fernando Valley

The Boys Club of San Fernando Valley was founded in 1966 by a group of community leaders who recognized the youth of Pacoima had a lack of activities and social services. They raised the initial funding to generate a joint grant from the Boys Club of America and Southern California Boys Club Foundation.

LeRoy Chase, along with the help of B'Nai Brith, a Jewish Women's organization, and a few others got the organization off the ground. The Boys Club's first location on Van Nuys Blvd was a building donated by the Pacoima Woman's Club.

First facility for the Boys Club of SFV on Van Nuys Blvd
(Courtesy Boys & Girls Club of SFV)

LeRoy Chase became the Boy's Club director in 1968 and remained involved with the organization for over fifty years. He was active with many causes and known by all the politicians and leaders in the Los Angeles area. He was a pillar in the community and always figured out a way to keep the doors open.

Educated at the University of Utah, Chase obtained his Bachelor of Science degree in health, physical education, and recreation. He also had political aspirations, once running for the Seventh District Council seat. His platform was for leaders to not focus on arresting and prosecuting offenders. Instead, he wanted to pull people out of a life of crime and prevent at-risk youth from getting in trouble. All the Mayors of Los Angeles throughout the years, as well as State Assembly and Council people, respected his work.

LeRoy Chase

Sugar Ray Robinson at the Boys Club with
Congressman James C. Corman in 1970.
(Courtesy of Boys and Girls Club)

Actor John Amos at Boys Club in the 70s. John Amos, who lived in Sylmar, had a successful CBS network sitcom called "Good Times," which ran from 1974 -79.
(Courtesy Camille Watkins collection)

Councilman Alex Padilla (future US Senator) and Leroy Chase at Boys and Girls Club event.

Perhaps LeRoy Chase's most notable success was his connection and concern for the youth of Pacoima. Countless Pacoimians give Chase credit for their achievements, including their first job, mentoring them, and providing a place to stay out of trouble. Most markedly was their exposure to martial arts and discipline.

In 1985, the Boys Club of SFV secured a new 30,000 square foot facility on Glenoaks Blvd, and in 1990 changed its name to the Boys and Girls Club of San Fernando Valley. Their after-school program provides a variety of activities for kids, helping them shape their future. Leroy Chase molded and led this organization through its hard times and good times until his passing in 2018. His wife Shirin and children Kymberly, Nicole, and Danielle survive him.

The Chase Family (L-R) Kymberly, Shirin, Danielle, Leroy, and Nicole

Leroy Chase leaves behind a legacy that Pacoima's history will always remember. The Boys and Girls Club of San Fernando Valley is the town's oldest nonprofit full-service youth agency. It operates under the leadership of his daughter Nicole Chase.

Many other countless individuals have served the Boys and Girls Club of San Fernando Valley. Dwayne Campbell, Art Director, has worked there since 1985.

(Photo courtesy Schvone Rouse)

He teaches art, including paper-mâché candle making, cooking, and woodcraft. He also takes the kids horseback riding as well as on fishing trips. Campbell has received awards from Mayor Tom Bradley for arts and achievements. His goal is keeping kids off the streets by giving them something inspiring to do. His children and now grandchildren have enjoyed the benefits of this organization.

(Pictured left is Dwayne Campbell teaching art at Boys Club in 1986.)

Today's Boys & Girls Club of San Fernando Valley

MEND

One of Pacoima's most prominent and well-known charity organizations is MEND, which was founded in 1971 by a group of people who recognized a need for individuals facing poverty. One of the co-founding members is Ed Rose, who, along with his wife Carolyn, tells the story of how MEND came about and what separates them from other charities.

"MEND is an acronym meaning, 'meet each need with dignity,' and it's our basic philosophy," says Ed Rose.

"We feel it is extremely important that all our clients be treated with respect and dignity. A person needs to have strong self-esteem and feel good about themselves. Otherwise, the chances of them succeeding are lessened. We're the largest nonprofit poverty agency in the San Fernando Valley, and through the years, we've expanded.

"We have dental services, medical services, acupuncture, zumba, all kinds of that type of activity, as well as we're the largest food pantry in the San Fernando Valley. We've gone into a great deal of effort for educational purposes, and we have one building set aside just for education. We have a couple of characteristics that most other nonprofit organizations don't have. One is we don't accept government funding. For all our 47 years, we've had to get funding from the community, foundations, businesses, and whatever. The other is we are volunteer-driven. So about 90% of the work is done through volunteers.

"We've talked about having our medical facilities — we have one man who is a doctor that heads that. But all the doctors and nurses and pharmacists are volunteers. Now we have connections with UCLA, USC, Yorba Linda, different colleges, and they all have internships and bring their students here to MEND. And like Concord and other schools where people pay to go to school, we have a connection with them so we can get their services for free. I was just thinking the other day that one of our big things, and we didn't plan it that way, is that we are really good at helping young people get an education in medicine and teaching. We have a lot of students from CSUN that come and assist us. Young students' mentor them and help them in their studies. Parents in this community, well some of them, quite a few, they really can't help their kids. They don't have the educational background themselves; maybe they don't speak or read English that well. So, the kids have kind of a difficult time. So, we have a lot of high school and college students, that help and mentor the kids. A mother will bring a son in, and he's doing D work. After three months, he's up to a C and quite often up to a B after a while. And it really makes the mothers happy and proud when they bring the report cards to the mentors."

Pacoima City Hall features trailblazers Ed and Carolyn Rose
Artwork by Ignacio Gomez

MEND began in a garage with Ed and Carolyn Rose, along with a few other people, that grew to three garages before they sought out a facility. They rented an old drapery cleaning building, but when the lease was up, they had to partake in some serious fundraising. They needed to raise $97,000, so they could purchase the property or lose the location. Ed Rose, Bob Von Frankenberg, and others hit the pavement fundraising. The old building needed renovation, but its location on the 13400 block of Van Nuys Blvd was perfect for their mission.

Despite the 1994 Northridge earthquake damaging the building, they still managed to repair it. However, they eventually outgrew that location and opened a new one on San Fernando Road.

Today the newest facility is a 40,000 square foot building, purchased in 2007, that serves the homeless and a wide range of Pacoima's community. Food, clothing, medical, dental, vision, and education are all channeled in this remarkable establishment.

MEND building on San Fernando Rd.

Other Notable Community Organizations

Pacoima Chamber of Commerce

Volunteers of America

Children's Hunger Fund

African American Leadership Organization

Pacoima Historical Society

Pacoima Neighborhood Council

Pacoima Community Coordinating Council

Pacoima Shrine Club

El Proyecto del Barrio

Youth Speaks Collective

CHRYSALIS

Pueblo Y Salud

Youth Policy Institute

Well Suited

Pacoima Kiwani's Club

Pacoima Woman's Club

Foothill Police Department

Foothill Police Department opened in September 1961. It is one of LA's oldest stations. Before its opening, all police services in the San Fernando Valley were dispatched from the Van Nuys station when needed.

The valley was transforming from an agricultural community to a populated suburb of Los Angeles when the city built the station. With an explosion of new homes getting erected in the fifties and significant population growth, the city decided to place Foothill Division Headquarters in Pacoima. The location chosen was on Osborne Street, near San Fernando Road. During that time, the station covered the areas of Granada Hills, Sylmar, Sun Valley, Sunland, Tujunga, and Pacoima.

In 1963, LAPD Captain Robert Richards was the commander of Foothill Division Station.

Sept 5, 1961 roll call performed by Robert W. Richards at opening of Foothill division.
(Veda James collection)

Foothill Detectives April 1965. Pacoima resident Veda James became the first female
to work in the detective unit for the Los Angeles Police Department.

Although Foothill Division is still best known for the infamous 1991 beating of Rodney King, the department has gone through a noteworthy makeover and now has numerous community outreach programs and a policing philosophy that engages with the culture of the town.

LAPD Cadets and Officers from Foothill Division hang out with California Secretary of State Alex Padilla (future US Senator) at Pacoima History Day on October 6, 2018.
(Courtesy Pacoima Historical Society)

Mural inside the Foothill yard painted by Levi Ponce, Juan Reyes, Leonardo Tejeda and Tomas Prado. (Courtesy Che Naveja)

Pacoima Library

Pacoima Library began its operation in 1926. Its first location was in the rear of Pacoima Dry Goods, where they rented space at the store. The first official library building came in 1945 and was run by librarian Agnes Eisert from 1945 until 1960.

Pacoima's first official public library opened in 1945. The community was proud to have a library when this branch opened.

On August 23, 1961, the Los Angeles Public Library opened a new facility to the public. More than 1,300 books circulated on that first day. The Librarian for the new location was Frances Miller, who helped make the library a cultural center.

Groundbreaking for new Pacoima library (above) and officially opened in 1961 (below)

Mrs. Frances Miller, Pacoima branch librarian, begins boxing of 13,000 volumes for move into a new $200,000 facility at 13605 Van Nuys Blvd in 1961.

Library aide Maria Barrigan, 17, works with children at Pacoima Elementary School in 1965.

United States Post Office

The US Postal Service in Pacoima began in 1913 with E. Q. Bransen, inside his general store north of the railroad tracks. Bransen was the first postmaster in Pacoima. In 1921, Morris Williams purchased the store located at 13132 Pershing St, which is today's Van Nuys Boulevard. In 1948, US President Franklin D Roosevelt appointed Lillian Friedman postmaster.

1950 Postmaster Lillian Friedman is congratulated on opening of new facility

The last postmaster appointed by a U.S. President was Nancy Avery, who headed up Pacoima. She was the first female African American to run a major post office. After her appointment by John F. Kennedy, postmasters received assignments through the civil service process. Nancy Avery retired in 1984.

Pacoima's U.S. Postmaster Nancy Avery with John DeRoo Jr. (right) in 1961. Avery was appointed postmaster by President John F. Kennedy

Morris Williams was postmaster from1922 to 1932. He also opened Pacoima's first general store in 1921. Williams and his wife Rose, who helped him with the daily operations, are shown in this 1964 photo.

Barbara Ann Woodhall was the first postal woman mail carrier in 1962.

US Post Office in Pacoima (Photographer Lorenzo Grandison)

Fire Station No. 98

Fire Station 98 was built in 1960, one year before Foothill police Station was built. It has always been open to the public for visiting and information. It is located at 13035 Van Nuys Blvd.

RTD

Rapid Transit District (RTD) was established in 1964 to serve the Southern California region. It replaced the Los Angeles Metropolitan Transit Authority and eleven other failing bus systems. It ran until 1982. One of the notable lines that ran down Van Nuys Blvd was the 93. However, the RTD numbering system changed a few times throughout the years as the population grew. It was a popular form of transportation for Pacoima residents.

Line 93 Bus Schedule - 1967

14

1957
Plane Crash

In 1957, Pacoima was experiencing mass migration from the new housing tracts. However, services had not yet caught up with the town. This story had nationwide consequences as President Dwight Eisenhower's administration had many questions to answer regarding this crash. It is a story Pacoima will never forget.

On January 31, 1957, Pacoima experienced a horrific tragedy when a Douglas DC-7B, operated by Douglas Aircraft Company, collided with a United States Air Force Northrop F-89 in midair. Students at Pacoima Junior High were practicing for their graduation in the auditorium at the time of the collision, while others were on the gym field. A total of three children died, with seventy-five injured as a result of this incident. The names of the students who died on the ground were Bob Zallan, Evan Elsner, and Ron Brann.

Four crew members also died in the crash, whose names were William Carr, Archie Twitchell, Waldo Adams, and radioman Roy Nakagawa.

Plane wreckage scattered over a two-mile radius. Witnesses to the crash described seeing two planes crash in midair and exploding.

Investigators determined the crash likely occurred over the Hansen Dam area at approximately 11:18 AM. The only survivor was radioman Curtiss Adams, who parachuted out landing on a garage roof in Burbank.

7 KILLED. 74 HURT IN SCHOOL AIR CRASH

SCENE OF TRAGEDY—Wreckage of DC-7B transport lies scattered over a Pacoima churchyard. Cross shows point of impact of planes and arrows trace the paths of the transport and the jet, which fell in La Tuna Canyon far to the right. Wreckage in the area of crashed transport covered more than two miles.

Jet, Transport Collide High in Sky; Pieces Slash Into Playground

Seven persons were killed and an estimated 74 injured yesterday when a new DC-7B transport collided at high altitude with a Scorpion jet interceptor and smashed into flaming bits across church and school yards in Pacoima.

Two of the dead were boys on the playground of the Pacoima Junior High School where the scores of youngsters were injured all boys in a gym class. Two 12-year-old girls were treated for shock.

Four crewmen died when the $2,000,000 four-engine transport plunged to earth at terrific speed in the yard of the Pacoima Congregational Church adjacent to the school. The collision occurred between 11:18 and 11:23 a.m.

The pilot of the Scorpion died in the falling crash of the interceptor in La Tuna Canyon, some two miles north of Lockheed Air Terminal, after his airman bailed out over Burbank.

Wreckage of the transport covered a path of more than two miles, with bits and pieces of the heavy liner

2 FULL PAGES OF PICTURES
Other photos and stories of Pacoima air tragedy will be found on Pages 2, 3, 4, 5, 6, 7, 8, 9, 14, 15 and 13, Part 1.

strewn across roof tops, hanging from trees and fences, littering lawns and streets.

The two children killed on the playground at 2810 Laurel Canyon Blvd. apparently were struck by hurtling chunks of metal from the fiery explosion that enveloped the scene when the main portion of the wreckage plummeted into myriad fragments.

Some 220 boys in four gym squads had been on the playground in free play (street) clothes moments earlier when they were summoned to the gymnasium by a class bell. Those nearest the building were inside when the crash occurred. Those farther out on the field were caught in the maelstrom of flying metal.

What made this tragic accident of national significance were the facts surrounding the crashed F89 Fighter. The plane had departed from Edwards Airforce Base in Palmdale at 10:50 AM and was conducting a radar equipment test at 25,000 feet above a residential area. The other aircraft was a DC-7B that left from Santa Monica at 10:15, earmarked for delivery to Continental Airlines on its first functional test flight.

President Dwight Eisenhower faced a storm of protests after the crash, regarding conducting tests in populated areas. A task force was assigned to investigate how to prevent accidents like these from happening in the future.

Teachers at Terra Bella Elementary attributed the "drop" exercise as a saving factor that helped prevent debris from hitting their students. That campus was adjacent to Pacoima Junior High, and the staff and students there suffered minimal injuries.

Debris was scattered across the grounds of Terra Bella Elementary School, located adjacent to the junior high. Pacoima Congregational Church, next door to the school also had debris.

Bernice Thompson was in the kitchen at her home on Terra Bella Street. She said the blast nearly knocked her down and blew out the kitchen windows.

"It was a terrible, horrible noise in the sky. It was black — I can't describe it…but I knew something was coming down… It was all fire and flames everywhere…I saw a woman screaming and trying to climb the school fence."

Bernice dashed into the yard and threw herself on the children to protect them from flying debris. Unfortunately, her five-year-old son had already been struck in the throat by flying metal. He luckily survived. However, the smell of gasoline and oil engulfed the area for quite a while.

The scene right after the crash at Pacoima Junior High was like a warzone as smoke swept over the schoolyard. First responders arrived quickly to an extremely chaotic set of circumstances.

1957 - Moments after the crash, people were assessing the damage on the schoolyard.

The seventy-five injuries consisted of amputations, severe burns, traumatic brain injuries, and more. Most people speculate that if there were not a graduation rehearsal, more deaths and injuries would have occurred.

At the time of the crash, there were a total of five hospitals in the San Fernando Valley, which served 750,000 people. First responders sent most of the injured to Sun Valley Hospital, but other nearby facilities received patients as well. Twenty-five ambulances arrived at the scene and transported 52 patients within minutes to St. Joseph's in Burbank and Valley Receiving in Van Nuys. The hospitals were aware of the magnitude of injuries and moved other patients to make room for the arrivals. Carts were waiting at the emergency entrance when the first ambulance arrived.

Pictured is debris that landed on a house after the crash

Even with all the emergency planning and swift work of first responders, the topic of discussion afterward was about no medical facilities in Pacoima. This tragic event led to the building of Pacoima Memorial Lutheran Hospital. Built at the cost of 2.5 million dollars, the facility opened in 1960.

Leading citizens of Pacoima visit site where Pacoima Lutheran Hospital will be erected. Photo taken in 1958

Director of Nurses Viola Carlson and Nurse Virgina visit the site of Pacoima Lutheran on Aug 26, 1960 as it nears final completion.

Pacoima Memorial Lutheran Hospital was dedicated to the dead and injured from the 1957 plane crash. Hospital opened August 1960.

Ronald Love was another witness to the 1957 plane crash and gave his recollection of what he saw.

"I was in high school (San Fernando) when the plane crashed. I was outside for lunch and looking up. One of the guys said that plane is going to crash. I said, 'no, it ain't. That plane is going to land at Whiteman airport or the Van Nuys airport. When I saw the wing fall off the plane, I then said, no its not gonna land. Then it went down, and I saw a puff of smoke. We knew it had crashed. As a matter of fact, we left the school trying to find it. We didn't know where it crashed. We just saw the smoke. We were driving around trying to find it.

"We didn't find out until later it was at Pacoima Junior High. I had a friend who was graduating from Pacoima, and they were doing their practice for graduation in the auditorium. The plane just missed the auditorium. It hit the gym field and maybe forty or fifty feet from the auditorium. There would have been even more damage had it hit where they were practicing. But it hit the field, and the kids on the field were the ones who got hurt."

Howard Huntsberry, a singer who played Jackie Wilson in the movie La Bamba, was a young boy in the car with his mother when the crash occurred. His mother had looked up and witnessed the collision. It looked to be in the same direction as Lockheed, where her husband worked. Huntsberry said she began screaming in her southern voice, "The plane done crashed on your daddy's job."

Pacoima icon Ritchie Valens attended Pacoima Junior High and was graduating with this class in 1957. He missed school that day because he had to attend his grandfather's funeral. This event had a devastating effect on the music icon and was an eerie premonition of what was to come.

15

Ritchie
Valens

Ritchie Valens, one of Pacoima's most celebrated icons, only lived to be 17 years old. Born May 13, 1941, Richard Steven Valenzuela arrived at 12:56 am at Los Angeles County Osteopathic Hospital to Joseph (Steve) and Concepcion (Connie) Valenzuela. They lived at 1337 Coronel Street in San Fernando, which did not have any hospitals at the time. Steve and Connie made the long ride down San Fernando Road to Los Angeles for Ritchie's birth.

Ritchie's parents separated when he was three years old but remained close. He mostly stayed with his father, who encouraged him to play an instrument and was said to have forced him to sing and play music at family parties.

Ritchie was known by neighborhood kids to always carry his guitar with him everywhere he went, including school. It began at Pacoima Junior High when he aimed to perfect his playing skills. By most accounts, Ritchie learned to play from family members and neighbors. He had no formal lessons

His father passed away in 1951, reportedly of diabetes or possible stroke. Ritchie was only ten at the time. His mother, older brother Robert (Bob), and two younger sisters Connie and Irma moved into his father's old house at 13058 Filmore Street in Pacoima.

Filmore Street was unique demographically. The homes closer to the railroad tracks had been there a long time and were predominately Mexican. Further up the block heading east towards Glenoaks, where Ritchie lived, it became mostly African American. However, the two communities got along reasonably well.

Although Ritchie spoke a little Spanish, the rule for many Mexican families was not to teach it to their children. His brother Bob did not learn Spanish until he moved in with his mother when he was a bit older.

Ritchie attended Pacoima Junior High, where the racial makeup was rather diverse. There were Whites from the west side, Blacks, Mexicans, and Japanese. Teachers from the school remembered mostly tolerance, and although there were episodes of occasional violence, it was more peaceful there than other places.

However, Ritchie mostly hung out with the Blacks and Mexicans.

Ron Love, an African American, remembers going to Ritchie's house and listening to him play rock n roll. "He liked to sing Little Richard songs," said Love.

However, he says, while they were at school and other places, Ritchie sang all the Black songs.

"I remember hanging out once, and we were sipping on wine that a relative's friend gave us, and Ritchie started blowin' all our favorite blues songs. We were friends, and that's something you never forget."

Ritchie's real irony happened on January 31, 1957, when he missed school to attend his grandfather, Frank Reyes' funeral.

Los Angeles schools had an A & B semester timetable. The A's were graduating in February and the B's in June. While the A's were practicing in the auditorium, the two planes collided. Ritchie was a B and would not have been in the auditorium but on the field with his friends.

He was already fearful of planes partially because of Whiteman Airport's low flying aircraft. However, this incident placed a permanent scar on the singers' psyche. He never wanted to ride in an airplane.

Shortly after entering San Fernando High School, Ritchie began singing in a group called the Silhouettes. The group included neighborhood friends he had known for a while. Ritchie was a slightly overweight, fair-skinned kid, who was known for his constant smile.

William Jones, Conrad Jones, and Gilbert Rocha were the organizers of putting the group together. They played at dances from October 1957 through May 1958. Ritchie was becoming known in Pacoima and San Fernando as an entertainer. He was also known as the "Little Richard of San Fernando."

Connie Valenzuela was struggling financially to care for her children. She lost her ex-husbands home on Filmore St, and they moved to a house on Gain St, where her mortgage was sixty-five dollars. In January 1958, Ritchie decided to throw a dance to raise money for the taxes on the property. He and his mother rented out Legion Hall in Pacoima and charged one dollar and twenty-five cents stag and two dollars per couple to get in. They had a fabulous turnout and made one hundred twenty-five dollars. More importantly, that is when Bob Keane of Del-Fi Records discovered Ritchie.

Keane, who had just started Del-Fi, sent a scout to look at the Silhouettes and some other singers. The scout returned with a recording of Ritchie, and Keane was very interested. Ritchie came in for an audition, and not long after that, he was recording in Keane's basement studio. He recorded the hits "Come on, Let's Go," "Donna," "La Bamba," and "We Belong Together."

Although his friends always knew him as Ritchie, it was Keane's idea to shorten his last name from Valenzuela to Valens. He felt the mainstream would accept Ritchie better without a Mexican name.

By fall of 1958, Ritchie was forced to drop out of school due to having a full schedule. He was booked in venues across America, appearing on television shows such as Dick Clark's American Bandstand. It was this success and stardom that forced him to overcome a fear of flying.

Ritchie was playing alongside the likes of Buddy Holly and Paul Anka. He played with Chuck Berry, the Everly Brothers, and Jackie Wilson. Ritchie also returned to Philadelphia for a second appearance on Bandstand. He completed two albums and made an appearance in the film "Go Johnny Go."

Ritchie was on tour with the "Winter Dance Party," in early 1959 with Buddy Holly, The Big Bopper, Dion and The Belmonts, and Frankie Sardo. The weather was brutal, with no heat on the bus. Ritchie, along with the Big Bopper, was sick with the flu, and frostbite had already hospitalized one band member.

After a performance in Clear Lake, Iowa, Holly, The Big Bopper (J.P. Richardson), and Ritchie boarded a plane chartered by Buddy Holly. Ritchie had won a coin toss against Holly's backup guitarist Tommy Allsup. The three-passenger plane departed at 1:00 am on February 3, 1959, and crashed shortly after for reasons unknown. The tragedy claimed the lives of all three passengers and the pilot.

Investigators look over the site of the plane crash that killed Ritchie-Valens, Buddy Holly, JP "The Big Bopper" Richardson, and pilot Roger Peterson on Feb. 3, 1959

The line of cars for Ritchie's funeral was unlike any seen in Pacoima. Irene Diaz, a friend of his since childhood, remembered the overwhelming sadness the community felt after hearing about his death. She remembered the massive cars and people who attended the funeral at San Fernando Mission Cemetery. His death was devastating to many. It is called "The Day Music Died" across America.

Paramount Pictures made a movie called "La Bamba" starring Lou Diamond Philips which told the Valens story. Moreover, as the years go by, his legacy continues to grow. Paxton Park in Pacoima changed its name to Ritchie Valens Park, and there is a section of CA Interstate 5 named after this Pacoima icon. Murals and monuments around the town also keep his legacy alive.

"The Day Music Died" is the name of this mural by artist Levi Ponce. It is part of the Pacoima Mural Mile

This mural was painted by Juan Hector Ponce. Located on Van Nuys Boulevard, it is part of the Pacoima Mural Mile.

Long-time Pacoima residents, who grew up and went to school with Ritchie Valens, continue to share their memories of the town's best-loved star.

"The way they portrayed him in the movie that wasn't him," says Irene Diaz, one of Ritchie's schoolmates. "He was heavier. He was always lively, a very happy person. Friendly with everyone, liked by everyone. I don't think anyone had a dislike on him.

"We went to elementary school together…we went to junior high together we went to high school together. We graduated together (Elementary and Junior High)," added Diaz.

"I remember I was driving over here to the Joe Louis tracts to a party with one of my girlfriends, and we saw him walking. He'd always be with his guitar. I said, 'Hey Richie, come on, jump in the car.' We had little side things on the Model A cars. He jumped up there, held onto his guitar, held onto the car, and we drove to the party.

"I dated his brother (Bob) for a little while, and he's not the kind of person they portrayed in the movie at all. He was as well-liked as his brother (Ritchie). I knew his family. My older niece married his cousin, and they were married until both passed away."

Diaz also remembered his death.

"It was sad when he passed away. I had never ever seen a line of cars that went to the cemetery the way I seen for him. I mean, you would look back, and the line of cars that were right behind you couldn't even see the end."

Another of Ritchie's friends was Tipy James, who lived around the corner, and he often hung out in her family's garage.

"He lived on the next street over. Everybody liked Ritchie. He was always happy. He was a heavy-set boy that always had a smile on his face. When he got popular everyone was so happy for him because he was so sweet. He kept his guitar a lot. Ritchie just loved singing, and he sang all the time. This garage, (interview location) where we are right now, he would sing for us. My mother actually had it so people come in and could get together in here. She had a couch and everything. We had dances and parties. So, this was, more or less, where people hung out. There was never a problem.

"He had a girlfriend named Donna, but she dumped him. He wasn't popular then, and he was crazy about her in school, but she never returned the feeling. He was kind of hurt. They were of different nationalities. When he got popular, she wanted him back. He didn't want her. He just wanted to make his music. At that time, that's all he wanted to do. Everyone loved him. He was a sweetheart."

James described the attitude of the neighborhood towards Ritchie.

"He was just Ritchie — to us, he was just Ritchie. We were happy for him…before he was popular."

She also reflected on his death.

"We felt bad when we heard about the crash. We just looked at each other. He was going on one of his tours, and that's how it had to end. It was really sad for such a sweet boy."

Singer Howard Huntsberry had a very unique story regarding his connection to Ritchie Valens. In addition to being from the same town of Pacoima, he played the role of singer Jackie Wilson in the film "La Bamba." He tells the events leading up to his role.

"Well, my brother actually went to school with Ritchie Valens. I remember him coming home and telling my mom a friend of his got killed. And of course, I didn't know who Ritchie Valens was. I was six or seven. When I joined the group Klique, we did a remake of the Jackie Wilson song 'Stop Doggin' Me Around.' My manager was having lunch with Taylor Hackford, who was the producer of La Bamba and said they were looking for someone to play Jackie Wilson. My manager told him I have the guy. They brought me in, and they played the track, and I didn't have to audition, I got the gig."

Huntsberry added, "What made it special is he was a young minority that came from a very small town and made a national impact. Who does that? Pacoima was very small, and for a minority to go on the national stage like Richie Valens, it just made it very special. He was like a hero to the community."

Connie Valens, Luz Rivas, Monica Rodriguez and Irma Valens at Highway dedication in May 2018 at Ritchie Valens Park.

"PacoimaStories" producer Crystal Jackson and Gil Rocha from Ritchie Valens old band The Silhouettes. Rocha often shares his collection of memorabilia with Ritchie Valens fans. He says he still misses his friend Ritchie.

16
Activism and Politics

Pacoima's role in civil rights, activism, and politics has been incredibly impressive. Over the years, the town has historically rallied and organized to deal with issues facing the community. Since the fifty's, residents have openly held demonstrations and protests on a variety of issues ranging from keeping the town clean and safe to police brutality and civil rights.

In the sixties and seventies, the town was a force, and Pacoima became the "go-to" place in the country for information on racial issues. NAACP chapter president Jose De Sosa became a national media figure with his activism on LAPD chokeholds and the battering ram.

Until the mid-eighties, unfair district lines prevented the town from having political representation reflective of its demographics. Several unsuccessful attempts were made by African Americans in the early eighties to run for city council positions. However, the lines were redrawn in 1986, leading to the election of city council and state assembly members of Mexican descent.

The activism mindset of the community has led some of the town's residents to pursue local and national politics. Stunningly, two US Congress members, Barbara Lee and Tony Cárdenas, as well as California Secretary of State Alex Padilla, are all from Pacoima and have served simultaneously during their tenures.

This chapter highlights the community's battles, and successes in the political, social justice, and activism arena.

October 20, 1958 - Members of Pacoima Woman's Club picketing on community streets for Pacoima Beautiful - All participants in strike dressed in mop-hats and raggedy clothes to promote cleaning up and enhancing appearance of neglected areas of community

1958 - Campaign associates in front of the Pacoima field office for the "No on Proposition 18" campaign, located at 13515 Van Nuys Blvd. (left to right): Otto Emerson, Joe Barrows, Mrs. Mary Munson, Richard Wakefield, Helen Rudd Owen, Bill Hoston, Mrs. June Sherwood, Robert Esch, John Morrisey

NAACP

By 1955, the Black population began to realize they needed to voice concerns about racial disparity. The whites still lived on the other side of the railroad tracks, and the Blacks and Mexicans were on the eastside. The Black community was still new, and they were starting from scratch.

Despite opening the San Fernando Gardens Projects, more housing tracts were under construction. The demand for housing, especially for people of color, was extremely high, and in Pacoima, the land was cheap. Some residents began to realize early on, the need to mobilize. One of the first steps they took was joining the National Association for the Advancement of Colored People (NAACP).

Getting an NAACP chapter for a town was not an easy task. There were stringent rules put in place. Most importantly, it required strong community support.

One man by the name of Jessie Mitchell took the lead along with other community members. They mobilized a door-to-door campaign to solicit supporters in April of 1955 and were able to get the fifty members needed to meet the qualifications. Next, they applied to receive their charter from the NAACP National Board.

The first elected officers were:

- Charles Ware — President
- Rosa L Broadous — First Vice-President
- Jessie Mitchell — Second Vice-President
- Georgia Durham — Secretary
- Dorothy LeFlore — Assistant Secretary
- Rev. Roy W. Bell — Parliamentarian
- John Mance — Parliamentarian
- James Pate — Youth Chairman
- Rev. Hillery T. Broadous — Chaplain

W. H. Coffin signs NAACP proclamation with Earl Erne and Pacoima NAACP Chapter member John J. Mance

On May 9, 1955, it was made official at Pacoima Junior High School, and they were able to address the concerns that faced not only Pacoima but the nation as a whole. Voting rights, fair employment, education, and housing were some of the significant issues. They changed the name from the NAACP Pacoima Branch to San Fernando Valley Branch in 1959.

The mission of the NAACP is to ensure the political, educational, social, and economic equality of rights of all persons and to eliminate race-based discrimination.

In 1908, a deadly race riot erupted in Springfield, Illinois, that resulted in violence and death. Lynchings and other anti-Black incidence were commonplace, but this was the catalyst that led to the creation of the NAACP.

Both Blacks and white liberals were appalled by the violence. They were determined to secure rights for all people guaranteed in the 13, 14, and 15th amendments to the Constitution of the United States.

Whereas Los Angeles had a substantial established population of Blacks, Pacoima emerged as a Black town.

Residents realized that in order to have strength, they must utilize established organizations and mobilize as a political force. The churches often helped the community with voting and assisted those unable to read.

With the signs of racial tension, especially when Blacks went outside of Pacoima, the quest for justice and the fight against police brutality began. For example, Blacks were discouraged from entering the town of neighboring Burbank. They would get chased out or worse. There were also Ku Klux Klan members living in the Lake View Terrace-Sunland area who made their presence known.

KKK parades down Van Nuys Blvd in the back of a truck in their robes and hoods on September 15, 1966.

The NAACP in Pacoima was a force in the community and across the nation for many years. They championed the cause for issues regarding housing discrimination and education disparities. Moreover, they stood on the front-lines whenever civil rights violations arose.

Jose De Sosa was perhaps the highest-profile NAACP president during his tenure. Under his leadership, police use of force and killing of unarmed people of color became the organization's top priority.

The case of Barry Evans in the seventies was the first publicized unjustified killing by law enforcement in Pacoima. However, the death of James Mincey and the beating of Rodney King had the whole nation focused on the town.

News media across the country interviewed De Sosa, who became a national spokesman on racial issues. Pacoima became a flash-point source for information on race relations in America, which gave it a considerable amount of recognition. Even national leaders like Jessie Jackson made visits to the town.

VALLEY NEWS

TODD BIGELOW / For The Times

The Rev. Jesse Jackson talks with the Rev. Dudley Chatman, left, and Jose DeSosa of the NAACP at a rally seeking support for Charter Amendment F. Jackson urged: "Vote for F. Vote for freedom."

MEChA

During the sixties and seventies, Mexicans in America began a search for their own identity. They began organizing, empowered through the political movements of the time, especially civil rights. Progressive members of Pacoima's Mexican community began calling themselves Chicanos and joined activist groups that fought for their rights.

Movimiento Estudiantil Chicanx de Aztlán (MEChA), which began during the 1960s, is a group that coalesced out of several organizations which had formed during that turbulent decade. In 1969, students from twelve universities met at a conference in Santa Barbara, California, and called for a unification of all student and youth organizations into one organization, MEChA.

1982 Photo - Xenaro Ayala (upper left corner), headed the MEChA Youth Program in Pacoima and worked with Chicano students to understand the movement and unify to fight oppression.

(Courtesy Xenaro Ayala collection)

One of the philosophies of the movement is:

"As Chicanas and Chicanos of Aztlán, we are a nationalist movement of Indigenous Gente that lay claim to the land that is ours by birthright. As a nationalist movement, we seek to free our people from the exploitation of an oppressive society that occupies our land. Thus, the principle of nationalism serves to preserve the cultural traditions of La Familia de La Raza and promotes our identity as a Chicana/Chicano Gente."

La Raza Unido Chicano youth 1985.
(Courtesy Xenaro Ayala collection)

La Raza Unida

The La Raza Unida Party is a Chicano nationalist organization founded in the early 1970s. Officially named Partido Nacional de La Raza Unida, the translation means National United People's Party. It was started to combat growing inequality and dissatisfaction with the Democratic Party that was typically supported by Mexican-American voters.

Xenaro Ayala established the local chapter in 1970 with an office on Maclay Avenue. Pacoima and San Fernando participated in organizing and marching in revolutionary fashion to promote building Aztlán, which is a symbol in shaping Chicano identity. This political party fought for the right to get recognition as the indigenous culture in America.

Although the La Raza Unida Party officially broke apart in 1978, Chicanos are still calling for ethnic solidarity under this umbrella. Brown people in Pacoima have fought for political and social standing for many years. Fighting oppression is a hard task, especially among the indigenous of the land. All have an equal place in society and must stand up for that right.

MECHA privately funded the La Raza Unida mural group to transform a graffiti scarred wall on Laurel Canyon and Van Nuys Boulevard into a multi-cultural mural. These young Latino artists are, from left: Benjamin Ruvalcaba, Francisco Ruvalcaba, mural supervisor Xenaro Ayala, Efrain Godianez, Angel Barajas, Ruben Ruvalcaba, Trancito Serratos.

Valley State 19

As Pacoima students, both Black and Mexican, began their quest for higher education, San Fernando Valley State College began allowing minorities entrance to the school.

Valley State, located in Northridge, opened in 1960, after nearly being built in Pacoima. Most of the students were local residents, and the Valley was predominantly white. In 1967, there were only 30 Black students at Valley State College out of an enrollment of 18,000. The Equal Opportunity Program (EOP) was still in its infancy, but the following year saw minority enrollment increase to nearly 300, due to EOP recruitment.

Japanese Americans did not appear to have the same restrictions in their college quest as Blacks and Mexicans. It is unclear if Native Americans had the same problems, but due to their last names being Spanish, it is reasonable to surmise.

Black activism on college campuses was beginning to emerge elsewhere but had not yet reached Valley State at that time. There were, however, several "activist" students that were trying to get Pacoima involved with Black issues at the college in 1967. They had organized the Black Student Union (BSU) and were trying to get the Pacoima community organized since it was the closest to the campus.

Archie Chatman Jr., who was from South Central Los Angeles, described the environment as hostile towards Black students.

"Black students there in 1967 and 68 were made to feel at best, ill at ease, and at worst, unwanted by the administration, faculty, and students. I came to the school in good faith and did not know what racism really was until I came."

Robert Lewis was from Pacoima and graduated from San Fernando High school in 1965. He changed his name to Robert "Uwezo" Lewis, a Swahili name. Eddie Dancer was from Levelland, Texas, and was offered basketball scholarships at several universities, but wanted to come to

California and wound up at Valley State. These young men would ultimately be central figures in what became known as "The San Fernando Valley State 19".

There were no Blacks on the varsity football team in 1968. However, a Black football player named George Boswell was on the freshman team that played Cal Poly of San Luis Obispo at Valley State on October 17, 1968. Twenty or more BSU students were there watching the game that night. During the second half, a brawl broke out between three white players from Cal Poly and one of Valley States Black players. George Boswell saw no one was going to help the Black player and ran from the bench to where the action was. By the time he got there, the officials had everything under control.

The freshman football coach, Donald Markham, followed Boswell onto the field. He told Boswell to run off the field, but instead, Boswell walked. Boswell explained, "He grabbed me around the neck, turned me around, and kicked me in the groin." Boswell returned to the sidelines, took off his helmet and uniform, and quit the team on the spot.

Outrage followed from the BSU students, who immediately went to the locker room for an explanation from Markham. The coach got belligerent, and the white players backed the coach. Things got heated, and fights ensued.

The BSU called an emergency meeting the next day and decided they would request firing Coach Markham, even though he was only a volunteer. A meeting was set up with the Athletic Director Arnett and three BSU representatives for November 4, 1968, at 11 AM. However, there were omitted details from the meeting, according to Archie Chatman's understanding of it.

Chatman, Uwezo, and Dancer sat down to talk, but the meeting did not go well. Dr. Arnett refused to consider firing Markham and had hostility in his voice as he condescendingly spoke to the BSU representatives. After many heated exchanges, Arnett said he did not have the power to fire Markham. They would have to take it up with the acting president Paul Blomgren.

Frustrated with the inaction of the Athletic Department, approximately 100 BSU members marched to the administration building where Blomgrem's office was. The staff claimed he was not there. When they entered the 5th floor, they ordered the staff to one room. No one in the BSU had seen the acting president and did not know how he looked. Approximately 37 administrators and staff were held up in room 509 with a few BSU students keeping watch.

While waiting for Blomgren, they decided that in addition to firing the coach, they would try to make things better for minority students and address other concerns. They made up a list of demands.

It turned out that Blomgren was among the staff in room 509, and he eventually stepped forward to identify himself. According to Professor Bill Burwell, the students were fed up with being marginalized and ignored by the school and presented their list of demands.

1. Black Studies Department leading to a B.A. degree

2. Recruitment of 500 Black students per year until racial population of the college becomes consistent with the national racial averages

3. Tutorial facilities to be operated by BSU to aid EOP students with study skills

4. No on Title V, and have college and Black studies representatives at meetings which are to be held

5. Investigation of employment practices on campus

6. Investigation of Black faculty for Black Studies Departments

7. Disarming of campus police

8. Set up grievance board by which students can bring grievances against faculty members

9. Fire Coach Markham

10. Conduct an investigation on Athletic Director Arnett; meanwhile Arnett to be removed from teaching duties

11. Weekly meetings with President to make sure these grievances are met promptly and receive the maximum college support.

By the time the meeting was concluding, it was approximately 3 PM. The BSU students were aware the police were lurking in front of the administration building waiting on word to move in. They made one final demand, amnesty to students involved in the confrontation. Blomgren signed the agreement, and the students dispersed.

Police initially made no arrests. However, the college president told the police he signed the letter under duress. They categorized this as being under seize and "John Doe" arrest warrants were issued for all the Black students.

The FBI got involved, and even the Governor of California, Ronald Reagan, called this a militant attack. Exaggerated stories began to surface that knives were involved, women harassed, and it grew like a wildfire. The Black students hid out in churches and homes in both Pacoima and Los Angeles to avoid being arrested.

Sharon Emory is one of the BSU students who participated in the take-over. She described the ordeal.

"Our immediate concern was to leave the building alive. Therefore, one of the demands was not being arrested or prosecuted for our actions in that conference room. The building had been surrounded by police, and news helicopters were flying all around. We were allowed to leave."

However, arrest warrants were issued the following day for 28 of the students involved. The white students were briefed to understand what happened and helped some of the professors get bail money and legal help for those arrested. Many were unaware of the treatment of Black and Brown students.

he Valley News

and VALLEY GREEN SHEET

WEST VALLEY EDITION

Established 1911

BY CARRIER
ORNINGS—75c MONTHLY ★ ★

TUESDAY, NOVEMBER 5, 1968

Mail Address: P.O. Box 310, Van Nuys, Cost. 91408
14539 Sylvan Street

340-0560   342-6101   786-7111   10c Copy

Valley State Demonstrators Hold Building for 4 Hours

Herd Administrators, Workers into Room

Students Seize Upper Floors, Show Knives Amid Threats of Violence

By PAUL WERTZ and BRAD RITTER

More than 150 students led by members of the Black Students Union yesterday occupied the upper four floors of the Administration Bldg. at San Fernando Valley State College for about four hours and threatened administrators and secretaries with violence.

Dr. Donald Krimel, executive assistant to the college president, said one student was bruised. He said the black students showed kitchen knives in ordering administrators and secretaries into a conference room where they were held for three or four hours.

Ordered Into Room

Some 60 black students controlled the fifth floor of the building, where Dr. Paul Blomgren, acting president, met with leaders of the BSU, while another 100 or so sympathetic white students held the second, third and fourth floors.

Dr. Krimel said a group of students wearing Black Student Union sweat shirts entered the fifth floor of the Administration Bldg. about 12:15 p.m.

"They ordered most of us, administrators and secretaries, into the presidential conference room and held us there three or four hours."

Blomgren was among the administrators herded into the conference room. The black students apparently failed to recognize him. The acting president remained in the room more than half an hour and then identified himself to the students.

At that point, Blomgren was escorted out of the room and taken to the negotiation sessions along with Archie Chatman, chairman of the BSU, and others.

Met With Officials

Dr. Krimel reported to newsmen that Blomgren would make no public statement until 10 a.m. today.

The college president met with college officials, representatives from State College Glenn Dumke's office, police and Dep. City Atty. Seton A. Myhrvold during the afternoon and evening, according to Krimel.

He said the only vandalism he knew of amounted to throwing some phones to the floor. He said the black students swept through the floor, rounding up the people in each office as they went.

There were about 31 administrators and secretaries on the floor, Dr. Krimel said.

Krimel said some of the secretaries complained that they had been bruised when black students grabbed their arms to get them into the conference room.

Black students remained in the room with the "prison-

Phone Calls on Tax Bills Flood County

Owners of Property Angry Over Boosts In Rate, Valuation

County switchboards were swamped yesterday with calls from irate taxpayers protesting record high property tax bills for 1968-69. The bills — totaling more than $1,500,000,000 — went in the mail Friday to homeowners, businessmen and landlords throughout Los Angeles County.

While about 2500 early birds called to complain Friday, the County got the brunt of the protest wave yesterday.

Bills Increased

Roy Heitzman, chief of the tax collector's real estate division, said the calls were pouring in to the assessor, the county auditor and the tax collector.

Many of them, Heitzman said, were from citizens whose bills had been increased because of higher tax rates imposed by the county, cities and schools.

Even more angry were taxpayers whose woes were compounded by increases in their assessed valuation as determined by Assessor Phillip E. Watson.

There were also some calls from property owners who hadn't received their bills and wanted to know why.

No New Misprints

County Tax Collector Harold J. Ostly and his secretary also fielded some of the calls when special tax switchboards became flooded.

"We've been pretty busy," he said.

However, Ostly said so far there had been no major problem with additional computer misprints on tax bills.

'NEWS' OFFERS RECOMMENDED BALLOT SLATE

The News today presents

SPEAKING to crowd from Administration Bldg. at Valley State College is Mike Lee, member of Students for Democratic Society and one of leaders in yesterday's demonstration at Northridge college. Demonstration erupted when Black Students Union members took over fifth floor of building and herded administrators and secretaries into conference room on top floor of structure.

MEMBERS of Black Students Union emerge from Administration Bldg. at San Fernando Valley State College after seizing and holding top floor of building for approximately four hours yesterday. An estimated 60 black students occupied fifth floor of building and white students took over second, third and fourth floors in demonstration which began shortly after noon.

Emory claims on January 8, 1969, two months after the incident, a peaceful demonstration took place in front of the administration building. Law enforcement officers beat and arrested Black students. One had his eye put out by a police baton. Undeterred by the police presence, students and professors of all nationalities resumed the demonstration the next day.

A peaceful protest turned into conflict between law enforcement and students two months after the administration take over.

In the end, officers arrested 286 protesters for their demonstration, and some were never allowed to return to college. For many of them, their transcripts mysteriously disappeared. On December 20, 1968, the Los Angeles County Grand Jury indicted 28 BSU students for their participation in the administration building take over. The trial did not begin until September 19, 1969, and charges against four were dropped, leaving 24 to stand trial. It was called "one of the most significant criminal trials in the state's history" by the Los Angeles Times. All of the twenty-four defendants got indicted on seventy-two counts, including kidnapping, conspiracy, and false imprisonment.

The students could see it was a sham from the beginning, and perhaps their biggest mistake was waiving the right to a jury trial. The news coverage on this portrayed the Blacks as militant and violent. A video on the CSUN web site had professors and witnesses describe the incident, and clearly, there was a disconnect. The witness accounts of what happened differed vastly from media accounts and portrayals.

The trial of the "Valley State 19" lasted nine months in the Los Angeles Supreme Court. Vincent Bugliosi, the prosecutor for the Charles Manson murders, prosecuted the case. The Law firm of Miller and Miller, which was provided by the NAACP, represented the students. 19 of the 24 charged were found guilty. Five were acquitted.

The nineteen students that were convicted got the stiffest sentences for campus activism in the history of America. Arthur J. Jones, Arrentia Holloway, Marion Kindle, Howard Johnson, Benjamin Caravo, Deardis Davis, Arnold Boyd, and Lidwina Apo got fines and probation. Robert Dyer, Michael Wrice, Jethro Collins, Yvonne Robinson, George Brady, Vaya Crockett, Sheldon Jones, and Sharon Emory received from 3 months to one year in County jail plus probation. The three "so-called" ring leaders, Archie Chatman, Robert Uwezo Lewis, and Eddie Dancer, were sentenced to serve one to twenty-five years in the state prison system. It was the most severe penalty ever given to individual campus activists and clearly designed to discourage future Black activism.

California Governor Ronald Reagan also sought to make an example of the students. He called it "a feeling of disgust" and said, "the students should have been taken out of (the building) by the scruff of their necks."

Life Magazine also covered this story in April of 1969, calling it "The Revolt at Valley State."

However, in the end, Pan-African (Africana), Mexican-American (Chicana/o), and Asian-American studies departments were formed in all California State Universities. More minority students enrolled in the UC system, and many more professors and staff (of color) received jobs. This progress is attributed mainly to the actions and sacrifice of the Valley State 19.

"We still got railroaded," stated Sharon Emory. "All the witnesses lied. This was an extremely trying part of our lives. We were so very young. We were elated for the opportunity to receive a college education, but never in our wildest dreams did we expect such brutality and raw hatred from people put in charge of our future — the racist deans, professors, board of regents, Ronald Reagan, Judge Mark Brandler, newscasters, and last but certainly not least, the police departments of Van Nuys, Devonshire, and Foothill Divisions."

Reflecting on the incident, Emory added, "I wouldn't have traded my opportunity to do my small share in the advancement of our people for the world. All suffering is not in vain."

Students protest with signs in front of the administration building. Their determination was strong to make the campus and curriculum color friendly.

Printes Hodges attended Valley State after the incident. He spoke about its impact.

"In the end, they decided we would have a Pan African Studies program, and they were going to allow more Black people in the school. But the people that did the staging of this take over were, a lot of them, banned from school for life. They weren't allowed to go to any college in California ever again. Why? Cause that's the way they wanted to do it. I don't know how many people were banned, but it allowed me to go to school.

"Some good things came of it. The Pan-African Studies Dept and during that time, they also started at UCLA, Cal Berkeley. Today, they changed the name. I have no idea what they are. They also started Chicano Studies."

Mexican-American Studies Departments were established along with Afro-American Studies.

Black Panthers

The sixties were turbulent times. The Black Panther Party began with good intentions as police brutality plagued Black communities. They wanted to offer protection, but the FBI targeted, discredited, and dismantled the group. They painted them as militant and made people perceive them as dangerous.

One Pacoima resident found himself on a losing end when he left Pacoima after college. Earl Anthony wrote several books on his Black Panther experience. His story shows how deeply rooted Pacoima people were in many aspects of activism, and for Anthony, how it had a huge twist.

The Anthony family moved from Roanoke, Virginia, in 1956 and headed to Los Angeles. They ended up in Pacoima shortly after that. James and Geraldine and their children William, Earl, Barbara, and Ronald lived on Weidner Street.

Earl Anthony graduated from the University of Southern California and went to San Francisco to study law. His sister Barbara Anthony Rhodes obtained her Ph.D. from USC as well. She became a professor at Cal State Northridge after marrying Russell Rhodes. It is unknown about the other siblings.

While in San Francisco, Anthony became very distraught at the state of Black America in the late sixties, as were many people. He saw poverty, police brutality, and oppression as an issue and became politically vocal and wanted to help make a change.

In April 1967, Anthony became an early member of the Black Panther Party. It began when he was participating in a rent strike movement and got wind of what they were trying to do. The Black Panther Party was formed in Oakland in 1966 by Huey Newton and Bobby Seale to patrol African American neighborhoods and protect residents from acts of police brutality. They very quickly became an FBI counterintelligence target and were considered by Director J. Edgar Hoover as a significant threat to national security.

As Anthony got to know everyone, he discussed his plan to write a book called "Picking up the Gun." He always talked about it and was offered a contract by Dial Publishing. However, the Panther leadership told him in no uncertain terms could he write and publish this book. They even put him under house arrest over this dispute. Despite this, he signed a deal with the publisher and released the book. According to him, after that, a hit was put on him and threats made on his family.

It was then that two FBI agents approached him from a special division that spied on subversive groups. Caught between the two, Anthony claims the FBI squeezed the hardest, as they knew everything about him and his family. He began providing inside information to the FBI about the group and their inner workings. The Panther's newspaper labeled him a traitor.

Ultimately the FBI systematically dismantled the Black Panther Party from the inside and by demonizing them with gestapo tactics. Anthony's second book, "Spitting in the Wind," clarified his story but never got him reinstated fully to the community. In one passage from the book, he wrote:

"Out of all the pain that followed, I came to the realization that taking to the streets to fight social revolution in this country is like "spitting in the wind, it will fly back into your face." - Earl Anthony

Black Panthers at John Sinclair Freedom Rally on December 10, 1971

Community Activism

In addition to nationally known institutions such as NAACP and MEChA, the smaller organizations in Pacoima began to take up issues plaguing the community in the eighties. Pacoima residents were vocal, political, and engaged when it came to their community. Even when drugs began to creep in and contributed to many residents fleeing Pacoima, the hard-fought battle for the town raged on.

Reverend Arthur Lee Broadous, who became director of the Pacoima Community Cultural Center in the eighties, spoke about community activism during that time.

"I was working for the Pacoima Community Cultural Center. The founder was Mrs. Jane McGlory. She had a vision of saving children. Her son died from the war, but he died here. I don't know if he committed suicide or what, but she was concerned about young people.

"Several people had become directors, but I became a director in 1986. From that, the Lord just started opening up some doors for us. I started working with the elected official's office and several organizations in the community. People were coming into my office saying we were having problems. A lady from the Lake View Terrace apartments off of Filmore said she was just inundated with the drug dealing in her area. She asked what can we do? Well, I said, I really don't know. Let's sit down and talk about it.

"So, myself, Rose Castenera, who was working for City Councilman Howard Berman's office, Connie Taylor Broadous, and I can't think of the lady's name who instigated us getting together — but we thought why don't we just start some marches to make people aware of what's going on? So, on weekends, we would go in different neighborhoods. We would have a few people who would just come, and we'd just walk down the sidewalk.

"The Lord blessed me with a voice, so I kinda used it like a pied piper situation. I would sing, "Save our children. We need our children!" I would sing things like that, and people would come out to see what's going on, and they were appreciative of what was happening. We were making people aware of their surroundings, that this is happening. Even if the dealers were there, we want you to know we don't want you killing our children. There was one event we did on Van Nuys Blvd by Rucker's Mortuary. I asked Joel Rucker can I use one of your baby caskets to make an impact as we go down Glenoaks. He said sure, and we carried that casket.

"This is going to happen to our children. Not just the drugs, but also the shootings. All the things happening that these children have nothing to do with. And we want you all to be aware you are affecting families. And so, the Lord blessed us to do that.

"We had elected officials with us on that day, and we went from David M. Gonzales Park marching down Norris to Van Nuys Blvd to Dronfield to Hubert Humphrey Park. It was just awesome all the people came out to join us. And from that, another gentleman whose name was Augie Maldonado, came in to help. He started AA meetings at the center when I was working there. All those people came out to do what was necessary to let people know that we want our city clean. We want to do better for our children. You have a problem, but don't do this around our children. We need to make it safer as they go to school. So that's what happened, and I got involved. We did some liquor license use permits. We used to go to hearings because there were too many liquor stores coming in here. Not only that, they were opening up so early in the morning and closing so late at night, we'd say, "no, let's minimize this time frame," and we did. We had good conversations with the owners. Some of them did not understand and were not sensitive to the cultures either. So, we had to say wait a minute — if we are coming in here buying stuff, you should have a better attitude. But you don't, and you wonder why certain things happen to your people, and we don't want that to happen. So, lets kind of talk together, let's have a good relationship. So, a lot of that started in the eighties and early nineties."

Rev Arthur Broadous marches through Pacoima opposing drug dealers in the town in 1988

Reverend Arthur Broadous was the son of Rev. Hillery T. Broadous, founder of Calvary Baptist Church. In addition to working in his father's ministry, he worked tirelessly behind the scenes, for the community. He did not seek publicity or recognition for his efforts.

A prime example was in May 2016, when a simple fight turned into what the media perceived to be a race war at Sylmar High School. Racial tensions were higher than ever before at the school. Pacoima's best-known actor Danny Trejo was asked to intervene in discussions. While Trejo was able to calm the situation, the fallout was harsh. The school suspended multiple students with some in danger of not graduating. With all the commotion, publicity and sensationalism by TV cameras and reporters, nobody had heard the real facts.

The grandmother of one of the boys reached out to Rev. Broadous for his help. Her concern was that her otherwise good grandson would not receive his diploma. Broadous stepped in, without hesitation, and requested a meeting with school district officials. He was able to resolve the situation without any fanfare and used productive dialog, which demonstrated his keen sense of community.

In other words, Broadous helped a young man graduate from high school and did not ask for publicity or acknowledgment. He just rolled up his sleeves and was able to articulate a side of the story that got lost in the mania. Many kids from Pacoima attended Sylmar High School.

Reverend Arthur Lee Broadous added nicely to his family's legacy in Pacoima and showed his love for the town in a multitude of ways. He passed away in 2018 shortly after his interview.

Crystal Jackson and Reverend Arthur Broadous after interview at Vaughn Family and Community Center in Pacoima June 2018.

Community vs. Law Enforcement

In 1980, the crack epidemic arose. Crack houses were a new phenomenon that neither the residents nor the police knew how to handle. People began to put bars on their windows and doors to prevent break-ins. However, this also prevented police from conducting drug raids on the crack houses. That is when law enforcement introduced their new crime-fighting weapon, the battering ram.

The battering ram was a tank-like vehicle used by SWAT law enforcement teams to gain entrance to a building or home.

In February 1985, Police Chief Daryl Gates authorized the use of this method on a Louvre Street home in Pacoima. His message was, "If you don't want a battering ram breaking down your wall, don't deal dope." However, the only things found in that home during the raid were two women and three children, two of them eating ice cream. There were no drugs or weapons found.

The tactics used and the potential danger to innocent people outraged the community. Religious leaders, community leaders, and the NAACP all pulled together to fight this battle. Rev. Jeffrey Joseph Sr. of New Heaven Missionary Baptist Church spoke about his outrage to the LA Times.

In the article, he stated, "This 14-foot armored vehicle is a brand-new toy, christened on blacks. We don't need new weapons to be tried out on us. Of all the methods that there are to arrest a person, they used a brand-new toy," Jeffrey said.

NAACP President Jose De Sosa stated his concerns as well.

"We want to find out why storm-trooper tactics were used in our community. We support the concept of removing harmful drugs but don't support actions that indiscriminately endanger the lives of children."

Ultimately the Supreme Court struck down the unauthorized use of the battering ram thanks to the community mobilizing, speaking, marching, and engaging with elected officials.

1985 Reverend Dr. Dudley Chatman, a prominent Pacoima religious leader, leads a protest march to stop police use of the battering ram outside Parker Center in Los Angeles.

Another significant victory for community leaders was the unlawful use of the chokehold. In 1982, Foothill Police Department Officers were involved in placing a chokehold on resident James Mincey Jr. causing his death. Around that time, law enforcement was deemed responsible for over a dozen Black deaths resulting from the use of that tactic.

Police Chief Daryl Gates added fuel to the fire in comments he made to the LA Times.

"We may be finding that in some blacks when it is applied, the veins and arteries do not open as fast as they do in normal people," said Gates.

He also said that he was investigating the possibility that controversial police chokeholds caused more harm to blacks than "normal people" because of physical differences. NAACP President Jose De Sosa held meetings and protests leading to a moratorium on that practice and, ultimately, the resignation of Chief Gates."

Rodney King (1965-2012)

Another incident that unknowingly put Pacoima in the headlines was the Rodney King beating. Although the community had faced police brutality and beatings, never before was it captured on video. Rodney King, who lived in Pasadena, had a blemished record and led police on a chase where he ended up at Baby Beef Burgers on the corner of Osborne and Foothill.

King said he tried to evade police because he would have been violating his probation. He eventually pulled over and was ordered out of the car. Officers beat him with batons, kicked him repeatedly causing multiple fractures, skull damage, broken bones, and teeth, as a dozen fellow officers stood by and watched.

As it was happening, a man across the street named George Holliday was on his balcony and began filming this injustice. He sent the footage to KTLA news station, and viewers saw it around the world.

In a rare move, prosecutors charged the four officers with excessive force. Sgt. Stacey Koon, Ted Briseno, Laurence Powell, and Timothy Wind stood trial for their behavior. A change of venue moved the trial to nearby Simi Valley, and temperatures began to rise as the verdict approached. Law enforcement began preparing for public discord, as did community leaders in Pacoima, who had a task force ready. A year after the brutal beating, on April 29, 1992, at 3 pm, the four officers were found not guilty. Three hours later, the unrest began.

South Central Los Angeles took the verdict extremely hard, and nothing could have prepared the city for the violence that erupted afterward. Six days of rioting caused 63 deaths, 2383 injuries, more than 7,000 fires, damages to 3,100 businesses, and nearly $1 billion in financial losses occurred. Pacoima did not see the level of violence and looting seen in other places. Other cities across the country, such as San Francisco, Las Vegas, Seattle, Atlanta, and New York City, also had civil unrest. On May

1, the third day of the riot, King made a plea to the country, asking, "Can we all get along?"

Mayor Tom Bradley said, "The jury's verdict will not blind us to what we saw on that videotape. The men who beat Rodney King do not deserve to wear the uniform of the LAPD."

President George W. Bush also commented on the verdict.

"Viewed from outside the trial, it was hard to understand how the verdict could possibly square with the video. Those civil rights leaders with whom I met were stunned. And so was I, and so was Barbara, and so were my kids."

In 1993, Federal prosecutors brought charges against the officers. Unlike Los Angeles prosecutors, their charges resulted in officer Laurence Powell and Sergeant Stacey Koon being found guilty and subsequently sentenced to 30 months in prison. Timothy Wind and Theodore Briseno were both acquitted of all charges. A civil lawsuit awarded Rodney King $3.8 million. Bryant Allen, one of the passengers in King's car on the night of the incident, received $35,000 in his lawsuit against the city of Los Angeles. The estate of Freddie Helms, the other passenger, settled for $20,000. Helms died in a car accident on June 29, 1991, at the age of twenty. Rodney King was found dead in his swimming pool in 2012.

USC Legend and Pacoima native Anthony Davis commented on how he viewed the event.

"I always say technology caught it on screen. It's been going on for years, and I always say they got caught on the camera. That was a bad depiction of the area, too, but also, what went on. I thought that was awful. I think that's when a lot of people started realizing that these guys can really do this. I believe in law enforcement. I've got friends in law enforcement. I have a highway patrol patch on my car. But there are bad apples everywhere. And that's the problem we're having today. Bad apples.

"I've got friends (in law enforcement), and they can't believe some of the clowns they work with. They admit it. That Rodney King situation opened the door, so everybody can see these people been telling the truth for years, and this actually goes on. I mean, they didn't have to do all that. If I'm 200 and something pounds, I don't care what this man's on. I'll grab him by the neck and tell him, dude, you not going anywhere. I can take two guys and hold him and kick him, and that's it. But they beat this man like he was a piece of meat. They beat him like a hog. Yeah, and got away with it. So, I mean you know that was a bad taste, it was unbelievable, the whole world saw that. Whereas years before, you never saw that. You just heard about it, no that can't be, that didn't happen — but it was on camera."

Today the site of the Rodney King beating, at the corner of Osborne and Foothill, leaves little evidence it ever occurred. The corner has changed, now home to Discovery Cube-Los Angeles. and the Lake View Terrace branch of the Los Angeles Public Library. However, it was the incident caught on tape there, during the early morning hours of March 3, 1991, that changed the city of Los Angeles for years to come.

Rodney King (1965–2012)

Pacoima Beautiful

Unbeknownst to many, because of Pacoima's proximity to the foothills of the San Gabriel mountains, the hills, and valley made for excellent industrial, residential, and petrochemical waste disposal. Two of the largest urban landfills in the nation reside near Pacoima. This environmental situation became the impetus for one of the oldest operating grassroots organizations in Pacoima.

Pacoima Beautiful began its operation unofficially in 1995. It started after a cleanup committee for Pacoima Urban Village (PUV), formed at Vaughn Next Learning Center on Herrick Aveneue. An urban planner named Marlene Grossman, who was not from Pacoima, volunteered with the PUV and was a pivotal person to getting this group together. Pacoima residents who worked on the PUV Committee included Liseth Romero, Evelyn Briceño, and Lupe Bello Hernandez. They joined forces with community leaders Marie Harris and DeeDee Barney, which took the committee to the next level.

Although told the community was hopeless, these six women stayed vigilant and met weekly to discuss the issues facing Pacoima. In October 1996, with the assistance of Los Angeles Urban Funders, the beautification committee engaged in short-term and long-term planning efforts. They began engaging volunteers and staff with the community to have clean up days along with grass and tree planting projects. Additionally, Grossman worked with CSUN to help identify environmental health safety issues such as lead, leaking septic tanks, and safe homes.

Pacoima Beautiful incorporated in 1999 with John Hunter as their first president. Twenty years later, Veronica Padilla-Campos continues the legacy for the only environmental justice organization in the Northeast San Fernando Valley. They also support art projects, one of Pacoima's trademarks with Pacoima Mural Mile.

Los Angeles Mayors

The relationship between a town such as Pacoima and its city mayor is significant. In the 1940s, Pacoima was mostly farmland and had a small population. Thus, there were mostly agricultural issues that would approach the mayor's desk. However, one known Pacoima resident Ethel Bryant did work with Mayor Sam Yorty in 1961. Yorty had the first mayoral office to integrate, with Asian, Latino, and Black staff members. He was also the first to have a female deputy mayor, as well. However, this does not negate the issues of race that plagued Sam Yorty's term.

Mayor Sam Yorty and wife Vicky takes photo with Ethel Bryant
(Courtesy of the Phillips family Celestine, Debra, Diana, Mike, and Monica)

Yorty was mayor of Los Angeles from 1961 to 1973. Although his staff had diversity, he did not fare well with Blacks. During the Watts riots in 1965, thirty-four deaths occurred, with forty million dollars in damages. In the eyes of many Black voters, Yorty failed to acknowledge the conditions that caused the riots. He also appeared proud of the military tanks that were used to contain the violence.

Many Pacoima residents came from Watts, leaving due to overcrowding and a lack of jobs. There were countless claims of police brutality that went unchecked.

After the riots, Martin Luther King Jr., who visited the city, partially attributed the riot to police brutality. Yorty accused him of performing a disservice to the people of Los Angeles and the nation. Yorty faced a barrage of other criticism as mayor, including from the Los Angeles Times, due to his excessive absence from the city. Even the 1965 Pacoima Little League World Series baseball team was not graced by his company when the mayor's office presented them with a certificate of recognition.

In 1966, a year after the riots, Yorty ran for governor of California and lost. Then in 1969, he faced opposition for his mayoral position by a Black man named Tom Bradley. During this campaign, Yorty used race-baiting and fear tactics as the theme. He used the Watts riots to invoke fear by claiming if Bradley was elected, more riots would follow. He made other claims saying Bradley was affiliated with the Black Panthers and claimed there would be a reign of terror if Bradley won. Yorty would defeat Bradley in the election.

However, four years later, in the 1973 election campaign, fear-mongering backfired on Yorty. Tom Bradley sailed through with a victory becoming not only the first Black mayor of Los Angeles but any major city in America.

Thomas Bradley was born December 29, 1917, in Calvert, Texas, to sharecropper parents. His grandparents were slaves. Bradley rose to become the highest-ranking African American LAPD officer as Lieutenant. He also served as a city councilmember before his mayoral campaign.

Bradley served five terms from 1973 to 1993. His mayoral connection to Pacoima was unprecedented. He visited the Boys and Girls Club, parades, special events and worked with community leaders on many occasions. The town of Pacoima was one of Mayor Bradley's biggest supporters.

Tom Bradley served 20 years a mayor of Los Angeles.

1975 Mayor Bradley meets with Junior High students Susan Fuller, Sheri (Cornell) Mahaffy and Crystal (Grandison) Jackson on pollution project. He was very accessible to the community.

City Council

Los Angeles City Council had a nine-district system until 1925 when a fifteen-member council replaced it. Each district was to be equal in population based on the gubernatorial election; thus, redistricting occurred every four years. The numbering system began with District 1 being the farthest north from the city, the San Fernando Valley, and ended with District 15 being furthest south in the harbor area. Today, redistricting is done every ten years with the US Census. Between 1923 and 1987, District 1 represented all or parts of the San Fernando Valley. District seven later became Pacoima's council area.

Charles Randall	1925-1933	District 1
Jim Wilson	1933-1941	District 1
Delamere Frances McCloskey	1941-1945	District 1
Leland Warburton	1945-1952	District 1
Everett Burkhalter	1953-1957	District 1
(City council voted to change district lines)		
James Corman	1957-1961	District 7
Ernani Bernardi	1961-1977	District 7
Bob Ronka	1977-1981	District 1
(City council voted to change district lines)		
Howard Finn	1981-1986	District 1
(City council voted to change district lines after Finn's death in 86)		
Ernani Bernardi	1987-1993	District 7
Richard Alarcon	1993-1999	District 7
Alex Padilla	1999-2006	District 7
Richard Alarcon	2007-2013	District 7
Felipe Fuentes	2013-2016	District 7
Monica Rodriguez	2017-present	District 7

*District lines were redrawn in 1986 allowing a Hispanic to be elected
*Richard Alarcon was the first Latino elected to District 7.
*Alex Padilla went on to become California Secretary of State
*Monica Rodriguez became the first female elected to District 7.

Councilmember Monica Rodriguez and Crystal Jackson at Ritchie Valens Freeway dedication. Rodriguez is the first woman to serve Pacoima's District 7.

Monica Rodriguez joins the Pacoima Historical Society in celebrating Pacoima History Day in June 2017

Tony Cárdenas United States Congressman

Antonio Cárdenas was born in Pacoima in 1963 and graduated from San Fernando High School. He obtained a degree in Electrical Engineering from UC Santa Barbara, however, decided to go into politics instead.

First elected to the State assembly in 1996, Cárdenas then went on to serve the 6th council district in 2003. He won the election to represent the 29th District of the 113th Congress in 2013.

Some of the significant legislation he has introduced includes:

- Gang intervention
- Youth detention regulations
- Immigration
- Education (several bills)
- Job/Economy
- Food safety
- Renaming Pacoima's Post Office in honor of Ritchie Valens

During his "PacoimaStories" interview, Rep. Tony Cárdenas talked about his family coming to Pacoima.

"My parents came to this country, after getting married in 1946 — both raised in Mexico and after getting married, they hightailed it to California. Starting off in Stockton, they had five children, and in 1955 moved to Pacoima, bought a home, and had (their) sixth child. I was number 11, the youngest born in 1963.

"I think what brought them to Pacoima was an opportunity for a better job. My father had a first-grade education... he was a farmworker. My mother was a homemaker, and she had a second-grade education. When he came to Los Angeles, he got a job as a union laborer, so those were the good times. He actually had a union card and got paid pretty well and was able to buy a home."

Rep. Tony Cárdenas (D-CA / 29ᵗʰ Congressional District)

During the interview at his Panorama City office, Congressman Cárdenas shared insight into coming from a working-class family.

"Back then, it was the 1950s...it was after World War II...the United States of America had the strongest economy in the world as far as growth and opportunity. The number of homes being built...construction was booming. Since my father was willing to be a laborer, he fit in quite well. It was a job opportunity as it was."

"I grew up poor, but I didn't realize it. We had a single income household. My father went to work every day to feed 13 people, and he did a wonderful job doing that. My mom stayed home to keep an eye on us, make sure things were nice and neat and orderly. It wasn't until later on that I went to college and realized how poor we were. But I don't mean that as a bad thing, I think it was a good thing.

"Our parents taught us the values of working hard and appreciating what you have. Going to church on Sundays and thanking God for everything and looking forward to opportunities and taking advantage of them. So, graduating from San Fernando High School like all my brothers and sisters did, we went off to college and were able to do things our parents only dreamed of. Getting elected into office, I quite frankly and my parents didn't think that would happen. So as a family, we exceeded the dreams of our immigrant parents."

Rep. Tony Cárdenas got selected to serve on the House Committee on Energy and Commerce.

Tony and Norma Cárdenas at premiere screening of "PacoimaStories: Land of Dreams" in February 2016.

Congresswoman Barbara Lee

Another Pacoima native serving in Congress is Rep. Barbara Lee (D-CA 13th District). Born Barbara Tutt, she began her activism at an early age. She received her Master's in Social Work from the University of California Berkeley.

Lee took an internship in 1975 working for Congressman Ron Dellums, where she worked her way to chief of staff. She was one of the first people of color to hold a senior position on Capitol Hill. Elected to the State Assembly in 1990, she served there until her election to the State Senate in 1996. In 1998, Barbara Lee became the Representative of the 9th Congressional District (now the 13th). She has served in Congress for longer than two decades.

Rep. Barbara Lee (D-CA / 13th Congressional District)

Congresswoman Lee was the first woman to represent the 9th district from 1998 to 2013 in Oakland. She has been both chair and whip for the Congressional Black Caucus. Lee is also a founding member and vice-chair of the LGBT Equality Caucus.

After the 911 attacks in 2001, Congress voted for the legal authorization of military force against those deemed responsible for the attack. All members of the Senate and Congress voted for it except Rep. Barbara Lee.

"I voted against that resolution 15 years ago because it was so broad that I knew it was setting the stage and the foundation for perpetual war. And that is exactly what it has done," Lee said.

She worked on bipartisan support to repeal this authorization. Her courage to stand up and hold her ground before the House and Senate, despite being a lone wolf on the bill, was highly commendable.

Rep. Lee was born in El Paso, Texas. Her family came to Pacoima in 1960, where she attended San Fernando Junior High and High school.

While attending San Fernando High, she had to work with the NAACP to integrate the school's cheerleading squad.

"It was John Mance and Carl McCraven. They were head of the NAACP during that time. And they helped change the rules because initially, it was a selection process. And of course, if you weren't blond hair and blue-eyed, you didn't get selected. So, they helped change the rules so the student body would elect you. And so, I tried out with the election, and I won. It was my first election. But also, during that same year, Jeanie Tanaka won, a Japanese American girl. So, I broke that glass ceiling for everybody, for girls of color."

Following her high school graduation, Lee married, moved to England, and had two children. After returning to the states, she attended Mills College in Oakland. While there, she became president of the Black Student Union and met the first African American Congresswoman Shirley Chisholm. Lee worked on Chisholm's presidential campaign in 1972 and ultimately served as a delegate at the 1972 Democratic Convention in Miami, Florida.

The Congresswoman is very proud of her decision to fight back at San Fernando High and pave the road for inclusion for people of color in scholastic activities.

The legislative bill, Lee says, she is most proud of is the Global AIDS Relief Act of 2000, which she co-authored in the Bush-era. She says this law saved millions of lives and helped end the AIDS epidemic.

Barbara Tutt (Lee) cheerleader San Fernando High 1964. She takes pride in helping pave the way for people of color to be given the opportunity to participate in activities such as cheerleading.

(Compliments Rep. Barbara Lee)

Alex Padilla

The political success of Pacoima natives reaches its pinnacle with Alex Padilla, who was sworn in as United States Senator in 2021. He also distinguishably served as the Secretary of the State of California from 2015 to 2021.

His parents emigrated from Mexico and settled in Pacoima in 1977. His father, Santos, worked as a short-order cook, while his mother Lupe cleaned houses.

Padilla graduated from San Fernando High School and earned a bachelor's degree in Mechanical Engineering from the Massachusetts Institute of Technology (MIT). Before running for office, he served as a field representative for U.S. Senator Dianne Feinstein and then-Assembly member Tony Cárdenas.

In 1999, at the age of 26, Padilla won election to the Los Angeles City Council. While representing the 7th District, in 2001, he was elected council president, becoming the youngest person and first Latino to serve in that capacity. In 2006, he was elected to the California State Senate to represent the San Fernando Valley and reelected in 2010.

United States Senator Alex Padilla

While in the legislature, Padilla authored legislation in a variety of areas. Some of these include:

- Requiring chain restaurants to post nutrition information on menus and menu boards
- Streamlining the process for community college students to transfer to four-year universities
- Phasing out single-use plastic bags
- Increasing access to broadband technology and computer science education for underserved communities.

In addition to elected office, Padilla has served on several boards, including the Governing Board of MIT, the National Association of Latino Elected and Appointed Officials (NALEO), the League of California Cities, and the Discovery Cube Los Angeles.

As the first statewide elected official from Pacoima, Padilla makes Pacoima proud and is an inspiration to young people. He and his wife Angela have three boys and live in the San Fernando Valley.

Alex Padilla received an "Excellence in Public Service" award from the Pacoima Historical Society in 2018.

Angela Padilla and their three boys at Pacoima History Day October 6, 2018.
(PHS archives)

California Secretary of State Alex Padilla receives award for public service from Pacoima Historical Society. (PHS archives)

Assemblymember Luz Maria Rivas is another Pacoima native that has defied the odds and rose to become a state lawmaker. She is a Pacoima native that attended Telfair Elementary, Pacoima Middle, and San Fernando High schools. In 2018, Rivas won election to the 39th California State Assembly.

California State Assemblymember Luz Rivas

From the early days of community action, Pacoima has influenced America. It began with grassroots protests to national political offices, which led Pacoima to be a force that many never recognized. Beginning with marches and ending with writing state and national legislation, the progress and impact Pacoima made defy all odds. In other words, being boxed into a one-sided narrative was not in this community's DNA. The poverty element has been overcome in many cases by education, determination, and persistence.

17
Houses of Worship

When studying the history of Pacoima, it reveals that religion and churches have been there from the beginning. When Jewitt Allin founded the town in 1887, he insisted on moral righteousness, even banning the sale of liquor. The area's only church was the First United Methodist Church in San Fernando, founded by Charles Maclay. During those years, most traveled to Maclay's church for services.

When the Japanese arrived at the turn of the century, they practiced Buddhism in private homes or traveled to Los Angeles until building their temple in the 1950s.

The same went for Catholics who had services in homes or open fields until building the first Guardian Angel Church in 1929. The majority of Mexican residents attended Guardian Angel or Mary Immaculate, the two oldest Catholic Churches in Pacoima.

Although there were African American Catholics, the majority were Baptist. When Blacks began arriving in Pacoima, Reverend T.G. Pledger established the first Baptist church in the San Fernando Valley.

Pacoima's history has seen places of worship for people of many faiths. Catholics, Baptists, Muslims, Jews, Buddhists, Methodists, Protestant, Jehovah's Witness, Christian Science, and many others have planted their spiritual roots in the town, and each has its own exciting story. This religious diversity represents an integral part of Pacoima's history. Unfortunately, some histories were not available, but this chapter encompasses those that were.

Guardian Angel Church

Built at 10909 Norris Avenue, Guardian Angel Church held its first mass on March 19, 1929, serving 100 people. The sanctuary was completed and dedicated in 1939.

In 1955, the church was displaced with the building of San Fernando Gardens and sat fenced up and unusable while the housing project was under construction.

However, after completion of the projects, Guardian Angel undertook a significant expansion of its facility. Parishioners constructed a two-story school building in 1956. Located on 10886 N. Lehigh Ave, the church served a substantial number of Pacoima households in the fifties and sixties.

Guardian Angel Church circa 1930
(Courtesy Lupe & Jesus Hernandez collection)

Faye Gayles-Hodges during mass at Guardian Angel Church in the early fifties

African Americans and Mexican Americans both attended Catholic churches in the fifties and sixties (Hodges Collection)

The Lozano family, dedicated parishioners, helped rebuild the church in 1959. Several buildings were added including a parish hall and rectory. (Courtesy Lupe & Jesus Hernandez collection)

1964 photo of Father Mattic and Jesus Lozano. Mr. Holmes behind them at Guardian Angel Church.

Guardian Angel Church is still located in the middle of the San Fernando Gardens Housing Projects. Numerous community meetings, weddings and events take place here.

Greater Community Baptist Church

Reverend Theodore G. Pledger and his wife Annie White Pledger helped organize the Greater Community Baptist Church (GCBC) in the forties. It was the first Black Baptist Church in the San Fernando Valley. The Pledgers had six children Brenda Ann, Marilyn, Ronald, Eugene Winfred Renee, Thergill Jr., and Theodore.

The church first opened in a small building known as Laurel Hall, located on Ralston Avenue and Penny Street. The church began with nine charter members Mrs. M. Parker, Mrs. A. White, Mr. & Mrs. C. Patton, Mrs. C. Leggett, Mr & Mrs. J. Perdue, Mrs. H. Johnson, and Mrs. A. Pledger.

Reverend Pledger was elected Pastor, Mrs. Hattie Johnson, Church Clerk, Mrs. Mary Parker, Superintendent of Sunday School, and Mrs. Ida Binyon, Choir President.

1956 - Wedding at Community Baptist Church (pictured left to right) Elva Mae Gandy, Julia Carter, Joyce Washington, Eloise Franklin, Nellie Bean Joseph, Al Joseph, Mac Franklin, Raymond Carter

The group started small, saved money, and pitched in. By 1960, they erected the sanctuary that still stands today. For decades, GCBC was a force in Pacoima's Black community, with one of the largest congregations. Whenever politicians were seeking the African American vote, one of their first stops was the church and congregation members helped by registering voters and filling out forms.

"The church was a community gathering place for religious and for social services," said Jim Smith, who worked with Rev. Pledger.

"All I know is he (Pledger) had a dream to build a senior citizen's place. I helped write the environmental impact report for Pledgerville. When we first submitted the report, it was turned down. They said there was no school, no bus line, no fire station. Well, the fire station was a block away. The bus ran right up Van Nuys. So, we got in touch with Congressman Corland, our congressman. It was through his efforts, through his office, that's how we got it passed. Pledgerville, the big building on the corner of Herrick and Van Nuys Blvd — right next door, the church is still there. Rev Chatman is the pastor now."

On June 22, 1986, Rev. Pledger passed away. Rev. Dr. Dudley D. Chatman became the church's new Pastor in 1987. Chatman was a new arrival to Pacoima at that time. He had big shoes to fill, and he accomplished that with great success.

Rev. Chatman not only filled the spiritual role, he actively participated in community issues, including marching against the battering ram and preventing riots during the Rodney King verdict. Chatman interacted with leaders such as Jesse Jackson and Jose De Sosa on social issues. His philosophy was, "I think the church has a moral obligation to keep its people informed so they can make the right decisions."

He was the first minority to head the San Fernando Valley Interfaith Council, which up until 1995, never had a Black President. The council praised Chatman for his work following the 1994 Northridge earthquake.

He and his wife Beth have a blended family of 6 children Kelley, Joshua Bradley, Deidre, Patrick, Dudley III, and Carnisa.

Beth, Rev Chatman, Joshua Bradley and Kelley Chatman 1988
(Courtesy Kelley Kali Chatman Rhodes)

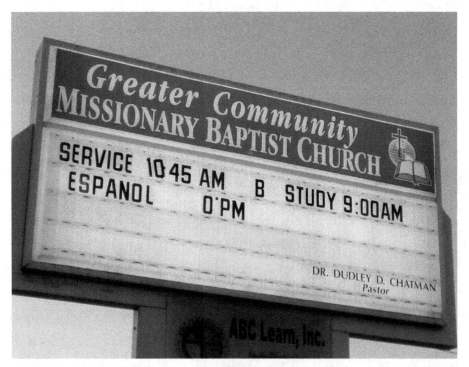

Greater Community Missionary Baptist Church has over 75-years of history in
Pacoima

Calvary Baptist Church of Pacoima

Calvary Baptist Church began in the home of Mrs. Marjorie Tucker at 12986 Montford Street on May 1, 1955. Located in the Joe Louis Housing Tract, it was there that Reverend Hillery T. Broadous began the process for organizing a council to get it started. The meeting was led by Rev. Percy Williams, from the Missionary Evangelist for the Western Baptist State Convention of California. The council consisted of Rev. R. White, Rev. William Brown, Rev. L.H. Clegg, and Rev. William Bradford.

In July 1955, they purchased property at 12928 Vaughn Street for $12,500. The land consisted of nothing but rocks, jackrabbits, and dirt. In November 1955, parishioners pitched a tent at the new site and broke ground to begin building the church in July 1957.

By 1969, they owned two-acres and built a multi-purpose room addition that included a daycare for working mothers. The church offered an extensive list of special interests and community services that addressed the issues facing Pacoima. The Broadous family has remained affiliated with the church for over sixty years.

1958 – Rev. Hillery T. Broadous with sons William Broadous and Arthur Broadous clear debris along with Trustee Charles Mozell during construction of the church

Rev. Broadous and Mr. Baugh hold a planning conference on the church's program for young people. Broadous was very active in the community.

Mother Rosa L. Broadous at Calvary Food Ministry during the holidays

One of the first members of Calvary when it was just a small house. Mildred Miller would bake cakes for all their events. (Courtesy Davina Conner)

Calvary Baptist Church of Pacoima on Vaughn Street sits on two-acres of land.

Christ Memorial Church of God in Christ

One of the town's most famous churches is Christ Memorial Church of God in Christ. Founded by Benjamin Crouch (1915-1993) in 1951, Crouch first began preaching in nearby Val Verde at the Macedonia Church of God in Christ. He preached at local jails, hospitals, and drug rehabilitation programs, as well as television and radio.

In 1951, Crouch began preaching sermons out of his garage. He and his wife Catherine worked side-by-side, building the attendance into a considerable following. Benjamin and Catherine had three children; Benjamin Jr. and twins Andraé and Sandra.

They moved into a new church location at 13333 Vaughn Street, across from Vaughn Street Elementary School. Reverend Crouch preached in nearly every major city in the country, including foreign nations. In 1983, he became a bishop.

His son, Andraé Crouch, became a Grammy Award-winning gospel artist who sold millions of albums.

After Bishop Crouch died, his children continued the operation of the church.

Bishop Benjamin Crouch is featured on the Pacoima City Hall Mural (artwork by Ignacio Gomez)

Muslims in Pacoima

Muslims first opened a house of worship in Pacoima on Mar 27, 1961. Located on 13209 Van Nuys Blvd, Pacoima had several hundred Muslim members during the sixties and seventies.

During that time, they followed the Honorable Elijah Muhammad and later Imam W. Deen Mohammed. Muslims in Pacoima were known for being well dressed and selling Muhammad Speaks newspapers and bean pies. For many years, Minister John Shabazz and Imam Sulayman Beyah led the Pacoima temple. There was another location where Muslims met on Paxton, as well.

As the Black community began leaving Pacoima, the Muslim community consolidated back to Los Angeles and closed the Pacoima temples.

This Nation of Islam was a powerful force in African-American communities across the US. It was started in 1933 by W. D. Fard and The Honorable Elijah Muhammad.

This photo was taken on the first day the Pacoima Temple was opened on March 24, 1961 on Van Nuys Blvd. A member of the F.O.I. (Fruit of Islam) stands outside as security during a meeting.

New Heaven Missionary Baptist Church

New Heaven Missionary Baptist Church first organized in Los Angeles in 1967 under Rev. Dr. Jeffery Joseph. It moved from LA to San Fernando and then ultimately to 13233 Pinney Street in Pacoima. With the purchase of surrounding property, the church has grown and celebrates over 50 years of operation.

New Heaven prides itself on helping crucial problems that face the community. From the police battering ram and chokehold issues of the eighties to the problem of homelessness, the church has been active and supportive.

Rev. Dr. Joseph has also been on the front lines during the civil rights movement. He participated in hunger strikes, sit-ins, and numerous marches and demonstrations.

His church in Louisville was the headquarters for protest strategy meetings with Dr. Martin Luther King Jr., Jessie Jackson, Rev. Ralph Abernathy, and US Ambassador Andrew Young.

Rev. Dr. Jeffrey Joseph, a community leader and Church founder

New Haven Mission Baptist Church Educational Building located on Van Nuys Blvd.
(Photographer Lorenzo Grandison)

Soul Winning Revival Center

George and Hattie Maunder opened the Soul Winning Revival on Van Nuys Blvd & Glenoaks in the early seventies. Hattie used to pick up the kids with a bus or station wagon that had a megaphone where she made announcements. Residents describe her as a devoted church person that cared about the children.

The couple lived on the corner of De Foe Avenue and Filmore Street. They taught Vacation Bible School in their home and were said to be extremely kind, giving snacks to all the kids. Sister Maunder also taught piano in her home.

Pamela Broadous of Calvary Baptist Church gave this description of her.

"Most of my life, she was the only female preacher I knew, and the only one my dad (Rev. Hillery Broadous) allowed to stand in his pulpit. I thought I remembered her last location was on the corner of Van Nuys and Glenoaks, where the Chevron station is now. She was a Pacoima icon. She impacted all our lives, and as a child, I did not recognize her value, but I do now. I loved her theme, "God's filling station."

Soul Winning Revival on the corner of Glenoaks and Van Nuys Blvd
(Courtesy Ed Rose)

Ed Rose, Hattie Mounder and George Mounder standing outside in the 1970s
(Courtesy Ed Rose)

Mary Immaculate Catholic Church

Mary Immaculate first began holding mass for parishioners in 1954 at Pacoima Moose Hall. After moving to the Panorama City Theatre in 1957, they opened a new church and school at their current location on 10390 Remick Street in Pacoima.

Father Luis Valbuena, the pastor of Mary Immaculate Catholic Church, began the first ESL (English as a second language) program in the San Fernando Valley. He also started the Santa Rosa Credit Union and was involved with Cesar Chavez's Farm Workers Movement.

FATHER LUIS VALBUENA
PASTOR OF MARY IMMACULATE CATHOLIC CHURCH
BEGAN THE FIRST ESL PROGRAM IN THE SAN FERNANDO VALLEY
STARTED THE SANTA ROSA CREDIT UNION
INVOLVED WITH CESAR CHAVEZ AND FARM WORKERS MOVEMENT

Father Luis Valbuena's image is on the Pacoima City Hall Mural

(Artwork by Ignacio Gomez)

Father Valbuena and Congressman Corman at Santa Rosa Church, 1972 before being reassigned to Mary Immaculate

Mary Immaculate mass for parishioners began in 1954 at Pacoima Moose Hall. They grew and a couple of years later this church was built. It's located at 10390 Remick Pacoima.

San Fernando Valley Hongwanji Buddhist Temple

In Pacoima's Japanese community, Buddhist services took place in its follower's homes until the building of the Hongwanji Buddhist Temple in 1961. According to the Temple, the Japanese have practiced Buddhism in the area for nearly one-hundred years. It is located adjacent to the San Fernando Valley Japanese American Community Center and serves hundreds of families. Buddhism is the world's fourth-largest religion.

San Fernando Valley Hongwanji Buddhist Temple located on 9450 Remick Avenue

1963 Kazuko Yoshiura and Ronald Doizaki get married at the Buddhist Temple in Pacoima, California. Jon Takeuchi performs the wedding ceremony.

Pacoima's religious leaders gather on Easter Sunday in 1965 at Roger Jessup Park on Osborne St. This cross was located at the top of Whiteman Hill, now known as Hansen Hill. Pictured are Rev. John C. Wetzel, Rev. Paul L. Kittlaus, Rev. Hillery T. Broadous, Rev. James Smith, Rev. James E. Brecheisen

Jehovah's Witness members have been a part of the Pacoima community since the 1960's. There have been several Kingdom Halls where they hold meetings. The newest is on Van Nuys Blvd.

Mount Zion Baptist Church first started in the home of Rev. William J Bradford Jr. on Louvre Street in 1956. After a year or so it moved to another home on Del Sur. In 1964, they were able to get this permanent location on Herrick Street.

First United Methodist Church of Pacoima

1956 Groundbreaking ceremony for the First United Methodist Church of Pacoima. (Left to right) Dr. George Moreland, Pastor Nathaniel Lacy.

Reverend John C. Wetzel, pastor of St. Philip's Lutheran Church in Pacoima, wanted to establish a congregation of people from different races and economic backgrounds at his church in 1963.

1949 - Evangelistic Tabernacle at 13232 Kagel Canyon St. in Pacoima opened in 1942 on land donated by Clifton Taylor.

Pacoima Mexican Baptist Church dedication in 1950 on Mercer St. and Lehigh Ave

Seventh Day Adventist Church

Rev. James P. Middleton of Seventh Day Adventist in 1965

Seventh Day Adventist Church is located on the corner of Glenoaks & Van Nuys Blvd.
(Lorenzo Grandison photographer)

1956 Parks Chapel African Methodist Episcopal Church choir

Parks Chapel African Methodist Episcopal Church group at Endsley home
on 13332 Fielding St. circa 1958. Rev. Young, Mr. Endsley, Cyrus Taylor

1959 - Rev. Herbert Johnson, right, president of Pacoima-Panorama City Ministerial Association.

Valley Advent Christian Church was built in 1956 to serve community needs for a worship center. This church opened for services at 12925 Branford Street in Pacoima.

Deacon David Johnson, a long-time Member of Lake View Terrace American Baptist Church which opened in 1963.

18
Jim Jones

Understanding how more than 900 people could die in a mass murder-suicide event is beyond the comprehension of most people. However, for people of color, the dream of racial equality and utopia, in a world of police brutality and poverty, can force some to take extreme measures to achieve that goal.

Religious faith has always been humanity's biggest strength and most vulnerable weakness. False prophets have corralled unsuspecting faithful followers for thousands of years. Sadly, for nearly a dozen Pacoima residents, trusting one of these false prophets and his vision for a racial utopia cost them the ultimate price.

Jim Jones was one of those who preyed on people who wanted to live in a better world full of love and not hate. Unfortunately, 918 people died as a result of believing in that vision, falling victim to the largest murder-suicide plot in American history. At least ten of these people were from Pacoima.

Jones was the religious leader for Peoples Temple Church, which began in deeply segregated Indiana, Indianapolis, in the fifties. During that time, the church division of races was clear. However, in Jim Jones' church, Black and White working-class people notably sat and intermingled together.

In 1962, around 80 members in Indianapolis packed up and moved to the San Francisco area. Jones took advantage of the civil rights era anti-government mentality to inspire people to follow his teachings.

The diverse group felt they were on a mission to make the world racially integrated, and letters revealed a sense of brotherhood throughout the temple community. They worked together to raise money as a unit and were able to recruit working-class Black professionals who saw the inequality of America's corporate and manufacturing sectors. Jones began infiltrating Los Angeles by speaking at African-American events, targeting revolutionaries and religious groups.

In the mid-seventies, Muslim leader Wallace D. Muhammad was looking to change the Black nationalistic image of American Muslims and join the interfaith religious community. John Shabazz, one of Pacoima's Muslim leaders, introduced Muhammad to Jim Jones. On May 23, 1976, Jones spoke at the "Spiritual Jubilee," held at the Los Angeles Convention Center.

Jim Jones enters the Los Angeles Convention Center with Imam Wallace D. Muhammad in 1976

Promotional flyer for Spiritual Jubilee featuring Jim Jones and Imam Wallace D. Muhammad (Courtesy of BAIT-CAL Archives)

Jim Jones speaks at the Spiritual Jubilee in 1976 at the Los Angeles Convention Center. Nation of Islam member Khalid Muhammad and a Peoples Temple security member sit side by side. (Courtesy of BAIT-CAL Archives)

During the sixties for Blacks, every attempt at justice and equality met with violence and death. The assassinations of leaders such as Malcolm X, Dr. Martin Luther King Jr., and others were devastating to the African American psyche.

By the seventies, many Blacks were looking for alternative ways to change their circumstances. Organizations like the Black Panther Party were under attack, and police brutality plagued their communities. Jim Jones was a psychologist and well-aware of the African American psyche. He presented himself, a White man, as their savior, and the Peoples Temple Church as a God-given path for change.

Showmanship and charisma were his appeal, which Jones used to create a unified communal environment. He convinced people to donate their property and earnings to the community. As his popularity rose, his wealth grew.

Jones opened Temple locations in both San Francisco and Los Angeles. In the early to mid-seventies, the church was aggressively targeting African American communities. Jim Jones brought his traveling Church to Pacoima during that time.

Jackie McCree, who grew up in Pacoima, attended one of Jones meetings.

"He had a tent set up on the corner of Van Nuys Blvd and Glenoaks for about a week. My neighbor, Mrs. Brown, took me and her daughter for one of the sermons. It was the most evil aura I ever experienced. I felt nothing good with that Temple. I was devastated when I found out what happened to his followers, but not surprised. That man was evil."

However, Jones enamored some Pacoima residents with his rebuke of racial oppression and talk of building a utopia. They began attending the Los Angeles temple, and later, a number became members.

The Peoples Temple Church condemned racism and promoted helping the needy and filled a gap that was appealing to minorities. Many people felt a sense of brotherhood and optimism as they began following the church.

However, a dark side emerged against those who defied his requests. Many followers strived to please him, but Jones would order aides to spy on temple members to test their loyalty. Sadly, his followers grew to become a cult. Some people from Pacoima who attended a few sermons described them as creepy and found the body search before entering the Temple unsettling.

During temple meetings, Jones used a perceived healing power he claimed to have. He staged rituals, miraculously healing broken legs and removing cancer through prayer. Jones even staged a shooting in front of the congregation and performed an act of healing the gunshot wounds. People believed it because he used fake blood and convincing props. Jones felt all this secured his power.

Jim Jones aligned himself with the most influential entity in the Black community, the Nation of Islam. He also interacted with Los Angeles Mayor Tom Bradley and developed relationships with other key people.

By 1974, the wheels were in motion for his big move. Jones had people cultivating and preparing a place in the Guyana jungle, not far from Venezuela.

However, defections had become a problem, and an angry Jones told one member wanting to leave, that she could go, but her son was staying. That member began contacting authorities, and Jones felt more of his followers would defect if the publicity and investigation escalated.

After news reports began to surface, Jones knew he could not continue in California under such scrutiny, and he moved up the Guyana departure date. In 1977, approximately 1,000 people rid themselves of their material belongings by selling their homes and valuable items — all for the dream of a utopian society in Guyana. Dedicating their lives to the "cause," they left in small groups as to not draw too much attention.

Those from Pacoima were said to have followed suit in hopes of a better, meaningful life with the man they called "father." Jones lured them to a land far away, with a promise of racial equality, prosperity, and justice for all.

Once in Guyana, people began to realize things were not as promised. The jungle was supposed to be a haven, but members described it as an "unfinished construction site." Long work hours, cramped housing accommodations, and a temperamental Jones also made life more of a struggle than they ever imagined.

They had to build everything from the ground up, including sidewalks, sanitation, electricity, housing, schools, waterworks, food preparation, and more. Everyone except the children was required to help.

Described as a prison camp, those who were dissident received cruel punishment. People were not free to leave, even though a few managed to get out.

Pacoima resident Juanell "Nell" Smart was a Peoples Temple member. She was interviewed for this book and discussed her ordeal.

"My mother (Kay Nelson), joined Peoples Temple first. She attended the meetings and brought my kids along, and they loved it. We were living on Mercer Street by Filmore Elementary. My two younger children, Scott and Teri, went to Maclay Junior High. Our family moved to Pacoima in 1964.

"My uncle, Jim McElvane, also joined the Peoples Temple with my mom, his sister. He was involved with real estate in Pacoima. He was 6'8 and went out for the Harlem Globetrotters, but got hurt."

Smart knew her mother believed wholly in Jim Jones' teachings but was not interested in getting involved, at first.

"One day, I went and heard Jones speak and found it intriguing. The message made sense to me. So, I became a member."

However, things became complicated for Smart when she got involved with one of the Temple's ministers.

"I became involved with one of the Temples ministers, and we got married. That's when I saw the real Peoples Temple and how they were misleading people. I also saw the real Jim Jones the fraud behind the scenes. Later I told my husband I wanted out. Jones said that if I left, I have to move 100 miles from Los Angeles. It was a very nasty meeting."

Shortly afterward, came the move to Guyana. Despite what Smart had witnessed, her mother was still a true Jim Jones believer and excited to be going.

"My mother had told my kids all about it, and they begged me to let them go with their grandmother. My older kids, Tinetra, she was married, and Alfred were also church members. They went too."

Despite the fraud, Nell decided to let her kids go.

"I couldn't compete with grandma, and I thought everyone would be safe. My mom always took great care of the kids."

It was a decision that cost her dearly.

Nell Smart's mother, Kay Nelson (center), and son, Scott Smart (front left), who attended Maclay Junior High, are seen here in Guyana. Neither ever returned home.

Children engaged in learning activities in Guyana. The FBI confiscated this photo, after the tragic deaths of the commune.

Children at play in Guyana.

Ariel view of the compound and cottages taken by the FBI

Jonestown, as they called it, became more of a cult environment, as Jones was obsessed with his power having members call him Dad or Father. He also feared the government was after him and had pre-planned the murder/suicide of the Temple followers with poisonous cyanide mixed in Flavor Aide (a cheap version of Kool-Aid). He was stocked up with it from the very beginning.

Congressman Leo Ryan went to Guyana in November of 1978 to check on the wellbeing of the Americans in Guyana. The congressman never received any warning about the weapons and mass murder threats that loomed there. Ryan and the news crew were caught entirely off guard. They only knew Jones did not want them there and may reject their entrance to the compound. Ryan did know that people were possibly being held there against their will. He was going to see for himself. Jones ultimately allowed them in the compound. A façade was put on by the members of joy and contentment, but some expressed wanting to leave. A note was slipped to Ryan, saying so.

Some of the members saw this as a way out and sought to leave with the Congressman. He welcomed them to do so. Approximately twelve to fourteen left with Ryan, and as they headed to the landing strip, a series of events happened. While walking toward the plane, an armed unit of gunmen pulled up and opened fire. Congressman Ryan and an NBC cameraman and crew were all shot. Everyone else ran towards the jungle when they heard the shots.

In the Jonestown archives, the diary account of Mark Lane mentions Jim McElvane, Smart's uncle, who was present when the congressman met with Jones. Lane was a Jonestown survivor and suspected Jones ordered his people to murder the congressman when they went back to the airstrip. Jones sent Lane to one of the cottages located away from the compound and asked McElvane to take him there. It is not clear how McElvane's death occurred, but his description in the diary was "a tall 300-pound man not displaying possession of any weapons."

Jones knew that the killing of Ryan was going to bring a close to Jonestown. He began having his crew mix up the cyanide drink and forced everyone to drink as he talked on the loudspeaker — what they call the death tapes. His speaking was often incoherent. Evidence suggests that the majority did not drink voluntarily.

In total, 918 people died, including ten of our Pacoima people, who dreamed of a better life without prejudice.

Nell Smart described how she discovered something was wrong.

"I was home when I got a call from a friend saying not to worry. I said, 'worry about what?' He said, 'Congressman Ryan got shot in Guyana, but everything is fine.' I turned on the television and found out everything was not okay."

In the agonizing days ahead, she learned the fate of her mother and children.

More than forty years since this horrific tragedy occurred, Smart has pieced her life together.

"All us survivors meet annually, and that sense of racial harmony and closeness returns. That was the good feeling that Peoples Temple brought that lured everyone into believing in a promised land. The survivors have bonded and learned to live with the pain of losing loved ones. Shedding the hatred of Jim Jones has also helped in the healing process."

Congresswoman Jackie Speier was an aid for Congressman Leo Ryan and accompanied him on that fateful trip. She was shot five times and hid out for 22 hours before help arrived. She went on later to win Leo Ryan's seat and continue his work.

Pacoima's connection with Jim Jones and the Peoples Temple Church is a sad part of the town's history. Moreover, the total number of town residents who died in this tragedy may never be known. However, these are the ones that have been researched and validated by the Pacoima Historical Society. The following pages are a memorial to those who perished in this tragedy.

Kay Nelson

"Mom, you always put the happiness of others before your own. You gave so much of yourself and you deserved so much more out of life than you got. I wanted you to be happy and you were not. You were not only my mother; you were my best friend. Had you not taught me to be strong and independent I could not have gone on. I am so fortunate to have had you as my mother. I know this world is a better place because you were here. Mom, you and the children were my life, my world but, I want all of you to be at peace." - Juanell Smart

James Nelson McElvane

"Jim was very tall and a very knowledgeable and good person. Soft-spoken and could handle any situation. Kind and always had a quiet laugh and smile for those who knew him as a friend. Always working for to help others." - Don Beck

"This man was my grandfather, and unfortunately, I never got the opportunity to meet him. I'm sorry for all the families and descendants whose lives are forever tarnished due to this tragedy." - Anonymous

Tinetra Fain

"Tinetra, 49 years ago today, I gave birth to you, my first-born child. What a beautiful baby you were, and you grew up to be an even more beautiful woman – inside and out. You were an artist; a designer and you could have done so much with these gifts. You were a gutsy strong-willed little girl. You always wanted everyone and everything to be alright and would try to do whatever you could to make it so. You with the heart of gold tried so hard at living life. I remember how you would tilt your head to the side and smile with your lips tightly closed - melted my heart because sometimes your eyes would be filled with sadness and at other times, happiness. Did I tell you enough how very much I loved you and how very proud I was of you? I hope so. When I last saw you, it seemed as if you had at last found the happiness you so longed for. You seemed at peace. Rest well, my firstborn. I love you - Mom" - Juanell Smart

Scott Smart

Teri Lynn Smart

Alfred Smart

The Pacoima community had an emotional reaction to this story about Scott, Teri, and Alfred, who attended Maclay Junior High. They left for Guyana with their grandmother rather abruptly, noted Donna J. Dungee, who was a neighbor.

"So sad, they lived down the street from us. My sister and l played with them. Then they just left!"

Anthony Travis posted, "Yeah, I was going to Maclay when it happened as well, Teri was a good friend of mine! It hurts today as much as it did when I first heard about it! I'm glad you posted their pictures I miss those faces! I'm getting teary-eyed all over again! They should not be forgotten!"

Dealing with suicide was new for Pacoima youngsters. It was a rarity in this town. Annette Carol Bailey explained how the school handled it.

"I went to Maclay with her when she died! They (the counselors) had to tell us about her death for it was the first suicide death we had to deal with. As children, we all remember 'til this day; we were in the 7th grade. It's was so sad! We were devastated. We went home confused, and our parents had to explain what happened to us as well."

Phillips-Mitchell Diana Dide remembered them well. "The Smart family were my neighbors. They lived on Mercer Street near Humphrey Park in Pacoima. There were two other siblings that died in the Jim Jones tragedy: Tinetra La Dese Fain aka Tinetra Johnson and Alfred Laufton Smart. I believe that Tinetra was married and her husband died as well. I will never forget when their mom came to our home on Mercer Street and broke the news to my family. Such a tragedy."

Oliver Morgan Jr.

Oliver Morgan Jr. was the loving father of two daughters named Rochelle D. Magee and Zelma A. Morgan. He also had a son, Marcus, and a relationship with a woman named Betty Daniel. According to his daughter, Daniel took the child to Guyana with her. Oliver went to Guyana to get them out but was unsuccessful and died with everyone else in Jonestown.

Beatrice Bell

Daniel Bernard Berry

Rori Lynette Bell Maddon

Pacoima resident Beatrice Bell, also known as Bea McCann, and her two children Daniel and Rori, all lost their lives in Guyana.

"That was my aunt," said Charles Brown. "Even though I had a chance to meet her only once, I know that she was misguided, and I pray that God forgives her for taking her life and the lives of her beautiful children."

Other Pacoima residents who escaped the Jim Jones tragedy had this to say:

Crystal Kaamilya Uqdah: "Growing up Muslim, the mosque we belonged to had been invited to Jim Jones's church. Scariest event I ever attended, and when we found out about Jonestown, I was devastated. It was scary because there were men and women dancing, screaming, and running up and down the aisles, with makeup and dressed in costumes. The location of the church was somewhere in Los Angeles."

Terrolynn Turner: "As a young teenager, I almost got caught up in the people temple out of fear. He was my monster; I was afraid of him. Things I witnessed at the temple were unbelievable. Reading about the killing in Jonestown saddens me deeply. I was only 15 years old at that time. I knew people from Pacoima that were getting ready to go over to the "promised land." Thank God they did not make it because of the massacre."

The final death tally in Jonestown was 918, which includes five killed on the airstrip with Congressman Ryan and four that died in Georgetown Guyana, the Temples headquarters. The majority were African American females.

69.2% Black
24.5 % white
3.9 % mixed
2.2 other unknown

Pacoima will always remember the tragedy of Jonestown and our beloved residents who perished there.

19
Baseball in Pacoima

Baseball was one of Pacoima's favorite past times. The town produced some incredible talent over the years, with Major League players, Negro League players, and a 1965 little league team that went to the World Series.

Baseball dates back to the 1800s in the San Fernando Valley. The leagues were mostly white until 1909 when teams began to let descendants from Californios elite families play.

Mexican baseball leagues began to appear in the 1930s. Potter's Milling Company of Pacoima sponsored teams, including the Aztecas. Decedents from the Pico family (Pio & Andres Pico) and Lopez family (Lopez Station) were notably in some of the photographs.

1909 baseball Frank Pico far left second row Edward D Lyon, Raul Chandelot, Albert Garcia, Fred Nemback, William Millen, from early Californio families.

Pacoima Athletics included: L-R (first row) George Villanueva, unknown, Pete Prieto, Raymond Pacheco Torres, Eddie Prieto: (2nd Row) Nacho Calzada, Simon Salas, Angel Luma, unknown, Poncho Torres, Del Rey, Ted Villanueva, unknown. Front row batboy Alfred J Calzada. (Courtesy Marsha Prieto)

Baseball has always been big in Pacoima. Mexican leagues were very popular for many years. In the late forties, one of the trendy teams was a Mexican team called the Pacoima Athletics.

In the fifties, when African Americans began settling in large numbers, they joined in on America's favorite sport. Although racism was still an issue, Mexican Americans were much more open to diversity.

Over the years, this sporting competition created interracial bonds between Pacoima residents, unlike anything else. The early years of baseball laid a foundation for sports excellence in Pacoima that still stands today.

This photo has some of the earlier (pre-Joe Louis) families. Fannie and Charles Macon (TOP RIGHT), who were brought to Pacoima by Rev TG Pledger in the late 40's, shown here as part of the Royals in 1958. And Eugene Pierfax (third from left top row) (Photo courtesy of Moses Guzman)

1965 North Valley Pony League Bottom L-R Gary Matthews, George Polo, Matthew Clark, Wilfred Chapron, Andy Thompson, Middle L-R Wilford Prevost, Chucky Liggens, Turner Kimball, Bob Calzada, Keith Roberts, Top L-R unknown, James Pate, unknown, Larry Woods, Tyrone Fontenot, unknown, Mr. Leroy Fontenot.

(Courtesy Bob Calzada) (Player information provided by Larry & Pookie Oliver)

One of the biggest untold stories in Pacoima sports is how a small group of Black fathers got together to launch little league baseball for their youth. During the fifties and sixties, all-white leagues in Pacoima, San Fernando, and other areas did not want Black kids to play. So, the fathers made a deal to lease land from the city of Los Angeles for one dollar, landscaped the property, and started the league. The final result was North Valley Little League Baseball.

Ironically the new baseball field was located right across the street from where Pacoima's White kids played. However, there was a stark difference between the two fields in terms of landscaping and baseball equipment.

What these Black fathers did with a group of kids learning to play organized baseball was unbelievable. Out of North Valley came Major League All-Star Gary Matthews and other amazing ballplayers. Astonishingly, in 1965, North Valley fielded an all-Black team of eleven and twelve-year old's that magically played their way to the Little League World Series in New Bedford, Massachusetts.

USC Football legend Anthony Davis played at North Valley and was on that all-star team. He recalled his experience.

"I remember when I was nine years old, 1962, 63, and went down to San Fernando Park, across the wash. My mother wanted me to play a little baseball there. That's what I wanted to do. I used to sleep with my glove and my bat, as my mother used to say. And the man said, 'no, your kind can't play here.' So, we had to go to the east valley, and that opened my eyes that I'm really different.

"And then years later, ten years after that in 1972, I had a great game. National television, Notre Dame vs. USC, six touchdowns, and that same man, not even knowing I was one of the kids he turned away, called my mother and wanted me to speak at his team banquet. My mother says, 'with all due respect sir, I don't know if you remember this or not, you were the coach at the time, and you told my son and I that he could not play here. So why would I allow my son to speak at the banquet when the same league said we couldn't play here.' That's one of the biggest memories I've ever had.

"They said we couldn't play in San Fernando, so all the Black fathers leased the land from the city and put the field together. They graded it, not to the best, I mean we used to tease each other that we're playing baseball with the gophers. Because they use to have gophers out there that would stick up their heads — they're watching the game too...But across the street, they had a very serene little league park, where all the whites played. I mean, this park was unbelievable we sort of envied it, but we knew we had the best talent."

In 1965 North Valley Little League proved their talent by advancing to the World Series. They called themselves the North Valley Broncos. According to shortstop Larry Oliver, one of the team's star players, they were all well-rounded athletes. He tells how the players departed Pacoima and went to San Pedro for the first round of the playoffs. The best two out of three games would advance.

Starting lineup:

Pitcher	Beanie Frazier
First base	Skippy Willis
Second base	Bobby Patton
Shortstop	Larry Oliver
Third base	Wayne Gibson
Left field	Ricky Chapron
Center field	Anthony Davis
Right Field	Lester Perkins

Larry Oliver

"That last game was memorable," Oliver says because he struggled to get a hit. "I fouled 17 times in one at-bat before grounding out. I could not seem to hit the ball. The last inning, we were ahead, but San Pedro was at-bat. There were two outs, and the ball got hit to center field. It was looking like a home run, then Anthony Davis reached over the fence and made a game-saving catch. That sh-t was so exciting. We all ran on the field. That catch saved the day and sent us to Utah."

While in Bountiful, Utah, the kids stayed in mansions, unlike anything they had ever seen before. The hosts, who were White, and had rarely, if ever interacted with Blacks, welcomed them openly. It was a very memorable and enjoyable experience for these eleven and twelve-year-old Pacoima kids.

"Here's a Black team going to Bountiful, Utah. Visualize that in 1965," added Anthony Davis.

"The way they had it structured two of us had to stay with families, and they happen to be White families. They treated us great. I found out years later that the families had been attacked verbally for 'allowing those N's in their house,' during the tournament."

The Braves won all the games in Utah. Oliver remembers hitting three home runs to advance them to the Little League World Series in New Bedford, Massachusetts.

Accommodations were much different in New Bedford. While there, they slept on a gym floor, which was a stark difference from Utah. The boys, by this time, were also beginning to get fatigued.

They played three games and won one before losing the next two. According to Oliver, they were all homesick and ready to leave. They had no one cheering for them and were missing their families. Also, the hard gym floors did not help.

Parents were delighted to have the children home safely. Mayor Sam Yorty's office held a luncheon for the team and presented them with certificates. However, the mayor personally did not show up to greet them. Office aides joined them in the celebration.

Strangely, the local newspapers barely covered this historic event. Pacoima's "all-Black" world series team received more press in other cities than in their home town. They were, however, competing with news about the Watts Riots, which were happening when the boys came home. In fact, says Oliver, when they were returning home on their flight, they could see the fires burning from the sky.

"Unfortunately, we didn't win. But the fact is that an all-Black team, in 1965 — Jim Crow... for us to do that — it's never been done," Anthony Davis reflected.

"That we were able to do that, accomplish that coming out of Pacoima, California — Black fathers put everything together. And you have this park right across the street that didn't do what we did."

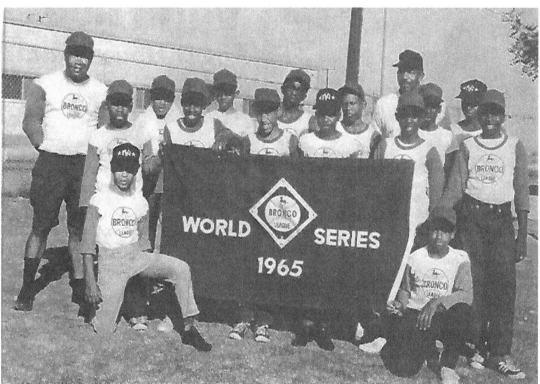

NORTH VALLEY BRONCOS EDGED OUT IN NATIONAL FINALS

Shown after returning from New Bedford, Mass. on Friday with souvenir of World Series are, kneeling, Jordy Hayes, left, and Larry Thomas. Second row, left to right, Larry Oliver, Ricky Chapron, Bill Davis (bat boy), Ralph Mountian, Dirk Clark and Eli Bryant. Back row, left to right, William Davis Jr. (team manager), Anthony Davis, Michael McCoy, Billy Savone, Bobby Pate, Sam Clark (president), Robert Willis and Beanie Frazier. Members of team not shown are Wayne Gibson, Lester Perkins and Jim Lewis (coach).

1965 – North Valley Broncos World Series team (courtesy of Michael McCoy)

Newspaper clipping showing 1965 North Valley All-Star Team
(Courtesy Michael McCoy & Ronald Oliver)

Broncos received a trophy for being in the world series.
(Courtesy Larry Oliver)

THE
CLUB SLATES PARTY FOR BRONCO TEAM

North Valley Mothers Booster's Club is sponsoring a welcome home party for the North Valley Broncos, currently participating in the Bronco World Series in New Bedford, Mass.

The Broncos are part of the Boys Baseball Inc. program, which includes Pony and Colt baseball.

North Valley sponsors 180 boys on 12 teams and new uniforms are needed.

The booster's club is looking for sponsors and money to carry out its projects.

Further information may be obtained by calling 365-6804, 896-4266 or 896-9936.

The team's mothers posted an article in the Daily News announcing a welcome home party.

Baseball was a significant factor in Pacoima regardless of gender, color, or ability. Some of the players were signed to an MLB team but did not get a chance to play, including Skippy Willis and Curtis Fontenot.

Anthony Davis spoke about Pacoima's baseball talent.

"Because of that park, our league produced a lot of guys that went on to the professional ranks and went high. I'm gonna give you some names, and I can tell you. Lawrence Marshall got drafted by the Cleveland Indians, me the Baltimore Orioles, we had a guy named Danny Cruz, Gary Matthews came out of the area, and Sammy Jones. These are notable guys that went on to do some great things."

Pookie Oliver clowning around at the North Valley ballpark in 1965

Pacoima Little League (Back row L-R) James Tipton, Brad B, Philip Tipton, Mr. Scott, Bobo, Ron Tipton, Barry Toliver. (Bottom L-R) Darryl Scott, Ely Bryant, Phillip Samuels, Lil Scott Clovis Scott, Skippy Willis, Jeff Bryant

Braves: Mr. Tipton, Philip Tipton, Michael Holiday, Jim Yancy, Daryl Scott, middle: Ovid Goode, Lester Linton, Darnel Holly, Larry Oliver, Bottom Jordy Hayes, Jimmy Davis, Clovis Scott, Bobby Holly. (Courtesy Philip Tipton & Ronald Oliver)

There are other great stories in Pacoima baseball history to be told. The boys were not the only ballplayers to enjoy the game; the Shamrock Lassies were the San Fernando Ponytail League champions in 1965. They won two championships in a row at San Fernando Park.

Left to Right (bottom row) Brenda White, Kathie Tapp. Christine "Pinki" Puga, Karole Puga, Vickie Holmes, Joanne Cruz. 2nd row top Charlotte Finch, Sharon Emory, Linda Armstead, Rosalyn Emory, Jackie Hill, Patsy Rodriguez. Coach Pete Puga and Chris Puga (team mother) (Courtesy Sharon Emory)

Tipy James 1948
(Courtesy Veda James collection)

Another story worthy of note is that of Elander Victor Harris, a Pacoima resident with extraordinary baseball history. He was a member of the Negro Baseball League. Vic Harris played 23 years with the Homestead Grays as an outfielder.

Between 1935 and 1948, Harris was also the manager for the Grays, leading them to nine championships. He guided them to six consecutive pennants from 1937-1942, then in 1948, they went to the Negro League World Series Championship. In 1943, when Homestead dominated the league, Harris led the team with a .380 batting average.

He played six East-West all-star games and managed the East team eight times. Harris became the first-ever Black elected to the Western Pennsylvania Sports Hall of Fame.

He settled in Pacoima, with his wife Dorothy, during the Black migration. They lived on Louvre Street and had two children. Vic Harris passed away in 1978 after working for the Castaic School District. He is a Pacoima baseball icon.

Vic Harris

20
Education

During the 1950s, Pacoima needed new schools due to the town's population explosion. The new housing tracts fueled the town's growth and migration from other areas. Mexicans continued to move into Pacoima as word spread and African Americans were on waiting lists as homes continued to be built well into the sixties.

Although Pacoima was still mostly fields, fruit trees, and houses with dark dirt roads, the need for schools was apparent. In 1954, four elementary schools (Vaughn Street, Montague, Beachy, Terra Bella) and one junior high (Pacoima), all opened their doors for learning that year.

The new San Fernando High School building began operation in 1952, two years before the other schools. It opened at 11133 O'Melveny Street in Pacoima.

San Fernando High (1896) was the only high school in the area for many years until the building of Poly (1957), Sylmar (1961), and Kennedy (1971). Later on, Arleta High (2006) and various charter schools opened. Some children also went to private schools such as Bishop Alemany High School (1956) and other Catholic schools.

This was San Fernando High School in the 1930's on Brand Blvd. (1906-1952) It was annexed to Los Angeles City High School District in 1914.

These students are in the courtyard at San Fernando High on Brand Blvd

This was Building "C" at the Brand Blvd campus that got demolished in 1955. It turned into a junior high in 1952.

The opening of the new San Fernando High building on O'Melveny seemed to coordinate with the opening of the Joe Louis homes. During the fifties, many Whites, who were the majority at the school, were introduced to African Americans for the very first time. There were already Japanese, and Mexicans attending, but the significant influx of African Americans created a previously unseen racial dynamic. Unique because the majority of the San Fernando Valley was Caucasian.

Racial tensions would rear its head from time to time in the fifties. Black youth complained about getting their lunch money stolen by the White students. They felt a need to stay in groups for protection. Samir Muqaddin then named Frenchy Grandison, described the situation as Blacks and Mexicans forming clubs for protection then uniting. He described his experience during the fifties and the racial environment.

"The Turks were something dear to my heart. We wound up with two groups here in Pacoima. The Saints, which was the Mexican group and the Turks, which were African American. We always united. When we had a club party, we invited them. We had to organize to keep the White gangs off of us. I remember one time when on Friday and Saturday nights, hundreds of them, use to gather at James Drive-in on San Fernando Road. And when they got through drinking, they would drive around the park and come down to Pacoima. They would find some people walking down the street or standing outside their house talking and jump on them. After about six months of that, we decided we had to do something. We got our clubs together and started protecting ourselves. When they came down, we had a way to get a message to all of us that they were cruising on the street so we could all organize. Now what we decided to do, was go up to James Drive-in, hide on the other side the railroad tracks and throw rocks into the drive-in restaurant, and we destroyed them.

"They stopped coming down. Blacks and Mexicans had to fight together. There wasn't enough of us."

The situation at San Fernando High was volatile, as well. Grandison described some of the challenges.

"We had to go to school. When we went to school, we were facing the same odds. They'd back us into corners, take our lunch money. No, it was serious stuff. So, we automatically came together to fight. And as our reputation grew, we were able to curtail the attacks from San Fernando and Van Nuys High kids. Our reputation spread to Polytech, once it opened up later on in the game. Canoga Park wanted to come mess with us too because we were the only people that didn't look like them in the valley. By 1962, 63, from the time it got started, about 1953, 54 — about a ten-year period of time — we had to struggle with White people."

The feeling of being unwanted outside of their community prevailed, and it was not just at school either.

"They didn't want us there. No, they didn't want us at the recreational places or social places, and I'd imagine on the job. Although it didn't really affect my experience. It didn't come up on the job. I mean, the adults understood what this process was. It was integration, and we had rushed upon them. The Pacoima movement came on them so quick that all of a sudden, five to six thousand African-Americans were in the valley. They never thought that was going to happen."

The school demographics changed when the Joe Louis Homes were built.

The campus on O' Melveny was very modern opening in 1951

1967 San Fernando High Class Officers

San Fernando High was initially a majority White school. The education was good. There was a small number of Japanese recognized for being smart and actively involved in student government.

In 1958, the Student Body President was Harry Muranaka, and Vice President was Nancy Fuluda, which showed the school's willingness to integrate Japanese into the mainstream student population. The education itself appeared to be exceptional by most accounts until the 1970s when it became a predominate minority school.

Patricia Takayama attended San Fernando High in the sixties.

"San Fernando High was very well integrated. It was probably like a quarter Black, a quarter Latino, a third White, and the rest Asian. Ethnically it was very diverse. The biggest dance used to be Cinco de Mayo. For me, it was a real interesting experience to be suddenly thrown into racial and cultural groups — to be able to learn about other people. I think, for the most part, people got along very well. Of course, there was your normal Saturday night fights...for the most part, things were pretty well integrated when I got there."

Printes Hodges graduated in 1965 and described the racial climate.

"I didn't feel it (racism) so much there at San Fernando High because there was a lot of Black people there. Of course, at this time there was a lot of white people there, there was a lot of Mexicans there. We would have fights with the white people. Yeah, there was no doubt about that there would be fights. But it wasn't as bad as it could have been. Maybe because that school was so mixed that it was easier to communicate to people there. But I didn't run into too much at high school. I enjoyed school."

Rolene Marie (Harris) Naveja graduated San Fernando High 1965 and shared her memories.

"San Fernando High was great. We had talent shows, and I had a good time. I met a group of friends who are still my lifelong friends. Five girls and we called our self the "Joy Luck" club. Because we are still connected, we still keep in touch with each other, and every year we have a reunion when everyone is back in Pacoima."

1965 B-10 Student Body Government

"Pacoima was a melting pot," said Naveja. "We had diversity. We had Caucasians...we had Mexicans...we had African Americans, but we blended. We had a good time. House parties were big — it wasn't like loud house parties. The neighbors knew the neighbor's kids. We had a good time as a community."

Congresswoman Barbara Lee was one of the 'Joy Luck' girls Rolene mentioned. She felt the education there was excellent. She went on to get her college degree and become a United States Congress member.

"It was great. It was really good. I was in GAA, Girls Athletic Association. I took music, Mrs. Selma Beckie was my music teacher. I didn't want to take typing because I told her (mother) I wanted to go to college and all, but she reminded me I needed to be able to type my term papers, so I took typing. My professor was Mr. Singer, and I got A's. I won typing contests and wrote the 'Val Vision,' which was a column for our newspaper. My class was called Val Perisian. The education was well rounded. I had music, sports, gym, and all the academics, and yeah, it was great."

Alithra "Tipy" James and Lionel "Frenchy" Grandison attend the SFHS Prom in 1957

Printes Hodges and Faye Hodges - SFHS Prom 1964

Russ Gonzalez 1964 Cheer Squad

1970 - San Fernando High School Class Photo

By the seventies, the educational experience had changed at San Fernando. While virtually all of the sixty's students interviewed went to college, students in the seventies spoke about a trend to discourage higher education.

Singer Howard Huntsberry explained.

"Dealing with education was a problem. We had teachers telling you, 'you don't need to study that. I don't think that's what you want to be.' Those kinds of obstacles. The people that got past that were people with strong parents that told you, 'you can be anything you want to be' and let you be anything you want to be."

High school educator Stan Leandro recalled his experience as a 1978 SFHS graduate.

"As proud as I am to have gone to San Fernando High School, I admittedly always state San Fernando High School did not do the job to prepare me for college. I was accepted to Cal State Pomona and Cal State Northridge, and by the sure grace of God, I went to Valley College (junior college). It was the best move I ever made. Quite honestly, I don't think I had the tools necessary to succeed in college. Valley College did give me those tools."

The eighties had the same mentality but still produced successful Pacoimians. US Congressman Tony Cárdenas discussed his experience.

"When I got to San Fernando High School in the 10th grade, that's when we started high school back then. I told her (counselor); I wanted to go to college and be an engineer. She looked at me and smiled and said, 'you know what Tony, you are probably good with your hands, you'd make a fine mechanic.' She tried to put me in wood shop, auto shop, metal shop. I was very fortunate... I already had older brothers and sisters who already went to college. So me, I knew I had to get through A through F requirement classes just to be eligible to be accepted to college. So, I had to argue with my counselor that I wanted to go to college and did not want to be trapped away from going to college. Luckily, I won that argument. I took the right classes and eventually got accepted as a senior to UC Santa Barbara. And then the story gets uglier. When I told Mr. Johnson, he cried with pride for me. And then I told my math teacher, that's when it got ugly. Before I could finish my sentence, 'I was accepted to UC Santa Barbara, and I was gonna be an electrical engineer,' he cut me off. He said, 'you can't cut it, don't even try it.' Those were his exact words.

"And so, luckily for me instead of me believing him because he had gone to college, I just got mad, and I said to myself, 'I'll show him.' But what really hurts me is that how many students were told something like that by a counselor or teacher, and that was the straw that broke the camel's back. They actually walk away saying 'gosh that person went to college and they know what college is like and if they said I can't cut it then they must be right.' Luckily for me, I was just more stubborn than willing to believe him and proved him wrong."

The seventies and eighties also ushered a change in the school's demographics. Although San Fernando HS was the most diverse school in the San Fernando Valley, fewer Whites were enrolling. The school became predominantly Mexican and Black, and tensions began to rise.

One of the first riots at San Fernando High School stemmed from a misunderstanding between two Black students. Ernest Lee Matthews was playing a practical joke on his good friend Alton Harris. According to Matthews, he had a balloon that he popped in his ear to scare him. As he was laughing, Harris, who was very upset, struck Matthews in the chest. The two began fighting, and a Mexican noon aid tried to break it up. He was holding Matthews while pinning his arms to his side. Harris charged at him full speed hitting Matthews while he was defenseless. Matthews, while fighting to stand-up and get his arms free, hit the aid in the nose. By then, students were aware that a fight was going on, but thought the fight was between a Mexican and a Black. From there, a mass Black vs. Brown riot ensued. The school was in chaos with students throwing items, blows exchanged, and multiple injuries.

The high school ended up shutting down until they could figure out what to do. Nora Belton had this account of her experience. She was one of the schools remaining White students and had friends of all colors.

"In 1972, we graduated from S.F. High. That year (or was it the year before?) there was huge anger, "racial tension," mini-riots and some violence...There was a lot of confusion and frustration, and my Mother, who always worked at the school, asked if I wanted to change schools. For me, it was out of the question. I had enemies, but my friends more than made up for it. By the way, my parents were friends with Nancy Avery, the Postmaster. I have a feeling there was some political affiliation, too. My Dad was an activist.

"It came to a point that it was impossible to hold classes anymore, and the principle, in his wisdom, opened the school for an ongoing forum. We gathered in sections. White, Black, Mexican, Boys, Girls — everybody got to talk, everybody was heard. There was so much love. It felt like we were actually getting somewhere, and then there was so much shared pride in that amazing Football team! Then the whole thing was eclipsed by the earthquake. No water, no electricity, aftershocks for weeks, a hospital collapsed, the freeway split, about 70 deaths; everybody was on the front lawn doing barbecues, standing in line for water...everybody helping everybody. More love. That is how I remember those days."

San Fernando High Pupils, Teachers Hold Conference

Classes Canceled in Wake of Battle as Groups Debate; Violence Almost Flares

The halls of San Fernando High School were empty yesterday, but the school cafeteria was jammed as 350 school officials, teachers, students and parents listened to debate on Tuesday's violent outbreak at the school.

Eight persons were injured Tuesday when about 150 to 200 youths, mostly Chicanos and blacks, became involved in a battle which began in front of the school and spilled onto campus.

Accusations Made

As a result of the incident, classes were canceled yesterday and a meeting was conducted in an attempt to resolve some of the issues which caused the violence.

The school also will be closed today.

At yesterday morning's three-hour session accusations were made by students and teachers and at one point the meeting appeared headed for another physical showdown.

Those attending the meeting forced television newsmen and other members of the press to leave the meeting at the outset yesterday, charging the media with aggravating feelings among students.

As a Chicano youth was speaking and demanding that blacks discontinue "harassment" of browns, groups of browns and blacks began forming on opposite sides of the cafeteria.

Gather Leaders

Principal Hugh F. Hodgens, who acted as moderator for the meeting, stepped in to cool the atmosphere and recessed the meeting for lunch.

During the break, Hodgens gathered leaders of the Chicano and black youths for a private discussion of the difficulties which hit the campus.

Witnesses to Tuesday's incident said the violence primarily was divided along racial lines, with blacks and Chicanos being the principal participants.

The school, 11133 O'Melveny Ave., Pacoima, was closed yesterday as a precautionary measure.

Tuesday's clash apparently was touched off while most of the school's

Continued on Page 18

Valley News - December 8, 1970

Nora Belton (center) and friends at SFHS 1972

Nora Belton calls her group of **diverse** friends the Fearsome Foursome (L-R) Verna Knight, Nora Belton, Inez Tanghal, Cecile Hill (Courtesy Nora Belton)

Anthony Davis spoke about his experience with the riots.

"There was a riot in 1970 here. And it was really serious. I didn't get it because we were the same beans from the same pot. Because at the end of the day, we're all going to get treated the same way outside the scope of San Fernando High School. The establishment is looking at us. 'Look at those…' I heard stories years later about the riots at San Fernando High School, at SC, and when I was in the pros. I used to meet retired cops who had patrolled the area. Some of the stuff they used to say about San Fernando High School — I never understood that clash, you know, I never understood that.

"It was pretty serious. We had battle lines. Blacks here, Hispanics over there. We were going at it. I had Hispanic friends. Bobby Chacon was a friend of mine; he became the lightweight champion of the world. I had Mary, my girlfriend. I didn't see it. A lot of people thought there was gonna be some…because of me crossing the line. It never happened. The point is I had a lot of Hispanic kids that were my friends…that I played baseball with. I never got that — because here you have two suppressed races anyway — why go at each other's throat? At the end of the day their going to say, let them kill each other. That pretty much was the attitude. As long as you don't go drifting off into the White area either north, south, east, or west, whatever it is, you're fine. Just keep them in that little area there. If they want to kill each other, that's fine."

This 1970 yearbook photo was just fun and games, but riots at SFHS were very serious

San Fernando High School - 1977

Maclay Junior High School

Named after the infamous Senator Charles Maclay, Maclay Junior High opened in 1960 and made enormous accomplishments throughout the years. When first opened, it was an equal split between White, Mexican, and Black. However, according to the school's head counselor, Jack Rosenberg, the demographics changed after the assassinations of Rev. Martin Luther King Jr. and Robert F. Kennedy in 1968. The White parents were afraid of retaliation and racial violence, and many pulled their children out of Maclay.

Despite the demographic shift, the level of excellence flourished. Thanks to the committed work of drama teacher Sarah Rosenberg and her talented students, they reached a status unheard of in minority schools. Mrs. Rosenberg taught at Maclay for 22 years, along with her husband, Jack. After working at Maclay for a year, she accepted a position teaching theater. According to Mrs. Rosenberg, the talent and skills of Maclay's students were apparent.

"It helped having a husband who was head counselor, and he would find kids who were very dramatic. But most kids found their way to room 6. My beloved room was accessible after school to everybody. We had a thriving program—after a year, we started beating every single theater department in the city. We're talking about Beverly Hills, Palos Verdes Peninsula, these amazing schools. Our little 9th graders were tremendous and beyond talented."

Students at Maclay Junior High competed in high school competitions and consistently won at the Shakespeare Festival. Mrs. Rosenberg explained that this didn't come without backlash.

"They competed with kids throughout Southern California, and there is a certain negativity that can follow competition. Most of the drama teachers were really cool. But it got on their nerve, I think, when you would win first or second place in every category. There were seven categories. And a few said, well, it's not possible that minority kids could or should (win). I know the majority of the Drama Teachers Association of Southern California were very supportive. They knew they were seeing something very special. That's why they made this movie 'Shakespeare High". To show all these great drama teachers that the talent will win out."

However, the big moment happened when they decided to create a play for Nancy Reagan's "Dreams Over Drugs" program. The concept was to create a tree with individual leaves from children all over the world. On each leaf, the child would write their dreams. They called it a Dream Tree.

Sarah Rosenberg in Washington DC for Dream Tree presentation. The tree can be seen in the background. (Courtesy Jack Rosenberg)

Maclay drama students pose with DREAMS banner
(Courtesy Jack Rosenberg)

The students also incorporated their Dream Tree into a slideshow and play. Rosenberg described the presentation.

"It started with a slide show. Beautiful little faces of children growing from babyhood to toddlers to middle school to high School — And all of a sudden, a hand reached out but instead of a diploma, with a bag of drugs. Then the slides went off, and the play started. It was upbeat, funny, and musical. It had culminated in the slideshow where my husband had been taking pictures of all the little kids throughout the day and all of a sudden they saw their face-up on the screen as a part of a dream of what they could do with their lives if they don't give in to negative elements. Then they would have every child sign a leaf. One side their name and the other side their dream — sometimes it was hard. 'I want my mother to come back to my father,' oh lord. But many times, it was I want to learn how to read, I want to be a cash register. I want to have a bike. And so, we would talk and interact with them."

After doing this for other schools' word got out.

"All of a sudden, we were sent up north to the governor, and the legislature wanted to honor us. Then we started taking our program to cities across the country. Then we were invited to the Senate, the Congress and got some big award. We presented the Dream Tree and then went to the Hubert Humphrey Memorial Building. Finally, we went to the United Nations, and there we put on the show for hundreds of countries around the world and their ambassadors. They then adopted the Dream Tree and what we were doing.

"We came back to LA, and we were honored with the hostages that were released from Iran. It was breathtaking. They all signed a leaf. I thought it was interesting that George W. Bush Sr. (vice president of the United States), had signed a leaf and told me, later on, he was announcing he's running for President."

The United States Air Force flew the towering tree to the Library of Congress and around Washington. First lady Nancy Reagan adopted the program for her "International Conference on Just Say No." She invited the Maclay Drama Students/Department to have lunch with her.

Rosenberg had many students who went on to colleges such as MIT, UCLA, and Cal State Berkeley. One of her students Vanessa Townsell, went to New York to be in the Broadway musical "Dream Girls," replacing well known Jennifer Holliday.

In 1989, a new principal came to Maclay and stopped all after school activities and even attempted to stop them from flying to Washington DC to be honored by Congress. Rosenberg contacted Roberta Weintraub, President of the School Board, who overrode his decision.

This principal believed the minority students should be placed in shop type classes and not prepped for college. After this, the majority of the teaching staff left. Although the school later demoted him, "the damage was done," said Rosenberg.

Opening ceremony for Maclay Junior High School in 1960

The first graduating class of Maclay Junior High in 1961 - (Courtesy Arturo Ramos)

Maclay Junior High 1962 boys home room class with Mr. Barr
(Courtesy Dan Tolentino)

Maclay Middle School, formally Maclay Junior High is located at 12540 Pierce Street in Pacoima

Desegregation Busing

Education in Pacoima evolved tremendously over the years. However, nothing could prepare Maclay Junior High and San Fernando High students for mandatory busing as a way to desegregate schools.

In 1954, a landmark US Supreme Court decision ruled that American state laws establishing racial segregation in public schools are unconstitutional, even if the segregated schools are otherwise equal in quality. In 1972, the Los Angeles Unified School District enacted a forced busing plan to accommodate this law. The entire city was in an uproar over this decision.

Although the mission was to desegregate, Whites in the San Fernando Valley did not want their students bussed, nor did they want students of color bussed to them.

Ronald Oliver, who is Black, explained that although San Fernando High had some racial tension between Blacks and Mexicans, they pulled together in times of need. The busing situation was one of those times.

"At San Fernando, you deal with the Mexicans from across the tracks. When we played sports, we were one family. In school, we had to deal with each other, but racial tensions would sometimes jump off.

"1972 came along, and I got a letter one day you will not be attending San Fernando anymore. They are trying a new deal of busing students out to this new school. It was Kennedy High School. My mother said, 'you have to go.'

"They chose one little area (in Pacoima) that everybody had to go to Kennedy. Then when we got there, that's actually when I was introduced to racism. The first day of school, they had "bus all n's back to Africa." They had it spray painted up on the front of the school, and we got off the bus and said, 'Wow, really?'

"Who's gonna take us (to Africa)? Come on, we're ready to go."

"About a week or two weeks later, we had a riot. We had to deal with all the Whites in the school and the Mexicans. They took a busload of

Mexicans out of San Fernando and bussed them to Kennedy too. We had two busloads of Blacks, and two busloads of Mexicans. The rest of the school was all White."

Oliver explained how the Blacks and Mexicans unified to deal with the hostile Black and Brown sentiment. The name-calling and tense environment helped bring them back together as a family during that experience. As for Oliver, the baseball coach refused to let him on the team, and he was able to return to San Fernando High.

"They didn't want us there. However, it was good because I got back into San Fernando," Oliver said.

Unfortunately, that left him with a negative attitude regarding school.

"As far as the street life that kind of turned me towards the streets. I didn't care anymore about school. They say I might have turned militant whatever and didn't care for dealing with those White folks."

Oliver ultimately received a degree from CSUN in computer science despite the challenges he faced in 1972.

Angela Cobb walks through Kennedy High School campus with Ronald Oliver (R) and Gary Commack (L) behind her – 1972 (photo courtesy of Ronald Oliver)

There were some bad experiences at Junior High Schools as well. Maclay teacher Sarah Rosenberg described how busing affected her students.

"We had to send a great number of our students out. None of the schools in the valley wanted to come to us. Finally, a junior high school, mainly Jewish, said we are going to send our kids there. Our Black kids on the other campus had a miserable time. They had painted circles out on the blacktop where our students had to stand during lunch. They couldn't even sit and eat with the other kids. Saying oh, you had this problem; you were tardy, or you weren't on task in some way.

"Our students, on the day they came, had huge banners welcoming individual kids from the other school. We accepted them right away. They put them in the theater class. That's how I got my name (Rosie). At the end we put on "Bye- Bye Birdie," and the parents got up and sang 'Everything is Rosie.' There are students that had such an important time at that school. These were wealthy parents from the West Valley. They saw the quality we had. Johnny Carson might not have, but you know."

The busing experience evolved, and tensions subsided over time. Robert Thomas, an African-American raised in Pacoima, felt he learned how to deal with this unfamiliar culture, which ultimately helped him in the corporate world.

"When you're at Maclay, in familiar surroundings, the pecking order is clear. I got used to that. By the time I was a ninth-grader, everyone knew me. I knew everyone. When I got to Kennedy, I knew no one. I knew absolutely no one. Like I tell my younger brothers, when I got to Kennedy, there were guys walking around with mustache and beards. This is not a high school; it's a college. But I was exposed to a different culture, a more Caucasian culture.

"It was interesting for me. It helped me to understand how to get along in a business sense in general, that exposure at Kennedy. I'm not downplaying San Fernando or Sylmar or any other ones, but I don't know if I would have got that type of exposure if I went to those. When you're with predominantly White, you learn things. You learn how to get along, and a different type of pecking order — a business type of pecking order — a pecking order that your type of intimidation didn't work there. And that helped me assimilate into a job culture that I'm currently in now.

Despite the good intentions of desegregation, forced busing eventually ended. Lawsuits, protests, and impact studies, mostly initiated by segregated White communities and politicians, have tackled this issue over the years.

Although many consider busing a failure, overlooking its successes could be a mistake. For many students of color, it provided access to a quality of education previously unavailable. Moreover, it gave segregated White children the opportunity to learn that most minority kids were just like them. For many, it made a positive difference.

Vaughn Street Elementary School

After the Basilone Homes closed, in 1954, its school relocated to the corner of Vaughn Street and Herrick Avenue. It was renamed Vaughn Street School and primarily serviced residents in the Joe Louis Homes. Although the student population was mostly Black, a number of Mexicans still attended in those early days.

Arvel Jackson was a Vaughn Street student in the sixties and shared this memory.

"Vaughn Street was a very together school. Mostly what I liked was some teachers made learning fun. Mr. Rider, Ms. King, Mr. Buck — they made you want to learn. We were also pretty bad in those years. But we did have fun learning."

Patricia Hodges had a very active mother, Essey Mae Hodges, who worked at the school.

"Vaughn Street, well my mother was a teacher there, so where most people could get away with stuff, I couldn't get away with nothing. My mother was in all the classes. She was a TA. So, for me, it was good cause it kept me in line, but it was bad cause other people could get away with stuff. I couldn't get away with absolutely nothing."

Vaughn Street School Kindergarten - 1960

Vaughn Street School - 1966 back L R Henry Williams, Shirley Shepherd, Patricia Smith, Diane Harden, Michael Webster Front Charles Robinson, Anita Prevost (Courtesy of Patricia Flowers)

Vaughn Street School First Grade Students - Mrs. Kennedy – 1970
Courtesy of David Johnson

Vaughn Street School First Grade Students - Mrs. Knight – 1981
Courtesy Diane Velarde Hernandez

While the community continued to grow and change, public schools faced the challenge of changing as well. However, during the eighties, a dark new landscape evolved. Hard drugs arrived in Pacoima, and the impact on its children was overwhelming. The situation became dire, but their solution changed the face of education in America.

Vaughn Elementary was suffering from the effects of a crack epidemic and gang violence, which saw education evolve from serious parental involvement to parental indifference. Grandparents were raising many children as their parents battled drug addictions and incarceration. The town was in a crisis.

The Los Angeles School District labeled it a Title 1 school, which meant test scores and attendance were far below standards. In 1990, they sent Dr. Yvonne Chan to become the principal of Vaughn. She explained how she faced parents battling each other over language, religion, and race.

"Los Angles built this school in 1950, and it's supposed to house 500 kids. By the time 1990 rolled in, we packed about 1200 minority students. In the beginning, it was predominately African American and Hispanic. There were no White kids. This school in 1990, was involved in huge busing. Twenty-six buses rolled in and out for desegregation. We bused out about 260 kids to the west valley, and bused in, over twenty years, four White kids.

"I moved here in 1990 because of racial, ethnic conflicts. The NAACP came in, and the principal was pulled out because of receiving death threats. She was Latina. She left in March of 1990."

Dr. Chan had a great deal of experience before Vaughn, but what she discovered was surprising.

"All I did was come to schools and try to help them set up a program for students with disabilities. I said oh my god, I started looking at the kids and noticed how capable they were. I've been a teacher at eleven schools. I started teaching in 1968. It's not they are disabled — it blew my mind that they were very talented in many, many areas. We just thrust the academic standards or cultural standards, and they are just not interested."

Unlike in Pacoima's past, language also became a problem for both the Blacks and Latinos. Dr. Chan explained her challenges.

"They can't speak proper English. That framed the need for a cultural relation structure facing the whole notion of poverty in this area. Not only to value and see what it's all about but develop family support.

"From the perspective of injustice, so many kids are identified and labeled as disabled, without facing the whole notion of poverty in this area. This whole neighborhood is surrounded by liquor stores. There's no JC Penny, no movie theatre, no sit-down Denny's, and up and down San Fernando Road quickie motels. These kids are in poverty with no opportunity. You look at these risk factors. How can you turn risk into opportunity? How can you do that? When Latinos started moving in, 'no, no habla English.' Now, this is another factor. What are we going to do with the fact that so many cannot speak English? Their parents cannot, and the school is trying to educate your kids to be proficient in English."

Dr. Chan explained how seeing these challenges and understanding how the school district worked, made her determined to resolve this issue and not just pass it on. She began strategizing on becoming a school independent of the district office, which she knew very well.

In 1993, Dr. Chan instituted the nation's first public Charter school. She explained the process.

"Don't forget, 27 years I was the one who made some of the rules. I knew what was good for kids and what's not. The refreshing idea of being independent with added autonomy, with added responsibility accountability — if you marry those two, you create additional and better education. That formula seems to work.

"We took about a couple of years to clean up the place. We developed the Pacoima Vaughn Street Gang. PBS did a 2-hour special on how we can talk to the gangs about safety and how they could help. I went outside and started talking to the gangs."

Dr. Chan later started a preschool, added a new middle school, then built her crowning jewel high school, Vaughn International Studies Academy. The high school graduation rate is 90%. Dr. Chan has had visits from former President Bill Clinton, first lady Hillary Clinton, and Governor Arnold Schwarzenegger. PBS and ABC's "Good Morning America" have both featured her.

Vaughn Next Century Learning Center is the only poverty school ever to win the Blue-Ribbon Award and started a trend of Charter Schools across the nation. Since Dr. Chan's effort, there are an estimated 7,000 charter schools nationwide, ten of which are in the town. Pacoima has once again been a pioneer in the United States of America.

This news article hangs on the wall in Dr. Chan's office. She was friends with both Bill and Hillary Clinton

Dr. Chan and former US President George Bush, when he was Governor of Texas

Dr. Chan and Calif. Governor Arnold Schwarzenegger (lower left) rally behind

Other Pacoima Schools

1954 Montague school opened at 13000 Montague Street 900 students pre-registered to attend this school. It was in Pacoima until this area changed the name to Arleta. The school was predominantly White when it opened.

Pacoima Elementary saw a reduction of students after Vaughn opened. It was still a very diverse school in 1954 after other schools opened. This is a second-grade class that shows the diversity. (Courtesy Dan Tolentino)

Pacoima Junior High opened in 1954. It was best known for the plane crash of 57 and the Ritchie Valens concerts. Ritchie had an album "Ritchie Valens Live at Pacoima Junior High." Teachers knew whenever a crowd of students got together, he was usually playing for them.

Pacoima Junior High 1957 kids line up to honor the flag. This was the first Junior High in Pacoima. Prior to this school kids went to San Fernando Junior High.

Beachy Avenue School opened in 1954 at 970 Obeck Avenue. Photo taken in 1958 in front of school (Courtesy Susan Boozer)

Guardian Angel Catholic School was located near the church by the projects. The school opened in 1956, a welcomed addition to the community.

(Courtesy Ida Cochran)

Mrs. Myrtle Hinssinger, office clerk, and Mrs. Joan von Klein Smid, principal at Sharp Avenue Elementary School which opened at 13800 Pierce Street Pacoima in 1959.

1969 Filmore Elementary (left to right, rear)) Deborah Jennings, La Tanya Milller, (left to right,front) Myra Kirk, Sheila Cannon, Roderick Williams aka Sonny, Denise Martin, Juaniki Franio

(Courtesy Sheila Y. Cannon)

Since Lopez Station school began in 1861, numerous schools have been part of Pacoima's history. Here is a list of the early schools up until 1960.

Public

• Lopez Station (school bunker)	1861
• Pacoima School	1888
• San Fernando Grammar	1889
• Morningside Grammar	1890
• San Fernando High Fifth/ Hagar	1896
• San Fernando High Brand Bl	1906
• Haddon Street School	1926
• Pacoima Junior High	1954
• Vaughn Street Elementary (Basilone Homes)	1954
• Montague Elementary	1954
• Terra Bella Elementary (Temporary)	1954
• Beachy Elementary	1954
• Vena Elementary	1957
• Sharp Elementary	1959
• Hillery T. Broadous (Filmore Elementary)	1960
• Charles Maclay Junior High	1960
• Telfair Elementary	

Private

• Guardian Angel School	1956
• Mary Immaculate School	1954

This list does not include schools after 1960.

21
S.F. Tigers

Nothing in Pacoima history has represented the town's spirit like Tigers athletics. The San Fernando Tigers have excelled as champions in numerous sports and has produced some of America's best-known athletes. The town's love for the Tiger's has been legendary, and its football program was once ranked number one in the nation. However, nothing speaks louder than the championship record they have amassed over the years.

San Fernando Football

City Champions: 1925, 1926, 1934, 1937, 1953, 1967, 1974, 1975, 2012, 2017

Basketball

1971 Perfect season 14-0
1981, 1988 League Champions

Baseball

1988 League Champions
2011, 2013 City Champions

Track & Field

1976 City Champions
1976 Co-State Champion

Wrestling

1977, 1979, 1980, 1982, 1983, 1987,
1991, 2001—2003, 2006—2009,
2012—2015, 2017 City Champions
Girls Champions 2014, 2015, 2017, 2018, 2019

Joseph Barney SFHS 1962
(Courtesy Adrianne Gilchrist)

Wrestling

The San Fernando High School wrestling team holds the largest number of city championships in Los Angeles. They were wrestling champions in 1977, 1979, 1980, 1982, 1983, 1987, 1991, 2001—2003, 2006—2009, 2012—2015, and 2017.

In 2006, Johnny Parada became the first-ever CIF Wrestling State Champion from the Los Angeles City Section, winning the 126-pound title.

However, one of the most memorable stories in Tigers wrestling is that of the Gilyard brothers, Rickey and Chris. In 1977, they were part of an unprecedented group of grapplers that powered San Fernando to their first-ever wrestling city championship. During the finals, the Tigers received first-place finishes from Terry Gillard, John Paez, James Cobb, and their All-City star Rickey Gilyard.

The 106-pound Gilyard led the team, being named "most outstanding wrestler" in the All-City finals. He finished becoming a three-year champion. Sadly, however, his brother and teammate Chris was killed in a car accident before graduation. Rickey attended Pierce College and later won the most-valuable wrestler award.

Wrestling Team — City Champs 1977

Top Row: Coach DeJohn, C Stokes, M. Perez, W. Lohman, J.Paez, T. Gillard, J. Rascon, Coach Tarin, Second Row: J DeLaCruz, C. Gilyard, G Widener, M. Velasquez, J. Henry, R. Gilyard, J. Lopez First Row; J. Widener, M. Paravato, L. Romero.

Football

SFHS football 1937 won the LA Championship title in a shutout. The school was located on Brand Boulevard then where the middle school is now.

There were some very noteworthy athletes throughout the years, as displayed by the school's ten city championship titles. The first documented football player to go pro was Frank Cassara, born March 22, 1928. He attended San Fernando High School in the forties and was selected all-city in 1946. He went on to play for St Mary's College and received induction into their Athletic Hall of fame. In 1954, Cassara was drafted by the San Francisco 49ers as a linebacker.

Look 'Em Over--1946 All-City Football Team--Tomorrow's College Heroes

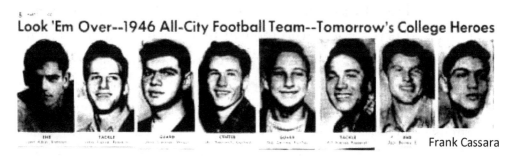

Frank Cassara

The next round of players consisted of Manfred Moore, who was a Tigers star in the sixties. He went on to win a Superbowl in the NFL. Also, William "Bill" Marsh, who was a standout "Player of the Year" fullback. Bill Marsh returned to become the head coach of Tigers football and win back-to-back city championships. Both of these players were multi-sport athletes.

There was also Allan Graf, who was an offensive lineman, co-player of the year in 67, who went on to play at USC. He was zoned for Sylmar High but chose SFHS because of their exceptional athletic reputation. He had a brief run with the NFL before going into the film industry.

Then came Anthony Davis, who put Tiger football on the national map. Many think San Fernando produced two Heisman winners because of the celebrity status Davis received. However, Davis never won the Heisman.

Anthony Davis recalled his days as a Tiger.

"San Fernando was my only choice. After 65 (Broncos World Series), all the kids joined up and played pop warner, but football was not my thing. It was going to be baseball.

"When I got to San Fernando High School, I was out in the baseball yard throwing the baseball, and a coach by the name of Pat Harrington saw me throwing the ball. He said, 'wow you have a strong arm. How would you like to be the backup quarterback on our team?' 'Varsity?' I said, 'Coach I never played, I just hung out at pop warner. I was never a starter.' He said, 'well, I like your arm. You know you don't have to worry about it come on out.'

"Academically I was struggling because I was having some tough times at home. And here's a guy who thought that much of me to make me his quarterback. He said, 'first of all you gotta do well in school, keep your grades up, and you can be the backup quarterback.' I said, 'you're giving me the position?' He said, 'yea, because we don't have anybody who's got an arm like you.'

"So, I remember we were playing against Polytechnic High School, my sophomore year, Poly was ranked number one in the city, San Fernando was ranked number 2. The first quarter we are doing fine. Second-quarter, we had a big quarterback by the name of Harvey Sneed, 6'2, 190 lbs. He was on his way to a Division 1 school as a quarterback — and in the second quarter, he breaks his leg. My teammate was Manfred Moore, who grew up on my street. He was our tailback. I looked at Coach Harrington, and he said, 'Davis, you gotta get in there. Harvey's hurt'.

"So really, I didn't take learning my playbook that serious, and I really didn't know all the plays, really. I was just happy to be hanging out with all the cheerleaders, band, and everything that was going on. I had to get in there and run this team. Manfred Moore literally coached me through the game. We ended up tying Polytechnic. And that was my beginning at San Fernando High School, both academically and as an athlete.

"Then we had a guy by the name of Mr. Cockrell, who actually went to USC, who started promoting USC to me. (He was) Putting the propaganda in my head when I was a sophomore in high school. He said, 'you need to go to USC.' That was my experience."

1971 – SFHS Yearbook Photos – (right) Anthony Davis, (top left to right) Ted Willis, Drake Conti, Robert Keith, (bottom left to right) Bruce Gima, Larry Porter

San Fernando High School won the city championship in 1968 led by future NFL Super Bowl champion, Manfred Moore — 1969 Yearbook Photos

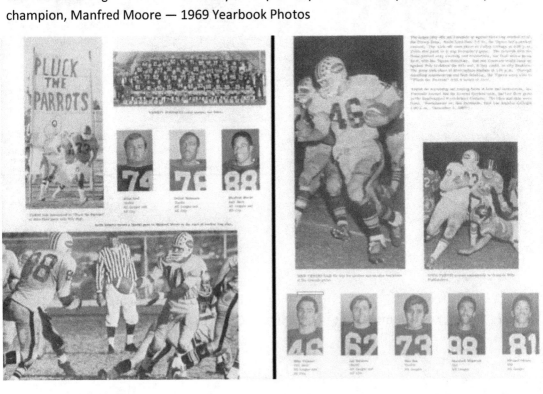

The magic years flowed after the Anthony Davis era. In 1973, a kid named Charles "Charlie" White entered San Fernando High. He was too young to play on varsity but had incredible speed and skill. Amazingly, he was not alone. During that year, a crop of ultra-talented children from Pacoima converged on the school. What followed was Tiger football's most celebrated legacy.

By 1974, this group of high school juniors featuring White, along with Kevin Williams, Raymond Williams (not related), Kenny Moore, and others, were ready to play varsity football. Most of these kids had grown up playing together in Pacoima, which was a close-knit community in the seventies. Their camaraderie and chemistry were explosive. Harnessed by the coaching tandem of Bill Marsh and Bill Hornbeck, they created an unstoppable team.

During that first season, things did not entirely start smooth. They lost their opening game to Gardena and quickly faced adversity. However, this extraordinary team of mostly juniors, came roaring back to win 11 consecutive games and earn a semi-final playoff matchup against perennial power Granada Hills.

It was Granada that dashed San Fernando's last hope of winning a championship when they defeated the Anthony Davis led Tigers in 1970. However, the Tigers prevailed 22-15, advancing to the city championship game. Granada Hills High coach Darryl Stroh said of their wishbone backfield, "that was the best backfield I've ever seen."

The anticipation was unbearable, heading into the matchup between San Fernando and Pacific Palisades on December 12, 1974. The Dolphins were a powerhouse team averaging 28 points a game. Bernie Milligan in the Valley News wrote, "Barring inconceivable developments, a Dolphin (Pacific Palisades) is going to tear a Tiger to pieces tonight in the Memorial Coliseum. I can just feel it in my bones." This attitude was prevalent in the media, who doubted this team of juniors could win a championship.

1974 Starting line-up

OFFENSE			DEFENSE		
Dwayne Jett	WR	Jr.	John Perez	T	Jr.
Steve Boyle	TE	Jr.	David Lopez	T	Sr.
Norman White	T	Sr.	Bill Benjamin	DE	Jr.
Pedro Arreguin	T	Sr.	Mark LaDue	DE	Jr.
Luis Estrada	G	Sr.	James Criner	G	Jr.
Tommy Hernandez	G	Sr.	John Contreras	LB	Sr.
Richard Flores	C	Sr.	Norman White	LB	Sr.
Kenny Moore	QB	Jr.	Charles White	LB	Jr.
Ray Williams	RB	Jr.	Kenny Moore	LB	Jr.
Kevin Williams	RB	Jr.	Ray Williams	S	Jr.
Charles White	FB	Jr.	Kevin Williams	S	Jr.

Before a crowd of 12,747 at the coliseum, the tables turned for this Pacoima team that had speed, precision, immense talent, and penchant for the big play. The Tigers battled hard in the first half, but could not score against the Dolphins. Fortunately, San Fernando's defense held Pacific Palisades to only a field goal. They trailed 3-0 at half time. Three plays into the third quarter, Kevin Williams took a handoff from Kenny Moore to score a 37-yard touchdown.

"I got past the line of scrimmage and then cut across," Williams said to the media after the game.

However, he did more than that. Once he cut back, he skipped over a fallen teammate, and using his speed never allowed any defensive players to touch him.

David Lopez, James Criner, Johnny Contreras, Charles White, and Kevin Williams anchored the Tiger's defense, holding the Dolphins to their lowest score that season. On a decisive fourth and goal situation at the two-yard line, Charles White blew across the scrimmage and nailed Palisades fullback Ian Rubin for no gain on the play. Coach Bill Marsh praised White's effort saying, "you stop Rubin, you stop Palisades."

However, it was Kevin Williams who made the game's biggest play. Late in the fourth quarter, he intercepted a pass and ran it back 47-yards for a touchdown. The Tiger's won 12-10 in a nail-biting game. This remarkable team, of mostly juniors, upset the landscape of football in Los Angeles and showed the non-believers what kids from Pacoima could achieve. They took the Los Angeles City Championship back-to-back years in 1974 and 75.

In 1975, Kevin Williams Kenny Moore and Charles White were named "city tri-players of the year." Legendary Banning High football coach Chris Ferragamo told the L.A. Times that year, "They have to be the best in the world."

The core members of the Tiger's football team also excelled in track & field. Kevin Williams, Charles White, Kenny Moore, and Raymond Williams led the San Fernando track team to multiple state titles.

Kevin Williams is the fastest runner in San Fernando High history. As a junior, Williams won the state championship and set a national high-school record for the 100-yard dash with a speed of 9.4 seconds. However, it was the state championship 400-yard relay that had people talking.

White, Moore, and both Williams' ran the 400-relay. With the championship on the line, they ran a storybook race to win the title. Hopelessly behind, with Charles White running the anchor leg, White unbelievably tracked down the lead runner to win the race and earn the championship.

All of them secured college scholarships with White, Williams, and Moore going to USC, and Raymond Williams to Washington State.

Kevin did exceptionally well at USC. He held the record for 25 career touchdown catches and NCAA record for the highest percentage of passes caught for a touchdown in a career. The New Orleans Saints drafted him.

Unfortunately, after his football career was over, Kevin Williams suffered an untimely death while working as a train operator when it crashed unexpectantly. He was only 37. San Fernando High School renamed the school's football field in his honor.

Kevin Williams (left), Charles White (center), Kenny Moore (right) make the cover of Prep Magazine, while preparing to defend their city championship in 1975.

Congressman Tony Cárdenas graduated from SFHS in 1981, well after the magic years. However, he remembers what his older siblings talked about, and the legacy they left behind.

"They are a little older than me. Charles White was there in the mid-seventies, and Anthony Davis was there in the early seventies. All my brothers and sisters went to school with all of those famous people. They talked about how they were the cool guys on campus, and everybody knew they were going places. Football and track — Charles White and Anthony Davis, they were great track and field athletes as well and wrestled and things of that nature. They called it three or four lettermen. And when Charles White was here, they were the state champions in the 4 x 100. Our backfield could literally run circles around everyone. Now that's how we were the city champions, and that's how they were able to go be Heisman Trophy winners, etc."

Vanessa Brown dated Charles White while in high school and talked about what a good time the community had during those magical years.

"San Fernando was great. For all three years I was there it was very good. I wasn't into any sports until my senior year. We had a great football team each year. Charles White, Kevin Williams, and Kenny Moore were our trio. And took championships a couple of years and after every football game, we would go up to Shakey's and have a good time. Work it out with nobody fighting. We would just enjoy each other.

"Those were the days. We didn't have to worry about guns. People weren't doing things like they do now. San Fernando was great. The teachers were great. I had a teacher, and I didn't know my own skill, and he knew it, but he was so hard on me. I chickened out... I could have been an architect, building homes and houses. I was very good at it. San Fernando, I have no regrets. If I could start all over, I would do that (again). Because I enjoyed my high school."

Arvel Jackson, whose family has been in Pacoima since the early fifties, also had fond memories of Tigers football games.

"Football games…what we did at the football games. That was the thing on Fridays. Actually, that was the only thing on Fridays that we had to do where we could stay out late. Watch the football games, root for our team, and beat Kennedy. San Fernando had to beat Kennedy and Granada Hills. Those were the nights. We had a ball. The games were like fantastic. Everybody was screaming and hollering and rooting for our team, knowing our teachers and seeing them there was fun. We had pop-locking things at San Fernando during the assemblies too. They would have Spudgy and all them doing the pop-locking concerts. And we loved those. It was really nice."

The half time shows at San Fernando High were just as entertaining as the actual football games during this era. The dance skills were phenomenal and in sync with the times. The marching band was award-winning as well. The seventies set the stage for admiration and excellence at San Fernando for many years to come.

Vanessa Brown talks about how involved the crowd was at San Fernando football games.

"San Fernando, oh my goodness — when you do the cheers against the other teams and your little squads (in the stands) were cheering loud. Our drill team was James Tolliver, Spuggy Walker, Corkey Hicks. We had a good drill team."

Patricia Hodges remembers the Tigers well.

"We had the pop lockers, African tribe dancers, at that time everybody at the school couldn't wait for Friday night football or basketball but mostly football. We were all there, and everybody knew all the cheers. We got up and cheered with them. Then it was Tommy's (Burgers) or Shoestring (food stand). Everything was on Van Nuys Blvd that you could go to. Nobody went to Denny's. That's the cool thing now. Nobody could afford to go to Denny's at that time. No Fatburgers, but we had Jack in the Box. Everybody hung out at the school before we went to get something to eat."

Thurman Hackett (L), Corkey Hicks (C), Rodney Foster (R) 1975
(Courtesy James Tolliver III)

Corkey Hicks (L), Rodney Foster (R)
(Courtesy James Tolliver III)

James Tolliver
(Courtesy James Tolliver III)

Corkey Hicks was the lead half-time performer for the Tigers. He graduated in 1975 and went to trade school to become a carpenter. He tragically passed away in 1977. (Courtesy Celeste Sarah Hicks)

The San Fernando Tigers Drill Team during the seventies was among the best

1977/78 San Fernando High marching band.

Patricia Nevarez leading the band and drill team

These USC Trojans were all San Fernando Tigers; (left to right) Anthony (Anky) Gibson, Charles McClanahan, Malcolm Moore, Kevin Williams, Charles White

(Photo courtesy of Malcolm Moore)

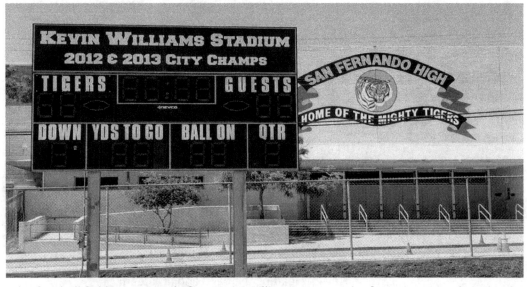

The football field was named after Kevin Williams. He was the fastest runner the school ever saw. He was tragically killed in a train crash in 1998 at the age of 38.

An early photo of San Fernando Tiger Baseball taken in 1960. The Tigers have won two city championships in 2011 and 2013

San Fernando Tigers Track & Field - 1978

Tigers Basketball was also extremely popular. Although they did not achieve the same success as football or Track, the games were still thrilling. Some of the players identified in this 1974-75 photo include #12 Lawrence Knox, #35 Keith Smith Sr., and #42 Charles McClellan.

San Fernando Tigers Basketball 1975-76 — Back row (L-R) Dan Sullivan, Mark Sutton, Dennis Seeley; Middle row (L-R) - Maurice Brown, Mark Sarpy, and Chuck McClellan; Bottom (L-R) - Eugene Burney, Haylock, Bill Benjamin

Pictured are a few members of the San Fernando High School marching band with their instruments. Photograph dated November 14, 1963.

San Fernando Tiger cheerleaders during the sixties

San Fernando Tigers Cheer Squad - 1972

22
Athletes

One of the most significant areas of talent in Pacoima is undoubtedly sports. Compiling a list of the town's successful athletes was most definitely a challenge. Many sports figures reference Los Angeles or San Fernando as their hometown. It was a daunting task, and some may still be undiscovered. However, one thing is clear, for such a small geographical area, the town put out an impressive number of world-class athletes.

Pacoima's list of professional athletes includes boxers, baseball, football, basketball, martial arts, and even Roller Derby.

Many of these athletes have battled adversity and challenges, which made their success an uphill climb. However, the raw talent and determination of these mighty Pacoimians have shined brightly, allowing them to overcome extraordinary circumstances and obstacles.

Anthony Davis, one of Pacoima's most noteworthy athletes, had this to say.

"I think it's in the water. It's in the culture. It's playing hard in the streets, competing with friends and siblings, no TV, no cell phones, fruit trees, clean air, and community. It allowed for the talent to develop and excel."

The Pacoima City Hall Mural and the Pacoima Mural Mile have captured some of the town's more successful champions. This chapter highlights these individuals and many others; however, some deserving athletes certainly may be missing.

Bobby Chacon

Bobby Chacon was born November 2, 1951, and grew up hanging in the projects, attending Pacoima Elementary, Maclay Junior High, and San Fernando High schools. As a youth, he played at North Valley Little League with Anthony Davis and always stayed true to the community.

Chacon attended Cal State University, Northridge, studying Liberal Arts and earning the nickname "schoolboy" by the boxing media.

He won world titles in two weight classes. Ricky Farris, president of the West Coast Boxing Hall of Fame, called Chacon, "One of the most exciting fighters in the history of the west coast. An amazing blood-and-guts brawler who took on the best fighters in three divisions."

Chacon began training in Pacoima with local people such as Calvin Woods and sparred with boxing champion Bennie "The Jet" Urquidez, also from Pacoima. However, his legend began to rise after a 19-0 run at the Los Angeles Forum, gaining him a title bout against world champion Ruben Olivares in 1973. Chacon lost that fight by knockout in the ninth round but came back with four consecutive wins afterward.

That run of victories created a stir in the boxing community and pressure for a match with another young Los Angeles fighter and future champion named Danny "Little Red" Lopez. Chacon won the fight by knockout in the ninth round before a sold-out crowd on May 24, 1974.

Later that year, on September 7, 1974, Chacon won the WBC Featherweight title by defeating former WBA Junior Lightweight champion Alfredo Marcano in nine rounds at the Grand Olympic Auditorium in Los Angeles.

In March of 1982, Chacon faced tragedy when his wife Valerie, mother of his three children, asked him to retire from boxing. She was concerned about his health and called Chacon the night before his fight with Salvador Ugalde. According to Chacon's good friend, Urquidez, while on the phone with her and arguing about it, he heard a popping type of noise. His friend Blinky Rodriguez told Bobby it's time to go, so he said, "I'll call you back" and hung up. Later, says Urquidez, Rodriguez went to check on Valerie and discovered she had shot and killed herself. That is when Bobby realized what the popping sound was. Valerie died at the age of 31.

Bobby Chacon ended his career 59-7-1 with 47 knockout victories. He won two world titles in two weight classes while defeating seven world champions. Boxing media hailed him, at his peak, the most talented, exciting, and popular fighter in the sport. 'Ring Magazine' voted his battles "Fight of the Year" in both 1982 and 83.

Chacon was a complete warrior, and legend, because of his enthusiasm to fight and never say die Pacoima spirit. He retired from boxing in 1988, but his success came at a cost. Doctors diagnosed the champ with pugilistic dementia, and in his later years, faced severe challenges. How much can be attributed to head blows will never be known, but over the years, Chacon fought in many fierce battles. Moreover, he boxed against some of the most notable fighters in boxing history including, Alexis Arguello, Ray "Boom Boom" Mancini, Rafael "Bazooka" Limón, Cornelius Boza Edwards, and a legendary trilogy of fights with Rubén Olivares.

In 2005, this Pacoima icon received induction into the International Boxing Hall of Fame. Attendees there noted his incredibly slurred speech.

Bobby Chacon passed away while in hospice care for dementia on September 7, 2016, at the age of 64. He left behind three ex-wives and three children. He had also lost a son, Bobby Jr., to alleged gang violence.

His legacy includes Ring Magazine "Comeback Fighter of the Year," "The 100 Greatest Punchers of All-Time," election to the International Boxing Hall of Fame in January 2005, and West Coast Boxing Hall of Fame in 2016.

The Pacoima City Hall Mural features a beautiful rendering of his image, and the town shall always remember his Pacoima legacy.

Bobby Chacon image on Pacoima City Hall Mural
(artwork by Ignacio Gomez)

Bennie "The Jet" Urquidez

Benny "The Jet" Urquidez image on Pacoima City Hall Mural
(artwork by Ignacio Gomez)

Bennie "The Jet" Urquidez was born in Los Angeles on Bunker Hill Boulevard, June 20, 1952. His ancestry is Spanish and Native American Apache. The Jet's family moved to Pacoima when he was young, and he lived in the projects attending Pacoima Elementary and Pacoima Junior High at times.

Both his parents were fighters; his father a professional boxer and mother, a professional wrestler. His life during high school had him headed down a negative path causing him to attend schools outside of Pacoima to stay out of trouble. He ended up at North Hollywood High due to his mischief at other schools.

The Jet talks about his constant fighting and the reputation the Urquidez family had in the San Fernando Valley. If one brother got messed with, they all got involved. According to Urquidez, he grew up fighting in the projects and had his first bout at the age of 5. He was always in trouble at school for fighting and had to learn at an early age the difference between street fighting and tournament fighting. Unfortunately, sometimes, those boundaries blurred.

By 14, he was the youngest to break tradition and become a black belt. During that time, achieving black belt status did not happen before the age of 18. As a result, he could no longer fight in his age group and had to fight with adult martial artists. He claims he used his speed as a weapon during his early fights and only had very few losses.

He met his wife Sara Mortero in 1970, who shared the Apache lineage with him. In his book "The Jet," he speaks highly of her extraordinary intuition, which made him nervous because, at times, she seemed psychic. They married in 1974.

Shortly after the marriage, he began working with Pacoima's featherweight boxing champion Bobby Chacon and another champion Randy Shields. It was in these early days of sparing with Chacon that he got his first bloody nose, and that was a deciding factor in him entering into the boxing arena.

He ended with nine black belts, eight world titles in 5 different weight divisions. He held his title from 1974 to 1993 with 63 wins 0 losses two draws and 54 knockouts and is the longest-reigning World Champion in the history of all professional sports. In addition to his fantastic career in the ring, he has choreographed and acted in numerous films. His sister Lily Urquidez Rodriguez was also a world champion kickboxer in the seventies.

Bennie says that although he has had many successes in the ring and films, his passion is teaching and training others. He has instructed law enforcement officers with the LAPD and laughs when he says, "I used to run from the cops, and now I coach them."

He was awarded the title "competitor of the Year" in 1978 by Black Belt Magazine and has been on the cover numerous times.

Bennie "The Jet" has never been defeated
(Courtesy Mr. Jet & Mrs. Jet)

Bennie and Sara Urquidez
(Courtesy Mr. Jet & Mrs. Jet)

Bennie The Jet and Jean-Claude Van Damme
(Courtesy Mr. Jet & Mrs. Jet)

The Jet also trained hundreds of actors, including Tom Cruise, John Cusack, Nicholas Cage, Jean-Claude Van Damme, and Mark Wahlberg, to name a few.

He worked on Jackie Chan films as well as Chuck Norris's and is a sought-out fight choreographer. His roles in over 50 motion picture films include acting, stunts, and fight choreography. He worked with fellow Pacoimian Sonny Barnes on the film "Force Five," as well.

Urquidez, who says teaching is his true passion, is the author of several books plus an autobiography called "The Jet." He is the most respected man in the sport. Bennie and Sara Urquidez have one daughter Monique and grandson Levi. At the age of 67, he and Sara still run and work out. The Jets' image is beautifully captured on the Pacoima City Hall Mural.

Gwen "Skinny Minnie" Miller

Gwen "Skinny Minnie" Miller grew up on Louvre Street and attended San Fernando High School. While doing gymnastics, she won first place on the Horse Vault, where she was the only girl in the city who could perform a straight arm handspring over the horse.

She tried out and gained a spot on the Los Angeles Thunderbirds (LA T- Birds) of the National Skating Derby League, also called Roller Derby. The league, which began in 1961, was very popular, and the LA T-Birds became a well-known team.

During the sixties and seventies, T-Bird games were one of Los Angeles' highest-rated TV programs. They skated at the Olympic Auditorium, which had excellent acoustics for the sound of skates and hits. The stadium sold out frequently. Whiteman Stadium in Pacoima also hosted Roller Derby matches. The sport became so popular that

Hollywood produced a roller derby film in 1972 called "Kansas City Bomber," starring Raquel Welch.

Gwen "Skinny Minnie" Miller won the title of T-Birds captain and was one of the most skillful skaters of her time. She was a local celebrity who became the unofficial queen of the roller games. However, the league changed its marketing and branding, and even though Gwen had a strong fan base, she got overlooked for high profile positions.

Some of her accomplishments include Roller Derby Hall of Fame Inductee, Roller Derby Most Valuable Player, Roller Derby All-Star, and Roller Derby Fastest Girl.

Gwen "Skinny Minnie" Miller was an elite Roller Derby skater for the Los Angeles Thunderbirds known for her innate skills and ability

Gwen Miller passed away in May of 2018. She was the mother of two children Jason Holmes and Jacolyn Holmes, who both became hugely successful in martial arts. Jason is a 6th-degree master black belt and has traveled the globe to win over 15 world titles. Jacolyn has four world titles, as well. Both say their mother instilled extraordinary values in them.

Jason Holmes and Jacolyn Holmes
(Courtesy Jason Holmes)

Gwen, Jason, and Jacolyn. They claim their mother taught them
how to compete and be the best.
(Courtesy Jason Holmes)

Sonny (Clarence) Barnes

Sonny Barnes came to Pacoima at 18 years of age in 1957. He lived on Eustace, Paxton, and Columbus Street until finally moving to Jouett Street in Lake View Terrace. In 1962, Barnes met a woman named Sarah at Kaiser Permanente Hospital, and the two married in 1967. He was a graduate of Hart High School, and it was Sarah who introduced him to Judo when he was in his mid-20's. Sarah and Sonny opened up Barnes Dojo in the garage of their Lake View Terrace home in 1971.

Barnes moved to Sylmar with a mission to help keep children off the streets and get them in the Dojo. By teaching them martial arts discipline, as well as self-respect, he fought diligently to keep young people out of gangs. He also began training the Los Angeles Police Department and the San Fernando Police Department in defense moves to help them with their dangerous job.

In between teaching, Barnes worked in the movie industry. He appeared in numerous films over the years including "House Party," "Batman and Robin," "Bad News Bears go to Japan," "Force Five," "Black Belt Jones," "Truck Turner," "Say, Say, Say" with Michael Jackson & Paul McCarthy and many more.

He earned his 10-degree black belt, becoming a Master of Karate, and later won the title of California's Heavyweight Karate Champion. His wife, Sarah Barnes, was a black belt as well, working as an officer at the San Fernando Police Department. They had three children Tony, Andrian, and Rachel, who were also black belts. He was very connected to Pacoima, training many people and helping them to become champions. His daughter Rachel says, "my father was a very kind-hearted man that wanted to help everyone. He always encouraged and pushed everyone to be the better version of themselves. He was always there for everyone that needed him."

Sonny Barnes & wife Sarah
(Courtesy Rachel Barnes Fines)

Andy Williams, Richard Moton, Floyd Shaw Jr., and Kenny Hayward were Black belts that trained with Sonny. He was friends with Chuck Norris and Bennie "The Jet" Urquidez, two powerhouses in martial arts. He also taught at the Boys and Girls Club of Pacoima with Bennie the Jet.

Floyd Shaw Jr, Clarence "Sonny" Barnes and *Tommy Singleton* in the sixties
(Courtesy Harold White)

Lily Urquidez Rodriguez

Lily Urquidez Rodiguez on the Pacoima City Hall Mural
(artwork by Ignacio Gomez)

Lily Urquidez Rodriguez grew up in a martial arts family where all her siblings were Black belts. The Urquidez family was known as the first family of Martial arts. The oldest brother Arnold was the first to put on a gi. Benny, Ruben, Smiley, and Lily all became champions of the arts. However, Lily, being a woman, set records beyond their highest dreams.

At five years old, her father took her to the gym, where she dressed like a boy and fought like one. Girls were not allowed to compete during those days, so Lily pretended to be a boy. She threw kicks and blows with the best of them, fighting her brothers and any challenger that came along. Every Thursday, the family would go to the Olympic Auditorium to box and box she did. However, officials eventually discovered her gender and banned her from further competition. Despite this, she continued working out with her brothers at home. She trained in Kempo, Shotokan, Judo then kickboxing. She was finally allowed back in the gym when she was 17.

Lily went into boxing and kickboxing, where she had 17 professional fights with two losses. At a young age, she married her brothers' friend Blinky Rodriguez, and they ultimately became the first husband and wife team to fight on the same card. They both won titles, and Lily was the first female kickboxer to be on the ABC's Wide World of Sports. She won belts in featherweight boxing and kickboxing as well as an induction to the California Boxing Hall of Fame.

Blinky and Lily had six children, five boys and a girl. After she retired from boxing, Lily opened a gym and started training. At the age of 59, she passed away from an infection. One of her boys died in a drive-by shooting. Afterward, when Blinky retired, he devoted his life to ending gang violence. Lily is on the Pacoima City Hall Mural.

Lily and Blinky Rodriguez were the only husband and wife kickboxing team. both champions.

Charles White

Heisman Trophy winner Charles White is one of Pacoima's most prominent sports figures. His legend began at San Fernando High, where he electrified crowds in both football and track & field with his dazzling skills. After winning back-to-back city championships at SFHS, he attended USC. While there, he was twice named PAC-12 "Player of the Year" and led the nation in rushing for both 1978 (1859 yards) and 1979 (2,050 yards). His stellar year in 79 earned him the prestigious Heiman Trophy, which somehow eluded Anthony Davis five years earlier.

Davis recalled meeting Charlie at a very young age.

"I met Charles White when he was six years old — his grandmother was walking him down the street in San Fernando heading to Pacoima. His grandmother raised him, his father wasn't around growing up, and his mother wasn't around. I always felt for Charlie in terms of that, male image and stuff like that. A lot of us didn't have that, but his was extreme. But what he's done, it was pretty phenomenal. I was always happy for him."

The Cleveland Browns selected White in the first round of the 1980 NFL draft. Later, he played for the Los Angeles Rams, where he led the league in rushing and earned a Pro-Bowl selection.

After the NFL, White appeared in seasons three and four of American Gladiator. His athleticism was remarkable, and he remained undefeated during his time on the show.

"I know he's had some struggles in his life. But in terms of what he had to work with, he did a good job," added Davis. "I mean, he went to USC, he's got five kids, healthy kids. One served our country in Iraq. So, he did something — him and his wife."

Charles White remains an iconic sports star in Pacoima, and his image lives forever on the Pacoima City Hall Mural.

Charles White won the Heisman in 1979

Manfred Moore

Manfred Moore was born on December 22, 1950, and graduated a San Fernando High football star in 1969. He went on to play successfully at the University of Southern California, where he played on the best team in USC history in 1972, along with Anthony Davis and Alan Graf. These athletes, all from San Fernando High, dominated the gridiron.

Moore was one of 4 brothers that attended San Fernando. His older brother Anthony and two younger Kenny and Malcolm, all played at there. Athleticism ran in the family. However, Manfred was the first to reach the next level. After starring at San Fernando, he earned a scholarship to USC as a running back. His specialty was punt returns, and his skills led the San Francisco 49ers to draft him in 1974.

Moore played for San Francisco during the 75 and 76 seasons. Both years he was named special teams' "player of the year." In 1976, he was selected in the NFL expansion draft by the Tampa Bay Buccaneers, which went winless that year. However, later, he joined the Oakland Raiders and won Super Bowl XI as a member of that team, making Pacoima proud.

Malcolm Moore

The youngest of the Moore brothers, Malcolm, was expected by the community to perform, and he did not disappoint. However, his success would come from a most unexpected place.

Malcolm Moore's oldest brother Manfred won a Superbowl, and his brother Kenny had just won back-to-back city championships, so expectations were high. Malcolm sailed through high school as a top athlete and got recruited by USC in the footsteps of Kenny, who was there 78-80. Malcolm, a wide receiver, compiled 37 receptions for 598 yards and two touchdowns at USC before leaving early to sign with the USFL. However, the league folded after the first year.

As a free agent, Moore signed with the Los Angeles Rams and later the San Diego Chargers, but injuries plagued him. After leaving football he found himself at a crossroads, and then suddenly, his path became clear.

Moore began working for a disadvantaged youth program with a man named Sean Porter. One day, a film director, Lee Stanley, said he wanted to make a documentary about their work. He followed them around for a year and called the project "Gridiron Gang." That project later became a movie with the same name starring Dwayne "The Rock" Johnson, who played the role of Sean Porter. Hip-Hop star Xzibit played Malcolm.

Gridiron gang originals and actors. Malcolm Moore, Xzibit, Sean Porter, Dwayne "The Rock" Johnson, Kevin Dunn, Ted Dexter.

The film depicts how Porter and Moore took a group of teenage felons and tried to turn their lives around by instilling football values. It highlights the Kilpatrick Mustangs 1990 season, and how the men channeled tribalism in the hood, to the football field. "Gridiron Gang" showed how pride, respect, and honor on the streets are remarkably like sports.

The documentary won an Emmy in 1994, and Sony Pictures released the movie in 2006. Malcolm's assistant coaching job, working with troubled youth, put him dead center for helping to inspire this film. Alan Graf, who played for San Fernando High with Manfred Moore, was a stunt coordinator.

More than the success of "Gridiron Gang," Malcolm Moore cherishes the experiences he shared at Camp Kilpatrick.

"I was thrilled as hell when I made my first professional football team," said Moore. "I played with Steve Young, Ronnie Lott, and Marcus Allen. But my days coaching at Camp Kilpatrick was the best job ever. I realized that I had something to give back. There's nothing like making a difference in a kid's life —I could save somebody else's life."

Malcolm Moore works as a deputy probation officer in Antelope Valley, California.

Crystal Jackson & Malcolm Moore 1978 at San Fernando High.
(Crystal Jackson collection)

Anthony Davis

Anthony Davis' family came to Los Angeles from Texas. During the sixties, they purchased a home on Vaughn Street, considered by many the border of Pacoima and San Fernando. While growing up, Davis' love of baseball would ultimately lead him to sports and legendary status in collegiate football.

After enrolling at San Fernando High School, a football coach saw him throwing baseballs, and Davis ended up as a backup quarterback. He came into a game after the team's starter was injured, and the rest is history. By his senior year, he was a football, baseball, and wrestling star.

Davis then attended USC, where his accomplishments stand alone. AD brought excitement to the game with his showmanship after each touchdown. His dancing was new and exciting, which brought many sold-out stadiums for USC football games.

Anthony Davis was known as the most electric college football superstar of all time and the Notre Dame Killer.

In 1974, AD was a unanimous first-team All American and led his Trojans to become what some have deemed, USC's best team ever. Many thought he deserved the Heisman in 1974, but he did not receive it. Unfortunately, voting for the award occurred before his historic game against Notre Dame, which is a part of Trojan lore. Davis scored an unprecedented six touchdowns leading USC to a legendary come-back victory against the Fighting Irish. Sadly, the Heisman voting did not factor this game.

Following the Heisman slight, in which Ohio State junior, Archie Griffin won, the NCAA voted to change the selection date. The action became a de facto admission that Davis should have won.

AD became known as the greatest kick-off return man in college. He was the first player in Pac 8 history to rush for 1,000 yards in three different seasons. His legacy at USC earned him the name "Notre Dame Killer."

Anthony Davis spoke about his days at USC as an athlete and student.

"I was a duel athlete. I had a B average, and it was really tough there. But I had the workings to be able to do that. Because most people just get through school and go to the pros. Everybody doesn't go to the pros. And then if you get there, you don't last long anyway. I was taught that years ago. My biggest mistake was I should've played professional baseball. It would last longer and made a career. But in those days, it was totally different."

Davis also reflected on why so many professional athletes came from Pacoima.

"It's one of those phenomena that I still haven't figured it out. But a lot of great athletes came out of here because they had the drive, and some of them did realize it was their only way out. Some realized that. Some didn't. Some just waisted it. I remember a kid named Michael Moore, unbelievable. Could play major leagues. I knew a guy named Billy Grout, major leagues — Sammy Jones major leagues — I mean these guys you never even heard of. But these guys were phenomenal, unbelievable. And I tell people to this day. You think I had skills! I got somebody that was better. I remember this guy named Tony Grace. He didn't go to San Fernando, but his family lived in Pacoima. He went to Alemany. But this kid was the fastest 14-year-old in the nation. He ran a 9.8 100-yard dash at fourteen. And I was his back up. Or two spots behind him at Valley Chargers. Tony Grace, unbelievable. Didn't happen. Didn't happen. I talk about that all the time."

The Minnesota Twins drafted Davis in the fourth round of the MLB draft in 1975. However, he decided to play football. The New York Jets drafted Davis also, but he chose to sign with the upstart World Football League. Davis performed well there, but the league folded after the 1975 season.

In 1976, Davis went to the NFL Tampa Bay Buccaneers with his former USC coach John McKay. He later played for the Los Angeles Rams in 1979. In 83, he played for the Los Angeles Express in the USFL, of which the league was also short-lived. Davis then moved on to real estate development.

Anthony Davis was one of the first wave of successful athletes to come out of Pacoima. He spoke about the pressure of being a role model.

"I didn't feel that pressure. Looking back, I hope I influenced some of these kids. A lot of people try to give me credit for the success of Charles White, Kevin Williams, and this clan of ballplayers, and I don't take that credit, but if I had some influence on them, then that was great. I've ran into some people from this area that said just watching you and your success inspired me to do well."

Here are some of the many accomplishments by Anthony Davis.

- Led in rushing, scoring and kick return yardage for three consecutive seasons
- Set NCAA record with scoring kickoff returns
- 6 touchdowns as sophomore in 72 in Rose Bowl win over Ohio State.
- 3 Rose Bowl victories
- 4 National Championships (Two in each sport, football and baseball)
- Inducted in the College Football Hall of Fame 2005

Crystal Jackson and Anthony Davis after their interview session for PacoimaStories: Land of Dreams. The interview took place at Vaughn International Studies Academy.

Anthony Davis hangs out with photographer David Aguilar
Courtesy of David Aguilar Photography)

Andrew Johnson

Andy Johnson was known to entertain and play with kids at Pacoima Park. Shown here with reporters, he dazzles them with his skills.

Andrew "Andy" Johnson was born in 1931 in Franklinton, Louisiana. His mother died when he was only six years old, and he moved to North Hollywood, California, to live with his aunt and uncle. As one of the early Black families in the area, they witnessed the migration from the South, into the Los Angeles area. Johnson was the first Black to attend North Hollywood High and excelled in basketball when he was there. The varsity coach provided him with his first pair of basketball sneakers as he played ball in his bare feet. He said playing barefoot helped him excel. Johnson, while playing at North Hollywood High, became a star basketball player and made All-San Fernando Valley League High School Basketball Team in 1949 and 1950.

He was noticed by some college players who informed their coach of the talented player they found. The University of Portland immediately whisked up Johnson before he graduated, to play at the collegiate level. While at the University of Portland, Johnson had quite a few firsts. He was the first African American admitted to the school, first to play basketball, and broke all the school records in basketball and high jump. Andrew Johnson received induction into the University of Portland's Hall of Fame. While playing at the school, the world-famous Harlem Globetrotters were scouting for talent and went to check out Johnson in 1953. The Globetrotters are an exhibition basketball team that tours the world, incorporating athleticism, theater, and comedy into their games. He signed with them but was interrupted by the US military for a short while. After his discharge, he went back to the Globetrotters in time for their 4th European tour.

He later moved to Pacoima, where he resided on 11142 De Haven Street. Andy Johnson was known to entertain and play with kids at Pacoima Park. Fans would gather to watch and interact with this local celebrity.

His niece, Lisa James, reflected on her Uncle Andy.

"He used to bring a few of the guys to see my son and his dad. We attended a few games too. Nice memories to share with my son and grandsons."

Johnson's son, Mark, wrote a book about his father's incredible life titled "Basketball Slave: The Andy Johnson Harlem Globe Trotter/NBA Story."

Harlem Globetrotters with owner Abe Saperstein (right) and team secretary W. S. Welch (left) during the fifties

The Holiday Brothers: Justin, Jrue, and Aaron

The Holiday brothers are a trio of NBA players with Pacoima roots. Their mother, Toya DeCree-Holiday, grew up on Welk Ave in Pacoima and attended Kennedy High School. She was a two-time all-city basketball star and played at Arizona State. She went on to be girl's athletic director at Campbell Hall in Studio City, where all her children attended, and excelled.

Jrue Holiday is an NBA all-star who helped lead the Milwaukee Bucks to a world championship in 2021 and later that same year won a gold medal with the U.S. national team at the Summer Olympics.

Justin Holiday is also an NBA world champion winning in 2015 as a member of the Golden State Warriors.

The youngest brother Aaron was a first-round selection in the 2018 NBA Draft by the Indiana Pacers. In 2019, Justin joined his brother, Aaron, also signing a deal with Indiana. There are only three other families in the NBA log to have three or more brothers playing in the league.

Steph Curry from Golden State Warriors with Jrue Holiday in 2015 at Oracle arena

Toya DeCree-Holiday grew up in Pacoima and attended Kennedy High School. All three of her sons have made an NBA roster.

Buddy Bradford

Buddy Bradford was born Charles William Bradford on July 25, 1944. Bradford played baseball at San Fernando High and graduated in 1962 then signed with the Chicago White Sox.

In a Los Angeles Times article entitled "Where Are They Now: Buddy Bradford," it chronicled how five childhood friends, from the same small town of Pacoima, defied the odds with incredible baseball talent. These young men that grew up on Judd Street would all have a brush with professional baseball. Then again, the reporter was unaware that this was more the norm of Pacoima than the exception.

However, in this case, all five were standouts at San Fernando High. Buddy Bradford, brothers Claude and Curtis Fontenot, Bobby Mitchell, and Gary Matthews. They all played in the minor leagues, but only two would make it to the major league, Buddy, and Gary Matthews.

Teams Buddy played with:

Chicago White Sox for 66-67, 72-75, and 1976.
Cleveland Indians 70-71
Cincinnati Reds 1971
St. Louis Cardinals 1975

Gary Matthews

Gary Mathews

Gary Matthews is another MLB player who grew up playing baseball in Pacoima. Mathews, who graduated from San Fernando High School, also played at North Valley Little League in the early sixties. He was drafted in the first round by the San Francisco Giants as an outfielder in 1968.

In 1973, after his first complete season, Matthews won the National League Rookie of the Year Award as a member of the Giants. During his acclaimed career, he also played for the Atlanta Braves, Chicago Cubs and Seattle Mariners.

In his 16 major league seasons, he batted .281 with 234 home runs, 978 RBI's, 183 career stolen bases, 1,083 runs scored, and 319 doubles. After baseball, Matthew's went into coaching and then broadcasting.

Gary Matthews baseball accomplishments include
- 1973 MLB Rookie of the Year
- 1979 MLB Allstar game
- 1993 Hall of Fame BBWAA

Matthews's son, Gary Matthews Jr., followed in his fathers' footsteps in baseball. Matthews Jr. played for the Los Angeles Angels, signing a $50 million contract in 2006. Both Matthews' were MLB All-Stars, making them the fourteenth father-son combination to appear in that game.

Gary Matthews Jr.   Gary Matthews Sr.

Gary Matthews (bottom left) playing for Pacoima's North Valley Angels in 1964

Garret Anderson

Garret Anderson was born on June 30, 1972. He graduated from Kennedy High school as a three-sport athlete; basketball, baseball, and football, receiving All-City honors and all-league honors. Drafted by the California Angels, he debuted in the major leagues on July 27, 1994.

Anderson was the first Pacoima major league player to win an MLB World Series, which he did in 2002. His accomplishments include 1995 AL Rookie of the Year, 3-time MLB All-Star, MLB All-Star Game MVP, and Homerun Derby Champion. Anderson finished his stellar career with over 2,300 hits.

In 2016, Garret Anderson was inducted into the California Angels Hall of Fame.

It is impossible to account for the number of successful athletes originating from this small town of Pacoima. However, one thing is sure, the success stories are still ongoing. From the past to the present, this town continues to be a breeding ground for athletic greatness. Pacoima remains proud of its sports legacy.

ATHLETES WITH PACOIMA ROOTS

MLB PLAYERS

• George Vico	1948	Detroit Tigers
• George Perez	1958	Pittsburg Pirates
• Buddy Bradford	1966	Chicago White Sox
• Frank C Rico	1969	Kansas City Royals
• Lawrence Marshall	1971	Cleveland Indians
• Gary Matthews	1972	San Francisco Giants
• George Page	1979	Los Angeles Dodgers
• Bobby Pate	1980	Montreal Expos
• Gene Lambert	1981	San Francisco Giants
• Danny Clay	1982	San Francisco Giants
• Larry David White	1983	Los Angeles Dodgers
• Tommy Barret	1988	Philadelphia Phillies
• Garret Anderson Jr.	1994	Anaheim Angeles
• Gary Matthews Jr.	1999	San Diego Padres
• Miguel Gonzalez	2012	Baltimore Orioles

NFL PLAYERS

• Frank Cassara	1954	San Francisco 49ers
• Marvin Montgomery	1971	Denver Broncos
• Alan Graf	1973	Los Angeles Rams
• Manford Moore	1974	Los Angeles Rams
• Anthony Davis	1977	Tampa Bay Buccaneers
• Charles White	1980	Cleveland Browns
• Raymond Williams	1980	Detroit Lions
• Dewayne Jett	1980	Detroit Lions
• Kevin Williams	1981	Baltimore Ravens
• Joe Kelly Jr.	1986	Cincinnati Bengals
• Mike Crawford	1987	Cleveland Browns
• Malcolm Moore	1987	Los Angeles Rams
• Anthony Gibson	1989	Cleveland Browns

- Latin Berry   1990   Los Angeles Rams
- Michael Pringle   1990   Atlanta Falcons
- Tim Stallworth   1990   Denver Broncos
- Dion Lambert   1992   New England Patriots
- Mark McMillian   1992   Philadelphia Eagles
- Russell White   1993   Los Angeles Rams
- Phil Glover   1999   Tennessee Titans
- DaShon Polk   2000   Buffalo Bills
- Manuel White   2005   Washington Redskins
- Derek Hagan   2006   Miami Dolphins
- CJ Gable   2011   New Orleans Saints
- Brandon Browner   2011   Seattle Seahawks
- D'Andre Goodwin   2011   Denver Broncos
- Rashaad Reynolds   2014   Jacksonville Jaguars
- Alani Fua   2015   Arizona Cardinals

NBA PLAYERS

- Andrew Johnson   1958   Philadelphia Warriors
- Jrue Holiday   2009   Philadelphia 76ers
- Paul George   2010   Indiana Pacers
- Justin Holiday   2013   Philadelphia 76ers
- Aaron Holiday   2018   Indiana Pacers

BOXERS

Bobby Chacon   1974-1988
Benny "The Jet" Urquidez   1974-1993
Lily Urquidez Rodriguez

ROLLER DERBY

Gwen "Skinny Minnie" Miller

23
Notable Peeps

This book has already highlighted many noteworthy individuals from Pacoima, and amazingly many more remain. Some who were born there, some still residing there, and some that have long since departed the town. Although this list is diverse, history must remember that for many decades, in this area, people of color had to live in Pacoima.

People like Kurt Russell, who practiced baseball at Pacoima Junior High, could live anywhere in the Valley he could afford. Those like Stymie Beard, one of the Black characters from the "Our Gang/Little Rascals" era, had few choices.

The good news is, Pacoima saw some exceptional talent reside within its borders. Some of whom are long gone, and some who are still thriving.

There are movie writers, directors, producers, actors, stuntmen, choreographers, comedians, and many more, who have called Pacoima home. The list is surprisingly diverse in terms of their talents. There is even a world-renown animal trainer who prepared rats for the movie "Willard," and the pig "Arnold" in Green Acres, who has roots in the town. Musicians have a chapter of their own. Here are the stories.

Danny Trejo

Danny Trejo was born in Echo Park, but his family moved to Pacoima when he was young. Best known for his starring film role as "Machete," Trejo has appeared in more hit films by far than any actor in Pacoima history.

Although his youth led him to prison, he overcame those obstacles through sheer Pacoima grit and determination. Recognized around town as an active community supporter, Trejo does fundraisers for local charities and makes appearances whenever he can.

Trejo's impressive list of film credits includes Heat, From Dusk Till Dawn, Con Air, Marked for Death, Anaconda, Spy Kids, Once Upon a Time in Mexico, Anchorman, Desperado, Blood In and Blood Out, Machete and numerous others.

Trejo has also become a hugely successful businessman, and his Trejo's Tacos restaurants are among the most popular in Los Angeles. In 2019, he made news headlines for rescuing a baby from an overturned car. More than just another success story, Danny Trejo is a real-life Pacoima hero.

Danny Trejo's mural on Van Nuys Blvd painted by Levi Ponce.

Danny Trejo attends screening of award-winning documentary "PacoimaStories: Land of Dreams." Shown here with the film's director Crystal Jackson.

William Marshall

William Marshall was a well-known actor in Pacoima during the seventies and eighties. He is best known for his role as Blacula but boasts a long list of credits.

Marshall was very active in the community and frequently allowed neighborhood kids to swim at his house on Dronfield Avenue. The Pacoima City Hall Mural features the image of this longtime Pacoimian.

His credits include Star Trek, Pee Wees Playhouse, Wild Wild West, Boston Strangler, and Man from U N C L E.

However, William Marshall was best known for his leading role in the 70's blaxploitation horror classics "Blacula" and "Scream Blacula Scream." In 1972, "Blacula" was a hit film for American International Pictures and became the top-grossing film for that year.

Jacob Vargas

Jacob Vargas was born August 18, 1971, in Michoacán, Mexico. His family came to Pacoima when he was a baby. He graduated from San Fernando High and has a long list of films including:

- Moonlight
- The Hills have Eyes 2
- Are We Done Yet?
- Dr Doolittle 2
- Traffic
- Next Friday
- Selena
- Mi Vida Loca
- American Me

Don Blackman

Don Blackman was a veteran actor of numerous films, television, and stage productions during the fifties and sixties. He was born May 12, 1912, in Alabama and moved to Pacoima with his wife Esther in the fifties.

He was best known for his roles in "On the Waterfront" (1954) with Marlon Brando and "Jungle Jim" (1955) with Johnny Weissmuller. He also appeared in numerous other films and television shows including, "Dragnet," "I Spy", "Twilight Zone," and many others.

In 1973, Blackman appeared in one of his last films "Scream Blacula Scream" with fellow Pacoima actor William Marshall. He passed away in September 1977 at the age of 90.

Cheech Marin

Cheech Marin, actor, comedian, and voice actor, was born Richard Anthony Marin on July 13, 1946. He attended Bishop Alemany High School and Valley State College.

Cheech began his career in the seventies doing the comedy act Cheech & Chong. "Up in Smoke" in 1978 saw him in the role "*Pedro de Pacas.*" They did several albums and feature film comedies. They ended their duo in 1985, and Cheech went on to star in "Born in East LA," "The Shrimp on the Barbie," "Tin Cup," and "Once Upon a Time in Mexico."

He did some film appearances until he made the full-time transition to television work. The "Golden Palace" spin-off from "Golden Girls," "Nash Bridges," and "Judging Amy" were some of his projects.

Cheech Marin has also become one of Hollywood's leading voice actors in animated films. He has voiced numerous hit roles for Disney and other major film studios.

His Disney voice characters included the Chihuahua in "Oliver & Company," Banzai the hyena in "Lion King," Ramone in "Cars," and Pancho in "Cisco Kid."

Cheech's other voice films include:

- Cheech & Chong's Animated Movies
- The Book of Life
- El Americano; The Movie
- Cars 3
- Coco

This Cheech Marin mural is part of the Pacoima Mural Mile. Painted by Levi Ponce

Matthew "Stymie" Beard Jr.

Stymie Beard, born Matthew Beard Jr. (1925-1981), was a child actor who played the role of Stymie in "Our Gang" short films from 1930 to 1935. Spanky, Alfalfa and Buckwheat characters later replaced his part when they formed Little Rascals in 1935.

Beards money supported his entire family of 13 brothers and sisters. He appeared in a few movies in the forties with minor roles. In the sixties, he moved to Pacoima. He did a few bit roles in "Sanford and Son," "The Jeffersons," and appeared in 1978's "The Buddy Holly Story."

Poncie Ponce and Starlet Darlene Tompkins

TV actor Poncie Ponce (1933-2013), lived at 13265 DeBell St. in Pacoima. Born Ponciano Hernandez, he was an actor, comedian, and musician. He played the role of Kazuo Kim in the television series "Hawaiian Eye," which aired on ABC from 1959 to 1963. Additionally, he appeared in the Elvis Presley film "Speedway."

Starlet Darlene Tompkins was born November 16, 1940, and lived at 13634 Chase St. in Pacoima. She was named "Miss San Fernando Valley" in 1957 and is a winner of 10 beauty contests. Tompkins appeared in three films during the sixties, including co-starring with Elvis Presley in "Blue Hawaii." She was named the honorary mayor of Pacoima in 1961.

Gilbert Esquivel

Gilbert Esquivel is a stand-up comedian who came to Pacoima in the winter of 1974 from Michigan. He attended both Maclay and San Fernando Junior High and both San Fernando and Polytechnic High School.

Gilbert lived in the Van Nuys Apartments on Borden and Van Nuys Blvd, which was predominantly Black at that time. He rose from gangbanger to comedian performing throughout the country.

He has appeared in several films The Holiday (2006), Tears of a Clown (2005), and Laffapalooza (2003).

In 2016, Gilbert appeared in the documentary film, "PacoimaStories Land of Dreams."

Kenya Barris

Kenya Barris is from a long-time Pacoima family. His father worked for General Motors and his mother in real estate.

He is a writer and producer of numerous television shows and films. He is best known as the creator of ABC's "Blackish" and the movie "Girls Trip." He has worked on "Sister/Sister," "Soul Food," "The Game," and "America's Next Top Model," among others. He co-wrote the screenplay for the 2019 film "Shaft."

His industry honors include NAACP awards for Outstanding Writing in a comedy series 2016 & 2017 and PGA visionary award for Outstanding Producer of episodic television in 2019. Barris was nominated multiple times for Primetime Emmy for Outstanding comedy series and also won the Rod Sterling Award for "Advancing Social Justice Through Popular Media."

In 2018, Kenya Barris received an honorary doctorate from Clark Atlanta University and donated a million dollars to the institution.

Kenya Barris and his wife Rania have six children. His sister is author Collette Barris, who wrote "Claretta Street," a novel about Pacoima girls coming of age.

Leslie Small

Leslie Small is a director and producer that grew up in Lake View Terrace, which is part of the Pacoima group. His family, including four brothers and one sister, were central in the Pacoima experience.

Small is best recognized for producing and directing several Kevin Hart films that include "What Now" (2016), "Let Me Explain" (2013), and "Laugh my Pain" (2011). Small has a Ph.D. in economics, a master's degree in statistics, and a bachelor's degree in physics from USC. His mentors, when he was first getting started, were Marvin Gaye and Barry White.

He and his wife Verani have a son named Justice. Small is a Pacoima success, who has not forgotten the town that raised him. He lends his talents on various programs to local churches and participates in the town's annual Holiday parade. His advice to young people is "pick something and become the best."

George Lopez

George Lopez is part of the Pacoima City Hall Mural

(artwork by Ignacio Gomez)

George Lopez is a comedian, actor, and producer born April 23, 1961. In 1979, he graduated from San Fernando High School in Pacoima.

Lopez has proved to be a force in the entertainment industry, and a respected spokesperson for Latino causes.

His resume consists of television, film, late-night talk shows and standup comedy. He is a producer, actor, and writer for many of his projects.

In 2006, he received a star on the Hollywood Walk of Fame and was named by Time Magazine as one of the 25 most influential Hispanics in America. Harris Poll named him one of the top ten television personalities.

Jimmy Velarde

Jimmy Velarde was born and raised in Pacoima and has worked in the entertainment business for over 35 years. He has earned 11 Emmy Awards and a Grammy nomination for his work with CBS Television Network. He also works on HBO's "Real Time with Bill Maher" and "Late, Late Night with James Corden."

In the eighties, Velarde worked with music legends such as Stevie Wonder, Buddie Guy, and opened for the Rolling Stones. He has produced programs for Fox Television and more. Velarde is an active member of The Academy of Television Arts & Sciences, National Academy of Recording Arts & Sciences, and Latin Academy of Recording Arts & Sciences.

Jimmy Velarde is also active in community work and serves on the executive board of directors for the Pacoima Historical Society.

Porscha Coleman

Porscha Lee Coleman was born into the musical Coleman family from Pacoima. Her mother, Betty Coleman, sang in the family's group "Coleman Reunion."

Porscha is an actress, singer, dancer, and TV host best known for her role on the UPN's "The Parkers." In 2014, she co-hosted the FOX TV series "Hollywood Today Live." Porscha also had a role in the Disney Channel original movie "Pixel Perfect" along with a 2017 film "You Can't Fight Christmas." Her list of film roles is long and impressive.

Porscha with brother John Diggs and mother Betty Coleman
(Courtesy Betty Coleman)

Kurt Russell

Born in Springfield, Massachusetts, in 1951, the Russell family came to Pacoima in the 1950s. Kurt and his sisters attended Sharp Elementary, and he practiced baseball at Pacoima Junior High with his father, Bing Russell. He played little league in the area as well.

Kurt began acting around the age of twelve when he debuted in the Elvis Presley film "It Happened at the World's Fair." His list of credits is long. A few of them include Escape from New York (1981), Big Trouble in Little China (1986), Overboard (1987), and Backdraft (1991).

Kurt Russell in 1974

Kurt Russell is here with Robert Vaughn in a segment of "Man from U N C L E" in 1964.

Kelley Kali

Kelley Kali accepts film award in December 2018
(Courtesy Kelley Kali)

Kelley Kali Chatman Rhodes is the daughter of Greater Community Baptist Church's Reverend Dudley Chatman and a rising star in the film industry.

Kelley earned her master's degree at USC School of Cinematic Arts and went on to co-direct a feature film, "The Adventures of Thomasina Sawyer." Then she directed, produced, and co-wrote a short film, "Lalo's House," inspired by real-life events of child trafficking in Haiti. The film earned Kelley awards at multiple film festivals, including the American Black Film Festival's Emerging Directors category and Directors Guild "Best Director" Award.

Kelley received the inspiration for Lalo's House while in Haiti. She heard the story of a Nun who ran a Catholic Orphanage and was allegedly allowing foreign men to assault the children sexually. Her path to completion of this film short took an incredible nine years. However, it earned Kelley her first programmers award for short film at the 2018 Pan African Film Festival. From there, it was all gravy.

Since winning the Student Oscars, Kelley has signed with Creative Arts Agency, where she wants to make message-based films. She is in the company of Spike Lee and Roger Zemeckis, who got their start winning the same award. She successfully pitched Ron Howard and Brian Grazer's company "New Form Digital" for a new fantasy film. The project is similar to Harry Potter, except the star is a little Black girl from Louisiana.

Kelley joins a group of other writers, directors, and producers whose story has helped Pacoima earn its name as "Land of Dreams."

Kelley Kali, her father Rev. Dudley Chatman, and mom Beth
(Courtesy Kelley Kali)

James "Buckwheat" Frazier

James "Buckwheat" Frazier, also known as Corkey, lived with his wife Ada, two sons and foster children, at 12893 Corcoran Street in Pacoima.

Frazier was best known for playing the role of Buckwheat during the "Our Gang" and "Little Rascals" era. Several actors played Buckwheat over the years, and Frazier was proud to tell people he was one of them.

This Pacoima man, who also coached little league baseball, was popular in the community. Many people in Pacoima knew Frazier, and he was pleased to give autographs whenever asked. Frazier was very active in the town and worked with the Pacoima Chamber of Commerce and Councilman Everett Burkhalter for street improvements in Pacoima. He was known for attending community events and engaging with politicians and local leaders. James "Buckwheat" Frazier leaves behind a nostalgic Hollywood legacy only overshadowed by his love and passion for the town he called home.

1964 Councilman Everett Burkhalter, James "Buckwheat" Frazier, Earle Erne, Pacoima Chamber of Commerce president. Ribbon cutting at Glenoaks and Vaughn for street improvements.

Tommy Kirt

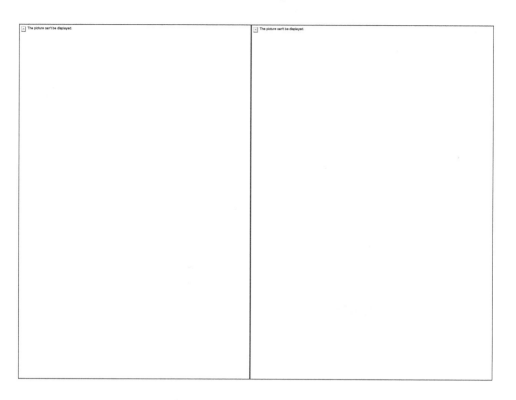

Born December 10, 1941, Tommy Kirt was a Disney actor who lived on Remick Street in Pacoima in the late fifties, early sixties.

He is best known for his role in the Walt Disney film "Old Yeller," a 1957 film about a boy and a stray dog in post-civil war Texas. Kirt also played in other Disney films including, The Shaggy Dog, The Swiss Family Robinson, and The Misadventures of Merlin Jones.

Colleen Richter, the author of "Mi Familia Loca," a trilogy about growing up Mexican in the sixties, was Tommy Kirt's neighbor in Pacoima. She remembers him and his brother Andy.

"It was a big deal having a star live nearby," said Richter.

Kirt also played on the Hardy Boys and a few Disney comedies, including "The Absent-Minded Professor," "Son of Flubber," and "Bon Voyage." Tommy Kirk received induction as a Disney Legend in 2006. He gave up acting in the mid-seventies.

George Clayton Johnson

Born in 1929, George Clayton Johnson was a Hollywood scriptwriter who became a local celebrity in Pacoima during the sixties and seventies. He was a science fiction writer best known for co-writing "Logan's Run," a popular MGM film released in 1976.

Johnson's writing career began with a story he wrote for "Alfred Hitchcock presents" in 1959. He also wrote episodes for "Twilight Zone," "Star Trek," and "The Man Trap." The box office hit "Ocean's Eleven" is based upon a story written by this talented writer.

George Clayton Johnson passed away in 2015.

Eddie Dean

Eddie Dean (1907-1999) was an actor and singer that made his name in the thirties as a country-western singer. He was also a well-known Pacoima celebrity during his time.

His career took off in the forties, and he was among one of the more popular cowboy stars. He appeared in one of the first color western films, but it was not standardized in the industry until much later.

Dean had a stellar music career. He wrote 80 percent of his songs, and they were played regularly on the radio. In 1948 he joined Mercury Records, and a song he wrote with his wife Lorene, "One Has My Heart (the other has my name)," made it to Billboard #1 country hit.

He and his wife Lorene Donnelly Dean (1911-2002) had two children Donna Lee Daniel and Ed Glosup.

Moe DiSesso

Moe DiSesso on the Pacoima City Hall Mural
(artwork by Ignacio Gomez)

Moe DiSesso (1924-2007) was an animal trainer known for training the rats in the films "Ben" and "Willard" in the early seventies. However, his work with Arnold the pig on "Green Acres" (1965), "The Raven" (1963), and his dog Sandy in "Annie" (1982) are also among the other 125 projects in his credits.

DiSesso was also the official animal trainer for TV shows, including "Seinfeld," "Murphy Brown," "3rd Rock from the Sun", and for films including "Swiss Family Robinson" and "The Gazebo."

His German shepherds appeared in TV shows and movies such as "The Bionic Woman," "Rin Tin Tin," and "Devil Dog: The Hound of Hell."

Moe DiSesso won 11 Patsy Awards for his expertise, and Jimmy, his talking crow, became an inducted member to the Pacoima Chamber of Commerce.

Animal Trainer Moe DiSesso with Ben and other animal cast members from the 1971 movie "Willard."

Howard Hill

Howard Hill (1899-1975) owned an estate on the corner of Laurel Canyon and Montague in Pacoima. He was often billed or introduced as "The World's Greatest Archer." In 1928 he set a world record for the farthest recorded flight shot with a bow and arrow, at 391 yards (358 m).

Leon Levitch

Leon Levitch was a holocaust survivor who became a notable music composer of classical music. He was born in Belgrade, Central Serbia, on July 9, 1927, and died November 26, 2014, in Pacoima.

He learned to play piano while at a concentration camp, with cold conditions. He was one of 1,000 Jewish refugees allowed in the United States. His compositions became known worldwide.

24
Music

Pacoima's geographical location made it somewhat easy for residents to pursue a career in entertainment. The town's proximity to Los Angeles and Hollywood, where many record companies operate, made breaking into the music industry one step closer. However, success could not happen without talent, and the successful musicians that come from Pacoima are many.

During the fifties, sixties, and seventies, garage bands were everywhere in the town. They were how many singers and musicians developed their skills. Ritchie Valens was known for playing in his garage and at his neighbors' homes. He sky-rocketed to a level no one thought a Pacoima boy could go. Valens was not alone. Andraé Crouch played at his dad's church on Vaughn Street and became a Grammy-award winning artist.

The fact is that Pacoima's music culture has been dominant, and its global influence is undeniable. The town has residents who have played Carnegie Hall, and inductees into various Hall of Fames.

Pacoima has a musical director, Greg Phillinganes, who orchestrated almost all of Michael Jackson's performances and other prominent industry talents. Andraé Crouch's choir played with Madonna and Michael Jackson as well. He also performed big movie scores for "The Color Purple" ('God is Tryin to Tell You Something') and "Free Willy" ('Will You Be There'). This town's contribution to the music industry is phenomenal. The bar is set high

Pacoima's first known song tribute was titled "Pacoima, I Love You," written and composed Phelps G. Allison in 1893 and recorded by Peggy Blake. The copyright year for the song is1923.

Allison dedicated the song to A.B. Widney, whom he referred to as "The City Builder." We assume he was referring to Judge Robert Widney, the nephew of Charles Maclay. Widney's name appears on numerous land documents during that era.

Cover Art for "Pacoima I Love You" by Peggy Blake (1923)

Lyrics for "Pacoima, I Love You"

Where linger the beautiful roses, where the Summerland stays on the screen
Where ev'ry new vision disclose, a peep of a fairyland scene
Where ev'ry one's heart beats so true, here's land that will love you and bless you
Pacoima, I love only you (chorus)
Where beauty of nature is thrilling, with orange and lemon groves there
And cascades of water fulfilling, the songs of the birds in the air
The school bell is joyously ringing, and children are frolicking too
Pacoima, I love only you
I love you, I love you Pacoima
Your mountains, your canyons and vales
I love all your beautiful shadows
And the sun as it purples and pales
A homeland of joy and contentment, the mass of riches untold
Pacoima, the tale of your future, will never oh never grow old.

Ritchie Valens

It was, however, Ritchie Valens, who put Pacoima on the map. Valens was a first-generation Mexican American whose professional career lasted just eight months, but his legacy has lasted over 70 years.

Ritchie was a self-taught musician whose raw talent allowed him to absorb the sounds of rock and jazz musicians of the day. He recorded his first song at a small studio in Del-Fi owner Bob Keane's home. "Come on Let's Go," Valens' first hit, was produced using a reel to reel, 2-track stereo recorder and two microphones.

Ritchie was forced to leave San Fernando High in 1958 when his career took off. His next recordings were "Donna" and "La Bamba," a 45 record, which sold over a million copies. The Recording Industry Association of America awarded it a Gold Disc.

Valens' song "La Bamba" received an induction into the U.S. Library of Congress' National Recording Registry in 2019. He has become known as the "Pioneer of Chicano and Latin Rock" with numerous groups following in his footsteps.

Ritchie Valens has more murals in Pacoima than any other figure. This one is located on the **Pacoima City Hall Mural** (artwork by Ignacio Gomez)

R&B singer Howard Huntsberry, who played the role of Jackie Wilson in "La Bamba," spoke about Ritchie.

"To me what made it special was Pacoima was a very small. For a minority to go on the national stage like Richie Valens — it just made it very special. He was like a hero to the community."

The Rock and Roll Hall of Fame inducted Ritchie Valens in 2001.

The Carter Brothers

The next known song about Pacoima came from the Carter Brothers with the "Pacoima Stomp."

Raymond and Julia Carter were one of the earlier Black families to settle in Pacoima. Albert, Jerry, Jimmy, and Roman, their boys, recorded their upbeat R&B instrumental "Pacoima Stomp" in 1959.

The Carter Brothers enjoyed a string of rhythm and blues hits in the sixties, including "Southern Country Boy," which reached # 21 on the R/B charts in 1965.

However, the US Army drafted Jerry and Albert. Roman, the vocalist, embarked on a solo career that would later win him the title of Best Male Blues Vocalist at the fifth annual Real Blues Awards in 1999.

The Carter Brothers were the earliest successful Black musicians out of Pacoima and were faithful members of Pacoima's Greater Community Missionary Baptist Church.

July 23, 1959   "'Pacoima Stomp,' by Carter Brothers of Pacoima, is accepted as official song of the Pacoima Community Fair July 29-Aug. 2 by the Chamber of Commerce. From left are Carter Brothers--Jerry, Jimmy, Roman, and Albert; their manager, Rex Stuart, and Mrs. Rossi Cutler, chamber director."

Andraé Crouch

Born in San Francisco on July 1, 1942, Andraé Crouch, his twin sister Sandra and family, moved to Pacoima in 1951. There, his father Benjamin and mother Catherine began preaching out of their garage.

Crouch began playing for neighboring churches but formed his first group while at San Fernando High School. The COGNICS (Church of God in Christ Singers), which was the name of the group, included legendary musician Billy Preston. He published his first song when he was only 15 years old.

In 1965, he formed "The Disciples" with Bili Thedford, Perry Morgan, and Reuben Fernandez. The group played locally and in 1968 released their first album, "Take the Message Everywhere." His sister Sandra joined the group in 1970 after Fernandez left, and two more albums came, "Keep on Singin" and "Soulfully."

Andraé Crouch and the Disciples appeared on the Tonight Show featuring Johnny Carson, performed at Carnegie Hall, Hollywood Bowl, and toured 68 cities. He went on to work with Michael Jackson, Madonna, Quincy Jones, Diana Ross, and Elton John. His film credits include "Lion King," "Free Willy," "The Color Purple," and "Once Upon a Forest."

Universally credited with merging gospel music and contemporary mainstream music, Crouch possesses a long list of awards and honors. He won his first Grammy award in 1975 and totaled seven by the end of his career. He earned an Oscar nomination for "The Color Purple" and became only the third gospel artist to receive a star on the Hollywood Walk of Fame. Crouch also received a Lifetime Achievement Award from the NARA's Inaugural Salute to Gospel Music and is an inductee to the Christian Music Hall of Fame and Museum.

Andraé Crouch passed away in 2015 due to congestive heart failure.

The Pacoima City Hall Mural displays Andraé Crouch as one of our Grammy Award winning and Hollywood Walk of Fame residents. (Artwork by Ignacio Gomez)

Sandra Crouch

Sandra Crouch, twin sister of Andraé, had musical talents of her own, including singing and performing with the Disciples along with her brother. She won a Grammy in 1984 for "Best Soul Gospel Performance, Female" and a Grammy nomination for "Best Soul Gospel Performance, Duo, Group, Chorus or Choir."

During the sixties and seventies, she worked with Motown records and wrote the song "Heaven Belongs to You" for the Oscar-nominated film "The Color Purple" in 1985. Additional films she has scored include, A Time to Kill (Take my Hand Precious Lord) and Once Upon a Forrest (He's Gone, He's Back).

Sandra Crouch also has acting credits on her resume that include "In Living Color" and "In Search of Dr. Seuss." She serves as pastor for her family's church, Christ Memorial Church of God in Christ.

On the day of Andraé's death, Sandra wrote this statement, "Today my twin brother, womb-mate and best friend went home to be with the Lord. Please keep me, my family, and our church family in your prayers. I tried to keep him here, but God loved him best."

Sandra and Andraé Crouch

Bili Redd Thedford

Bili Thedford is an accomplished musician from Pacoima. Born in Los Angeles, his family migrated to the town in 1957, living on Bromont Street. His career began in 1960, working with Johnny Otis, who was a well-known musician at that time. Otis went on to have a weekly variety television show that lasted eight seasons.

In 1964, Thedford, along with Perry Morgan, Howard Neal, and Andraé Crouch, started the Disciples at Christ Memorial Church. He traveled the world with the group for twelve years, touring forty countries and every state in the US, except Alaska.

When asked, Thedford offered this characterization of Andraé Crouch.

"He was a complex yet simple person. Andraé didn't think people understood him and preferred they only know the professional side of him. But he was a very nice person."

Thedford became an acclaimed music arranger-composer, lyricist, musician, and singer who went on to work with George Benson, Quincy Jones, Melissa Manchester, Minnie Riperton, and others. He has won two Grammys with six nominations.

His resume also includes international performances for the Queen of England and the Prime Minister of Australia. He played Carnegie Hall in New York, Usher Hall in Edinburgh, Scotland, Queen Elizabeth Opera Houses across Canada, and numerous venues in the Orient. The list is massive.

Through all of his world travels, Thedford was proud to say, "The hometown feel of Pacoima always made it nice coming back." However, he joked, when he came home, he was always greeted with, "When are you leaving again?"

Bili Thedford received an induction to the Gospel Hall of Fame in 1996.

Bili Redd Thedford

Bili Redd Thedford at Pacoima History Day 2018

Al Mckay

Al Mckay was born Feb 2, 1948, in New Orleans, Louisiana. His family moved to Pacoima, and he graduated from San Fernando High in 1966.

His first professional experience happened when he was 18 years old and was hired to play guitar for the Ike and Tina Turner Review. He later got picked up to work with Sammy Davis Jr. and then Stevie Wonder.

However, Mckay is best known as lead guitarist for the legendary group Earth, Wind & Fire. He won 6 Grammy's and 17 nominations while with EWF. They also won 4 American Music Awards out of 12 nominations.

The group has a star on the Hollywood Walk of Fame and gained induction into the Rock & Roll Hall of Fame, as well as the Vocal Group Hall of Fame. They sold 90 million records, which made them one of the bestselling bands of all time.

Earth, Wind, & Fire lead guitarist Al Mckay

Howard Huntsberry

Howard Huntsberry is a true Pacoima man, who drove low rider cars and played in garage bands. His family arrived in Pacoima from Louisiana during the 1950s.

Huntsberry had a successful music career as a solo artist and as a member of the eighties R&B group Klique. However, most people remember him for his role as Jackie Wilson in the hit film, "LaBamba."

He first began playing in the school band after his mom bought him some drums and other equipment. Huntsberry says that back in those days, they would listen to the radio, mimic the music, and learn the songs.

He was discovered by a guy named King George, who heard his group practicing in his friend Danny Duplechan's garage. George was coming down the street, and he heard them playing, knocked on the door, and picked the group to be his opening act.

"Everyone wanted to be in the music business in those days," said Huntsberry. "I was in a group called Five Shades of Black…a Temptations kind of group. We used to sing at house parties."

The Five Shades of Black was Howards first group. They were the first group to play at half time in LA Unified School District at San Fernando High. (photos courtesy of Howard Huntsberry)

The Huntsberrys in Pacoima during the 1950's
(photos courtesy of Howard Huntsberry)

Howard Huntsberry (second from right), with one of his early Pacoima bands.
(photos courtesy of Howard Huntsberry)

"There was a family in Pacoima that I owe a lot to, the Colemans. They had a group called Coleman Family reunion. It was two groups. The younger siblings and the older — I was the drummer for the younger. We wound up going to Japan backing up Karla Thomas and Rufus Thomas."

Huntsberry tells how he got started with the group Klique and behind the scenes stories.

"Klique was founded by a good friend of mine, Isaac Southers. I was with a group called The New Experience, and we were opening act for a night club here in Los Angeles called the 'Total Experience,' owned by Lonnie Simmons. He is famous for the Gap Band and Yarborough and Peoples. I was doing background for the Gap Band albums. When you are a struggling musician, you have to do all kind of things to make ends meet. I took a job at a stationery store in Inglewood called Sanders. The manager of Klique, George Murphy, owned it. They were auditioning for a member that they had kicked out of the group. I was sending people over there to audition, and my wife said, 'what's the matter with you? You know you love this, and you want to be on stage. You want to continue to sing and entertain. Why don't you go over and audition for the group?' And I did. We signed for MCA records in 1980, we did our first album Winning Time and had a little success with it.

"We hooked up with Thomas McClary from the Commodores, who became one of our producers. We were at rehearsal one day, and all of a sudden, this Jackie Wilson thing came up again. Someone came in and said, you sound like Jackie Wilson. Of course, I didn't think I did and said common man I'm doing my thing. My manager George said we are going to do a Jackie Wilson song. It wasn't going to be a single — we were just gonna put it on the album. We were at Motown fixing it, and we saw Berry Gordy peek his head through the window at Mo West Studios, which had portholes in it. He stuck his head in when he heard the song. Berry wrote 'Stop Doggin Me Around' with somebody. He poked his head in, and he called Thomas McClary outside the hallway and said, 'if you don't pick that up as a single, you are a fool.' Thomas came back in and told our manager that Berry Gordy wants that as a single, and so who argues with Berry Gordy? We made that as a single. Number two on Billboard and number one on cash box. We toured off that for a good while."

Collage of Howard Huntsberry 's discography. He had a successful career as a part of the group "Klique" and as a solo artist. (courtesy of Howard Huntsberry)

Singing Jackie Wilson songs would pay even bigger dividends for Huntsberry, when he landed the role of Jackie Wilson in the Ritchie Valens movie, "LaBamba." He had this to say about getting that part.

"There is only one Jackie Wilson. I didn't really think I sounded like him. You don't know what you sound like to other people. When I saw it in the movie, and I heard it back I thought ok maybe they were right. It was a very exciting time and to be linked with that kind of person was just incredible."

The Colemans

The Coleman family moved to Pacoima in 1960. Garfield "Pops" Coleman" and Christine "Moms," along with their eight children, got involved in music and performed all around the city, state, Canada, and overseas.

Pop's Coleman was a professional boxer from 1941 until 1953. His career was interrupted after being drafted during World War II. Following his service, Coleman resumed boxing, but with children in tow, he redirected his career. He set up his garage for music.

"There wasn't a musician in Pacoima and surrounding cities that didn't come over to practice and jam," says Betty Coleman, his daughter. "Everyone in Pacoima knew him. He assisted many musicians with learning about music."

All the Coleman kids attended San Fernando Junior High and San Fernando High School. The group was well-known and very popular in the area. During the seventies, they also toured successfully in Europe and Asia. Their first European tour lasted for nearly a year. They left Los Angeles on November 5 of 1972 and returned home in October of 1973.

Clarence, Bruce, Betty, Garfield, Rebecca, Milton Carol and Rodney Coleman. The group was popular in Japan and Europe. (Courtesy Coleman Family)

Pops Coleman sparring in the 1930's. He went into professional boxing in 1941 and fought for 12 years. (less two years in the service)
(Courtesy Coleman Family)

The Colemans 1972 photo shoot at Hansen Dam

Sal Rodriguez

Sal Rodriguez has been drummer for the group War for over thirty years.

Sal Rodriguez has played drums for the group "War" for nearly 30 years. Born in Tijuana, Mexico, his family moved to Pacoima when Sal was very young. His father influenced his early music beginnings with a drum set when he was nine years old. Sal saw his uncle play and knew that was what he wanted to do. By eleven, he started playing gigs on Van Nuys Blvd with his family.

Sal attended San Fernando High for the tenth and eleventh grades, but transferred to Kennedy High as a senior. He talked about that experience.

"I went to Kennedy because of the big band orchestra. It wasn't cool to be in big band at San Fernando. It was more lowriders and like that. This was like back in 74. I loved the school (Kennedy). It was great. They all thought I was Jewish cause they called me Sol. 'Hi Sol.' I didn't know why. They were all Jewish…it was a predominately Jewish school back then. There were like 10 Latinos in that whole school at that time."

When Sal finished high school, he went to Texas and played with Grammy award winner Little Joe and the Familia.

In the early eighties, Sal toured with Jose Feliciano then spent five years with the legendary group Tierra ("Together," "La La Means I Love You"). In 1990, Sal joined the group War ("Low Rider," "Cisco Kid," "Slippin' in the Darkness"). While with War, Sal also toured with Duke Ellington, which was a surreal experience for a kid from Pacoima. He played at Carnegie Hall, where he says he kissed the building in awe of the magnitude of playing there. He performed at an event that honored Ella Fitzgerald, where all the jazz greats were in attendance. He says he was in "jazz heaven."

Sal also worked with Three Dog Night's Chuck Negron, Tower of Power, and toured with Tom Jones. Despite his grueling tour schedule, Sal takes time to give back to the community with inspirational faith-based speeches and support. He and his wife Madeline have three children, Andrea, Sal Jr., and Sheila. The Pacoima City Hall Mural features a beautiful image of Sal Rodriguez as one of the town's great musicians.

Sal Rodriguez hangs out with fellow Pacoima native Cheech Marin (right) and his comedy partner Tommy Chong (left) (courtesy Sal Rodriguez)

Rodriguez family 2014 (L-R) Sheila, Madeline, Sal Sr., Sal Jr., and Andrea.
(courtesy Sal Rodriguez)

Sal Rodriguez and his wife Madeline attend screening of PacoimaStories: Land of Dreams at Pan African Film Festival in 2018. Pictured L-R are Sal, Madeline, the film's director Crystal Jackson, and executive producer Lon Grandison with his wife Chanelle

Sal Rodriquez is featured on the Pacoima City Hall Mural. (artwork by Ignacio Gomez)

Michael O'Neill

Michael O'Neill is a Grammy-nominated, award-winning composer, and producer. He is a multi-instrumentalist that has released five solo albums as a musician and vocalist. He has performed throughout the world and worked with the best in the music industry including, Barbara Streisand, George Benson, Stevie Wonder, Aretha Franklin, John Legend, Earth Wind & Fire, Al Jarreau, Michael McDonald, Al Green and many more.

During his early days, O'Neill played music regularly in both Pacoima and San Fernando, taking in the influences that thrived in that area.

"I owe a lot of my career success to the years I played music in Pacoima," he says.

Michael O'Neill has two children named Joseph and Sadie. Joseph is a lighting designer in the entertainment industry, who lives in Sherman Oaks and Sadie heads up an Indie Rock band named "City Ghost."

Greg Phillinganes

Greg Phillinganes was born May 12, 1956, and is a singer/songwriter, musical director who lived in Pacoima. He learned piano playing by ear before he ever enrolled in formal lessons.

His musical career began when Stevie Wonder heard his demo tape and hired him. However, his real fame started when he became the musical director for Michael Jackson and the Jacksons in 1978. Phillinganes contributed to virtually every album Michael ever made, including "Thriller." He performed the synth bass part, high pitched synth parts, and the pipe organ that Vincent Price rapped over. Phillinganes was also the musical director for Michael's "Bad" and "Dangerous" tours, as well as his 30th-anniversary special.

Phillinganes worked and toured with a montage of artists including the Bee Gees, Donna Summer, Quincey Jones, Aretha Franklin, and Anita Baker, to name a few.

Printes Hodges was Phillinganes' neighbor in Pacoima for a short while. He said, "Lionel Richie was there all the time when they were making an album."

Greg Phillinganes performing with Herbie Hancock in Warszawa, Poland.

King T

Born Roger McBride, King T, aka King Tee, is a hip-hop rapper and producer with strong Pacoima roots. He was born December 14, 1968, in Pacoima and raised on Louvre Street. His grandfather, Arvel Jackson Sr., was one of the original members of the Pacoima Property Owners Association.

King T was one of the West Coast's pioneering rappers and recognized as one of the biggest influences in gangsta rap. He made his debut in 1988 with "Act a Fool," which is considered to be a rap classic.

Signed to Capitol Records, he mentored young rappers such as The Alkaholiks (also known as Tha Liks). He also helped Lilwit Crew, which featured Xzibit, and brought him closer to Dr. Dre. After several albums that went certified gold, King T left Capitol to join Dr. Dre's 'Aftermath' record label.

King T says, "he came in the game young, and it was people in Compton that helped him get started." However, there is no doubt this legendary rap icon left a Pacoima imprint on the hip hop world.

King T was a pioneering rap artist with hits like "Act A Fool," "Bass," and "Payback's a Mutha"

Al McKibbon

Al McKibbon (1919-2005) was a jazz double bassist known for Bop and Latin Jazz. He played with greats such as Dizzie Gillespie, Miles Davis, Count Basie, and Thelonius Monk, among others. These jazz giants highly regarded McKibon as a bassist.

His first album in 1999 was "Tumbao Para Los Congueros De Mi Vida."

His second album, "Black Orchid," was released in 2004. He also wrote the afterword in "Latin Jazz," a book by Raul Fernandez for the Smithsonian Institution's series of exhibitions of jazz.

Photo above is McKibbon with his wife Classy (second and third from right) in his yard on Filmore Street. (photo by George Skipper, courtesy Camille Watkins)

521

James "J-Ro" Robinson

Pacoima's own James "J-Ro" Robinson founded The Alkaholiks (Tha Liks), a talented hip-hop trio that formed in 1991. The group featured J-Ro, Tash (Rico Smith), and E-Swift (Eric Brooks), who toured the world in the nineties, releasing several albums and their hit song "Make Room."

J-Ro's grandparents Samuel and Helen Ford moved to Pacoima in 1952. His grandfather, Samuel Ford, was a Tuskegee Airman. Growing up on Gain St, J-Ro attended Pacoima Elementary. "I was born in Pacoima and have many good memories of growing up there," said J-Ro, whose parents are Butch Hayes and Pat Ford.

The McCrary's

The McCrary's moved from Youngstown, Ohio in the seventies to Pacoima. Their biggest hit was "You" with Stevie Wonder on the harmonica. They had several albums and collaborated with other artists such as Michael Jackson, Andraé Crouch, Angela Bofill and Philip Bailey.

Issac Avila

Issac Avila was lead vocalist for the group Tierra in the 90s and early 2000s. He also played with The Company Band and his own group, The Pirates. Availa grew up in San Fernando and was lead singer for Tierra for 10 years. He passed away on August 31, 2009.

Terral "Terry" Santiel

Terry Santiel was one of the original members of the R&B group Rose Royce that was formed in the 70's. He played Congo's for the group, which had hits such as "Car Wash," "I'm Going Down," and "I Wanna Get Next To You." The soundtrack for the movie "Carwash" earned the group Best Motion Picture Score "Album of the Year" in 1976.

Charles "Smooth Jazz" Biggs

Smooth Jazz Biggs was raised in Pacoima since the age of 5. He first started music while at a Maclay Junior High School. He learned to play drums and guitar, but it wasn't until his 20's he engaged in the piano and keyboard. He joined a band called "805" and has played venues throughout California specializing in smooth jazz.

James Wesley (Jim) Smith

Jim Smith was born on October 18, 1943. He began his music career during the 1950s, playing in a group started by Danny Sanford Coggins called The Tangents. "When Danny, who also formed The Moonglows, began assembling The Tangents, performers from all over converged at his house," said Smith. "Everyone wanted to be in the group. We played at El Monte Legion Stadium and Long Beach Municipal Auditorium."

Smith did openings for The Impressions, Four Tops, and Del Reys. He also went on to do back up for Martha & The Vandellas, David & Jimmy Ruffin, The Spinners, and more. He later worked with Gladys Night & The Pips and made appearances on Johnny Carson and Ed Sullivan shows.

"Pacoima was the hub for music. At Dee's, which was a beer joint on Van Nuys Blvd, Sam Cooke's brother, and Eugene Dozier made deals there," Smith added.

He and his wife of over 54 years, RJ Anthony-Smith, have three children, seven grandchildren, and two great-grandchildren.

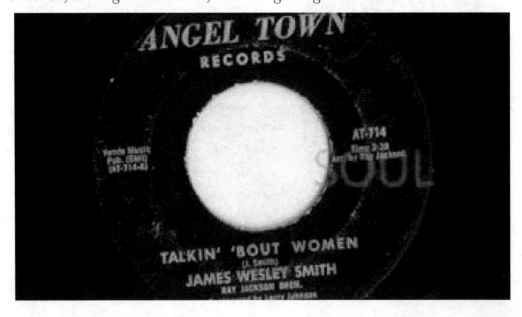

25
Earthquakes

In 1971, many Pacoima residents had never experienced an earthquake. However, that changed on the early morning of February 9, when buildings crumbled, freeways collapsed, and lives ended in the blink of an eye.

Pacoima had never experienced damage this profound, and town records show no recorded quake damage in Pacoima's history, before this. It was an introduction for many to California earthquakes.

California has a well-documented history of earthquakes. Whereas Pacoima has felt some nearby shaking, nothing could have prepared it for the 6.6 magnitude quake that struck the town. Then, 23 years later, the violent shaking repeated itself. Northridge, just a few miles west, was the epicenter. However, fences still came tumbling down, and people were injured. Those that lived through it will never forget.

San Fernando Earthquake 1971

On the morning of February 9, 1971, at 6 am, Pacoima felt the wrath of a 6.6 magnitude earthquake that lasted only 12 seconds. Officially listed in neighboring Sylmar, the town was virtually at the epicenter of the quake. Pacoima, along with much of the San Fernando Valley, took a beating.

Sixty-five deaths and over 1000 injuries resulted from the quake. To people experiencing the jolt, 12 seconds felt like more than a minute. The aftershocks were almost equally as terrifying with more than 200 of them and four with a magnitude 5.0 or greater.

Massive destruction was done to infrastructure, hospitals, businesses, and homes, totaling $553 million, which would be the equivalent of $3.4 billion in 2019. The damage included 180 schools, 62 freeway bridges, four hospitals, and five dams, one of which forced the evacuation of 80,000 people.

Local hospitals suffered tragic devastation. Pacoima Memorial Lutheran Hospital, Olive View Medical Center, Foothill Medical Building, and Veterans Hospital, all were damaged. However, the VA is where most of the deaths occurred.

First opened in 1926, the Veterans Hospital consisted of 45 individual buildings that were 3 miles off of the Sylmar fault. When built, these buildings did not require seismic-resistant designs. As a result, they suffered the most damage, with four collapsing, resulting in loss of lives.

The 1971 San Fernando Earthquake caused the collapse of four buildings at the Veterans Hospital in Sylmar.

Thirty-one patients and ten employees died in the quake. Six others died later after being moved to another location, and the last body was not found until noon February 13, after they sifted through the debris. Eighty percent of the deaths attributed to the 71 Sylmar quake were from the VA Hospital.

In 1972, they decided to demolish the entire location and transformed it into what is today called Veterans Park.

This entire VA Hospital was demolished and became the very popular El Cariso Park

Olive View Medical Center also sustained massive damage and casualties resulting from the quake. First opened in 1920, the main building had been newly constructed in 1970 and had reinforced concrete earthquake-resistant construction that failed.

The hospital had just become a county facility with 888 beds. The quake hit six weeks after the opening and caused the collapse of 4 stairwell wings, the parking structure, and the shifting of the entire five-story building with the buckling of the first-floor columns. The whole building nearly came down and was damaged beyond repair.

It was demolished by implosion on May 31, 1973. At the time of the quake, Olive View had 98 employees and 606 patients. There were three deaths from this location, two from loss of power to life support equipment and one who was struck by the collapsing building as she tried to escape.

1971 earthquake Olive View Hospital partially detached stairway

Fallen stair towers and damaged basement at the Olive View Hospital

Pacoima Memorial Lutheran Hospital suffered severely as well. It was designed in 1958 under the Los Angeles building code to resist horizontal forces of 1 percent gravity. It contained 98 beds and 30 bassinets.

There were 109 patients in the hospital at the time of the quake. As a new nursing shift was coming in, the shaking began. Windows broke, and there was a loud explosion heard nearby. Three patients were in the false labor room as IV bottles and glass were breaking around them. They were forced to evacuate. One patient was delivering her baby, and one was non-ambulatory, so transporting was not possible.

The damage to the structure ranged from minor to major. The nursing unit, which has four levels, including the basement, was heavily damaged. Although it did not collapse, there was widespread cracking in the concrete walls and one stairwell. The supporting beams also had structural damage. The primary power was out, and there was significant damage to the water systems, boilers, shelving, and piping. Leaks were spouting all over the place.

Critically injured victims were being routed to Pacoima Lutheran, not knowing of the hospital damage.

After 30 minutes, the emergency power came on, but still, there was no phone service. Within 45 minutes, the administration decided to evacuate the nursing area. The emergency room continued to operate, but preparations were underway for evacuations, which they completed by 9 am.

The Emergency Room ended up treating 400 patients. However, months later, they began demolition of the top three floors of the nursing tower. The hospital was repaired but suffered financial problems over the next ten years and was ultimately closed down.

1971 San Fernando earthquake – Scarp at Foothill Nursing Home – Street level view

There was substantial damage done to a ten-mile stretch of freeways in the San Fernando Valley. Total collapses, cracking and buckling left the overpasses and roadways in shambles. Twelve overpass bridges collapsed onto freeway lanes. The I-5/ 210 interchange caused two deaths when it fell. The recently completed Newhall pass saw a complete failure at the Interstate-5 Antelope Valley interchange. The Newhall Pass was rebuilt in 1973 only to suffer the same fate 23 years later.

1971 San Fernando Earthquake – Collapse of Newhall Pass interchange

Pacoima residents had vivid memories of the San Fernando quake. Inde Murphy remembered getting shaken out of bed at 6 am that morning. Her father was calling out, asking if everyone was ok. Her sisters' bed had literally hopped towards the door to the hallway.

"What I most remember is how all the neighbors came together on Corcoran Street to help each other out even with all the damage. No water, no power. We had our front yard set up like a campsite with the stove, ice chest, even a porta-potty. We were being neighbors, and' that's what it was like back in 1971."

Betty Jean Coleman also had vivid memories of that day.

"I will always remember that dark morning as though it was yesterday. I was shaking, rocking, and rolling in the bed like 'Reagan' from The Exorcist. I was grown, but I could have sworn that King Kong and Godzilla had come over the foothills and was shaking the house (near Foothill Blvd and the S. F. wash) like a toy (roaring)."

Craig Jones remembers his experience.

"I was living in Pacoima, being thrown out of the top bunk of the bed I shared with my brother. When it was over, our whole family walked around our house and checked out all of these cracks. The whole neighborhood was out. It was scary as a kid."

"My mom was up already up getting ready for work," said Tonya Garrison, who was nine years old living in the Van Nuys Apartments in Pacoima. "It was the scariest thing ever."

Another interesting story came from Annette Carol Bailey.

"I lived in the Van Nuys apartments & my mom was getting ready for work. I was laying on the couch, and she was in the kitchen! The earthquake hit, and I remember holding onto the couch. Mom jumped on top of me, my sister came flying from her room, and all the hallway doors opened up & she avoided splitting her head open. I was terrified! What I remember the most is when we went outside, the moon was blood red."

Former councilman Richard Alarcon remembers both the 71 & 94 quakes.

"It was my first day as Student Body President at Poly High. I think I was the only one who showed up to school that day. Then six months after being elected to City Council, we had the Northridge quake. I guess you could say being the first Latino elected at Poly & the first elected in the Valley to the City Council was an earth-shattering experience."

1971 San Fernando Earthquake - The lower Van Norman Dam was very close to breaching, and approximately 80,000 people were evacuated for four days while the water level in the reservoir was lowered.

1994 Northridge Quake

Following true to form, in the early morning hours of January 17, 1994, at 4:30 am, a 6.7 magnitude quake once again struck the San Fernando Valley area of Los Angeles. This time the epicenter was Reseda, but it is known as the Northridge Earthquake. It lasted 10 to 20 seconds with peak ground acceleration of 1.8g, which was the highest ever instrumentally recorded in an urban area. The aftershocks numbered in the thousands with some registering as 6.0 and lasting up to a minute. The death toll in this one totaled 61 with more than 18,480 injured and 1,533 admitted for care. The property damage totaled between $13 and $50 billion, making it one of the costliest natural disasters in US history at that time.

This quake left 25,000 homeless, 1.2 million without electricity, 150,000 without water, and 40,000 without natural gas. Over 55,000 structures were deemed uninhabitable, with thousands of long-term evacuations. Over 13,000 were housed at emergency shelters while others stayed in makeshift shelters, cars, or camped outdoors.

As with the San Fernando quake, Olive View in Sylmar, Holy Cross in Mission Hills, and the Veterans Administration building in North Hills (newly built after the 1971 earthquake) closed. Kaiser in Panorama City sustained damage and had to evacuate some of their patients.

Kaiser Permanente Building after Northridge Earthquake in 1994

Some of the residents rejected staying in still-standing buildings after their walls collapsed, opting for parks. Some left the area altogether. However, many Pacoima residents now had previous earthquake experience, including the town's fast-growing Central American (Guatemala, El Salvador, and Nicaragua) population. Many of them had also faced major earthquakes before. By the end of the week, the National Guard had set up canvas army tents with cots, blankets, and a Red Cross comfort kit.

The Los Angeles School District, the second-largest in the country, was closed for a week after the event. With 800 campuses and over 100,000 students, the district suffered structural damage to approximately 300 schools. Thousands of students found themselves in makeshift classrooms. Counselors were sent out to help the students deal with the stress of this disaster.

Northridge Earthquake, January 17, 1994 -- An aerial view of destruction caused by the 6.7 magnitude earthquake.

Unlike the Sylmar quake, where most of the deaths were at the VA Hospital, this one had various locations. Northridge Meadow Apartment complex had 16 deaths.

Northridge Fashion Center and Cal State University Northridge suffered extensive damage, and the early morning hour of the quake may have saved many lives.

Freeway damage was just as severe in this disaster. The same interchange at the Newhall Pass, where I-5 meets the Antelope Valley Freeway (Hwy 14), collapsed. One life was lost when a motorcyclist fell 40 feet from the connector.

Northridge Earthquake, CA, January 17, 1994 - Many roads, including bridges and elevated highways were damaged by the 6.7 magnitude earthquake.

Despite repairing the damage from these horrific quakes, the memories still haunt those who experienced them. Moreover, knowing that earthquakes are a real-part of Pacoima life, residents remain mindful of what may come again someday.

Prudencio Miguel Gomez

Anyone who frequented Gomez Market knew the kindness and spirit that this family ran business exemplified. Known as only Gomez, he was born in a small village named Alconada, located in Salamanca, Spain, on March 29, 1900, and was an only child. His family emigrated from Spain to Hawaii when he was only nine years old. Shortly after that, they went to San Francisco, where they picked fruit to make a living. Slowly they crept down the state until they ended up in San Fernando in 1916.

Gomez was a very hard worker, and at the young age of 12, he was awarded a championship prize for picking the most and best apricots. His only formal education was when he was a young boy in Spain because he was needed to help the family. Not deterred by circumstances, he learned reading and writing from his boyhood friends in San Fernando and practiced reading while watching silent movies.

Working in the agricultural arena for local landholders, Gomez aimed for something more and landed a job at Southern California Gas Company, where he met his wife. She was a Mexican girl from Texas named Mercedes Morales. They were married at the San Gabriel Mission in 1921 and settled in Pacoima. He then began working in the orange industry, which was prominent in the area. The landscape was made up of orange and lemon trees among a host of other agriculture. It was not long before Gomez realized his ambition to own his own business. By this time, he had five daughters Frances, Rosalie, Mary Ellen, Virginia, and Mercedes. He also took in and raised Carmen, their niece, from his wife's side.

Despite his lack of formal education, Gomez opened his market on Judd Street in 1926. He knew all his customers and treated them like family. During the Great Depression of 1929, Gomez was one of only a few that extended credit to his customers. Not only that, he fed hungry travelers, which coincided with his kind nature.

His wife, Mercedes, was instrumental in the success of the business. While Gomez sought to improve the community, she very meticulously handled the six children, ran the household, and managed finances at the market.

As a savvy businessman, Gomez began to purchase real estate in Pacoima, which was very cheap at that time. When the economy improved, he began working actively to secure civic and home improvement loans to develop the shanty landscape that plagued Pacoima. There were mostly shacks and outhouses, except for the few Victorian houses built in earlier years. There were no paved roads except for Van Nuys Blvd, so there was much work to be done.

Gomez later moved his store from Judd Street to Filmore Street on property he had purchased in 1927. The building of new homes in Pacoima, including the Joe Louis and San Fern Manor housing tracts, generated business for his store. Gomez embraced the Black community as he did everyone else.

He got involved in many community organizations as the town grew. He was a director for the Kiwanis Club of Pacoima and president of the Pacoima Chamber of Commerce as well as backing many youth groups. Gomez was also instrumental in getting street lights, sidewalks, and paved roads in the town. He received the "Pioneer of the Year" award in 1961 from the Pacoima Coordinating Council for his active part. He was credited for his progressive leadership in the community's betterment and for guiding youth on the path of honesty and success.

In 1960, Gomez suffered the death of his oldest daughter Frances. He took her death extremely hard. Gomez demolished the store on Filmore Street, rebuilt the property, and decided to retire. His daughter Rosie and her husband Ralph Roman opened a new store on the corner of Pala and Filmore in 1961. They changed the name to Roman's Market. In 1981, Gomez's grandson Prudy took the reins.

It was a time when parents could send their kids to the market with a note to purchase cigarettes or alcohol. They continued the small community atmosphere and personal interactions. As large grocery store chains began to dominate, small establishments started to suffer. Prudencio Gomez passed away in 1984 at the age of 84. Perhaps the first true trailblazer in Pacoima history, the community recently honored him. His daughter Mercedes accepted the Pioneer Award from the Pacoima Historical Society in October 2018.

Prudencio Gomez (center) shown here in the late thirties butchering fresh meat he sold at his market (Courtesy Mercedes Salazar collection)

PM Gomez with his mother, Maria Piedad
(Courtesy Mercedes Salazar collection)

Prudencio Gomez accepts Pioneer of the Year award from Pacoima Community
Coordinating Council 1961. (Courtesy Mercedes Salazar collection)

Deputy Axillary Police awards presentation 1962. Gomez shown with awardees.
(Courtesy Mercedes Salazar collection)

granddaughter Francesca Brooks and his only living daughter 86-year-old Mercedes Salazar accepts the award.

(Courtesy Fernandeño-Tataviam Band of Mission Indians)

Rudy Ortega Sr.

The citizens of the Fernandeño-Tataviam Band of Mission Indians are the original inhabitants of the area now known as Pacoima, which derives from the traditional word Pacoinga. It would be remised not to list trailblazers from that community.

Rudy Ortega Sr. was born in 1926 and, as a young man, sought to learn more about his heritage. After the European invasion and unsuccessful genocide of his people, it was not uncommon for Indians to downplay their culture due to possible repercussions. However, Ortega was encouraged by his Aunt Vera Salazar to research, organize and form an Indian cultural club in the 1940s. She wanted him to learn their history.

Ortega began the research process of learning his family, community, and lineage history. He also learned about the enslavement of his Tataviam ancestors at the Mission San Fernando Rey in present-day Mission Hills.

Placing his research on hold in1943, he enlisted in the US Army during World War II. Ortega served in Korea and the Philippines until the war was over. However, when he returned home, he resumed his tribal history research.

Meanwhile, a voluntary coalition of Mission San Fernando associated Indians was maintained. It consisted of three main families identified by the surnames of their Tribal leaders, which were the Ortega, Ortiz and Garcia lineages. The Spanish names came from the Padres at the San Fernando Mission, who renamed the natives after baptizing them. This practice of forced naming was common during the mission era, but inter-marriages with Spanish settlers also played a role.

In 1928, the Department of Indian Affairs had a California Judgement Indian Roll call where Indians were asked to register. The leader of the tribe at that time was Antonio Maria Ortega, his grandfather, who urged the community not to register. He feared they would be stripped from their families and relocated to reservations outside of the San Fernando-Santa Clarita area. Therefore, most of the Ortega family did not register in 1928, severely crippling the tribe's goal of government recognition.

After his father James Ortega died in 1951, Ortega was appointed as the traditional leader of his lineage by the elders and elected as tribal president. He came to be known as Chief Little Bear, and eventually led the community to register with the Bureau of Indian Affairs. Little Bear hoped to finally achieve federal recognition and establish a reservation where future generations can maintain their sacred connection to the land.

His campaign intensified, and he sought to share the history of his people with the external community. Specifically, his goal was to reclaim the lands granted to his great grandparents in the Mexican period, such as one square league at Rancho El Encino, present-day Encino, California. Due to deceitful business practices, the property was stripped away from them by encroaching settlers. Siutcanga, now known as Encino, went unprotected as the US government failed to protect their land as promised under the 1848 Treaty of Guadalupe Hildago.

Throughout the decades, the voluntary coalition of lineages named their tribe Fernandeño-Tataviam Band of Mission Indians and Chief Little

Bear continued leadership as the elected tribal president. He dedicated his life to his people and establishing cultural enrichment programs, as well as reclaiming traditional lands and a land base. Little Bear also fought for health services for local Native Americans and scholarships for all Native American students in Los Angeles County. He founded a non-profit organization now called Pukuu Cultural Community Services, which still operates today.

Chief Little Bear passed away in 2009 at the age of 82 after suffering a heart attack while driving. Before leaving, he fought hard for the "settler government" to recognize his tribe as a sovereign native nation and establish a government to government relationship with the United States. His ancestors first communicated with federal government agents in 1892. However, it was not until 2015, almost 120 years later, that the Department of Interior initiated a formal review of the tribe's petition for federal recognition. This review began under the leadership of his son and current elected tribal president Rudy Ortega Jr.

Rudy "Chief Little Bear" Ortega Sr. displayed qualities of good leadership that followed in the footsteps of his forefathers. He left behind ten children, 49 grandchildren, and 54 great-grandchildren. His son Rudy, appointed new Captain by the elders, continues his people's legacy.

To honor their former leader, the tribe established a park in partnership with the City of San Fernando. Rudy Ortega Sr. Park is located on property originally inhabited by and granted to tribal leader Rogerio Rocha in the Mexican period. On this historic land, the tribe gathers to reclaim their culture, practices, and legacy, in the memory of Chief Little Bear.

The Pacoima community had fond memories of Chief Little Bear. He and his wife Celia were known to go to Denny's every Saturday Morning. Described as "bright" and "happy," he would give all the food servers peppermint candy.

1920s - Manual & Vera Salazar Rudy's Uncle & Aunt who convinced him to research the tribe. (courtesy of Fernandeno-Tataviam Band of Mission Indians)

1975 - Rudy Ortega Sr. (Courtesy Fernandeño Tataviam Band of Mission Indians)

Rudy Ortega Sr. gets drink from son 1958
(Courtesy Fernandeno -Tataviam Band of Mission Indians)

Rudy Ortega Sr. was the father of 10 children, with 49 grandchildren and 54 great-grandchildren. (Courtesy Fernandeno- Tataviam Band of Mission Indians)

Rudy Ortega Sr. and Steve Ortega in 1990
(Courtesy Fernandeno -Tataviam Band of Mission Indians)

Dr. Sanbo Sakaguchi

Dr. Sanbo Sakaguchi lived to be 95-years-old and practiced medicine for over 55 years. He devoted his life to medicine and helping the community alongside his sister Dr. Mary Sakaguchi Oda.

For over 30 years, he served as a team physician for local high school football. He also served on boards for the Japanese American National Museum, JACCC, and the Little Tokyo Service Center. He did this all while being a well-respected practicing physician.

Sakaguchi earned a bachelor's degree from UCLA in 1939 and then attended medical school at Marquette University in Wisconsin. During that time, the government incarcerated his family in North Hollywood, along with nearly 120,000 other Japanese Americans on the West Coast during World War II. He was classified by the FBI as a 4C, enemy alien, and not allowed to be in the US Armed services.

Upon his return to the Los Angeles area following the war, Sakaguchi married Kazuko (Kay) Furuta, whom he met after a chemistry class while he was a student at UCLA.

Dr. Sakaguchi gave generously to community organizations. His medical school, Marquette University, reported he was a generous contributor to their program. However, he and his wife Kazuko "Kay" also gave to UCLA, who has a display recognizing him for his generosity.

Dr. Sakaguchi settled back in the Valley in 1955. It was when he returned that he discovered no hospitals would accept his patients of color. So, he and his sister, Dr. Mary Oda, founded Serra Memorial Hospital, as a non-discriminatory facility.

The image of Dr. Sanbo Sakaguchi is on the Pacoima City Hall Mural and the meeting hall at the San Fernando Valley Japanese American Community Center bears his name. (artwork by Ignacio Gomez)

Sakaguchi Family in 1925. All were sent to Manzanar Internment camp in 1942 where three died.

Kazuko and Sanbo Sakaguchi

Jose De Sosa

Jose De Sosa served as President of the NAACP San Fernando Valley Branch from 1978 to 1994 and led campaigns that resulted in significant changes in practices in the Los Angeles Police Department. He also rose to state NAACP President and served on the National Executive Board.

Born in Panama, De Sosa migrated to New York in his early years. He met his wife Juanita while stationed in Omaha, Nebraska, and they married in 1959. After serving in the US Air Force, he retired from the military and moved to Pacoima, where he and Juanita raised three children.

De Sosa began his activism in the sixties and later was a key figure in placing a moratorium on the chokehold, which was killing African Americans in the 1980s. He also got the Los Angeles Police Department banned from using the "battering ram," which targeted the destruction of homes thought to be crack houses.

De Sosa said his first task was to get Police Chief Daryl Gates out of his position. "Gates was a racist," he said. Mayor Tom Bradley had appointed him as chief in 1978, and he remained there throughout the majority of Bradley's term. De Sosa led marches along with Congresswoman Maxine Waters and Congresswoman Diane Watson until Gates finally resigned in 1992.

De Sosa has also held statewide positions in the NAACP. In 1988, he was elected state president for the NAACP in California, which involved overseeing more than 88 adult branches and 30 youth and college chapters. Also, on the Board of Directors for Boys and Girls Club, he assisted in a multitude of community projects. Additionally, De Sosa served on the board of directors of San Fernando Neighborhood Legal Services.

Jose De Sosa's dedication to the community was well respected, but the historic magnitude of his contributions may never be truly understood. However, his local and national dedication to addressing race relations in America makes his story as compelling as any in Pacoima's history.

Jose De Sosa and Juanita De Sosa join Crystal Jackson at the premiere screening of "PacoimaStories: Land of Dreams" in 2016

Rosa Lee Broadous

Rosa Lee "Mother" Broadous, born December 8, 1918, in Gould, Arkansas, was a powerhouse in Pacoima. Her birth name was Effie Rosa.

She married Hillery T. Broadous in 1937 and ultimately moved to Los Angeles.

In 1946, they were informed of military housing and ultimately ended up at Basilone Homes by Hansen Dam. In 1953, they purchased land in Pacoima and laid down their roots after building their home.

Mother Broadous was known to be motherly but also managed to hold her own in activism. She co-founded Calvary Baptist Church with her husband in 1955 and was on the first board of directors for the Pacoima NAACP as Vice President. Her legendary involvement in Community faith-related activities included San Fernando Valley Interfaith Council and San Fernando Valley Chapter of Church Women United. She was also the first to organize Negro History Week programs in the SFV and volunteered at the Braille Institute, Boy Scouts, Girl Scouts, PTA, and YWCA. She served on the board for the Northeast Valley Multipurpose Senior Center, named after her daughter Alicia Broadous Duncan. Duncan was Executive Director of the center when she passed away in 2003.

Mother Broadous had a total of eleven children. One passed away as a baby, and 6 of her children became Baptist ministers. She went on to graduate from Los Angeles Mission College as Liberal Arts major and then attended Cal State Northridge.

In 2000, the LA Times named her "One of seven 'Great Dames' who helped shape California." The article stated, "These were women who came of age at a time of limited expectations and found a way to acquire power regardless… and use it for the better good."

Mother Broadous believed wholeheartedly in the "total" community as she ministered and worked with people from all walks of life. Her philosophy was "make a difference."

She passed away in 2008 at the age of 89. Her image is on the Pacoima City Hall Mural along with her husband's, but Mother Broadous is a trailblazer in her own right.

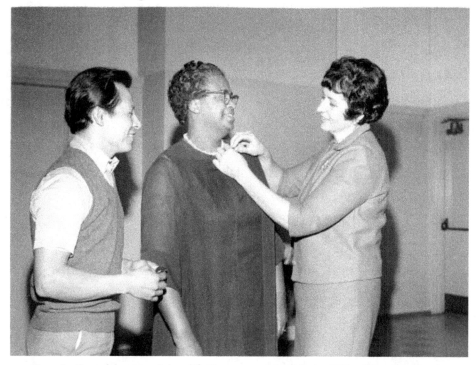

Rosa L. Broadous receiving lifetime membership to PTA of San Fernando

Marie Harris

Born October 10, 1922, in Houston, Texas, Marie Harris is Pacoima's most legendary Matriarch. Her effort to build Pacoima into a Los Angeles powerhouse town was relentless over the years. She became a force to be reckoned with in local and state politics.

Marie Harris arrived in Pacoima in 1960 with her husband Alvin and their three children. Rolene Naveja, Marie's daughter, spoke about her family arriving to town.

"We came here in 1960, my father worked for US rubber in Detroit, and the plant started doing a lot of layoffs. Our Uncle Tony lived in San Fernando, so we packed up and moved to California. We had my younger brother Alton and older brother Sydney. I went to San Fernando High and graduated in 1965.

"My mother rolled up her sleeves and decided to get this community going. She used to love telling people she was designing a community. And she did."

Harris became active on various committees, and in 1979 founded the Pacoima Property Owner's Association. She served on the Pacoima Chamber of Commerce Board of Directors and the Board of Economic Alliance of the SFV.

In 1981, she ran for Los Angeles City Council's 7th district, where she was narrowly defeated. Harris spearheaded the "Back to Pacoima Expo," which took place at Hansen Dam from 1980 to 1987. Her daughter, Rolene, produced the event, which became a star-studded yearly community gala.

Rolene Naveja and her mother Marie Harris (R) in the 1970's

Marie gets award from LAPD Chief Willie Williams for her community service
(Courtesy Marie Harris collection)

(From left) Leroy Chase, Miguel Garcia, and Councilman Alex Padilla with Marie Harris
in 1983 (Courtesy Marie Harris Collection)

Marie Harris worked tirelessly to build and design Pacoima. During the eighties, she co-founded Pacoima Beautiful, to beautify and change the town's image. Harris also forged a relationship with the Piken Company to develop the town's largest shopping center at that time, located on Van Nuys Blvd. and Glenoaks.

"She found a developer willing to come and build a shopping center," said her daughter Rolene. "She teamed up with the city, and that's how we got the Pacoima Plaza of the Stars, and it's still on the marquee. And that's the name my mother came up with to have that shopping center named Pacoima Plaza of the Stars."

Pacoima Plaza of the Stars is the crowning jewel for Marie Harris. Working with the Piken Company, this shopping center on Van Nuys Blvd and Glenoaks was built in the 80s. It has become a town fixture and among its busiest plazas.

Mrs. Harris served as a delegate to the California State Democratic Party Convention for ten years and was honored by the California State Legislature in 1994 and 2004 as "Woman of the Year."

Marie was named the honorary mayor of Pacoima, and the corner of Van Nuys Blvd and Glenoaks is now named Marie Harris Square in her honor.

Mural at Foothill Division Police yard. Marie Harris is towards the back.
(Mural painted by Levi Ponce, Juan Reyes, Leonardo Tejada, Tomas Prado)

CITIZENS
to ELECT

Marie Harris

FOR

CITY
COUNCILWOMAN

★ She has lived and worked in the First Council District twenty-three years—she knows the problems first hand and has been working on solutions in response to the voters' requests.

★ She has been a member of countless committees, organizations and groups through the years—working constantly to secure improvements for the betterment of the lives of the residents who live here.

★ She will continue her efforts to bring about benefits for the District's Senior Citizens—who deserve so much more—in Housing, Police and Fire Protection, expand Paramedic services, keep cheap convenient public Bus Transportation and "close-to-home" health facilities.

★ She will work to rid the streets of crime, muggings, rape, burglary by recruiting dedicated plainclothes Police Officers and more Police Foot Patrolmen to Patrol our streets to capture the criminal in the act in our neighborhoods. This is the **strongest** deterrent to criminals.

★ She will immediately conduct a street-by-street, complete survey of the entire First Council District street lights making sure all streets are lighted "bright as day" as a further deterrent to crime, so once again our families can drive and walk the streets safely.

★ She will bring an era of cooperation between our district and the cities of Burbank and Glendale in quicker, more massive responses to devastating fires in the foothills. She'll join them all together in the fight to save lives and property.

★ She will focus special attention in the canyon areas and elsewhere towards prevention of floods and mud slides.

★ She is determined on jobs to work to fill the need for more work in the skilled, semi-skilled and unskilled areas. More jobs mean much higher wages for the working man and woman as they share in the profits of business from the use of their labor.

★ On Housing—she will bring in affordable housing so young families, through small subsidies, can buy their first home, rather than rent. To give them an opportunity to take part in The American Dream—owning a house. The pride of accomplishment through ownership.

★ She will reverse the trend in the First Council District of thirty (30) years of neglect. She will see that the residents share equally with the rest of the City of Los Angeles in the "horn of plenty" so that all share in the future benefits equally.

★ The future looks bright. The First Council District areas are in for an unprecedented boom and we must all be ready to prosper and benefit by being ready to take advantage of any opportunity. Marie Harris is the ONE qualified Candidate who has the vision and has the force and the power to shape it so all the residents can share in the bright future that is coming. Give Marie Harris your vote.

Marie Harris ran for City Councilwoman in 1981. This flyer is from her campaign
(Courtesy Marie Harris Collection)

Los Angeles County Board of Supervisors member Michael Antonovich (L), Marie Harris, and Mel Wilson (Courtesy Marie Harris Collection)

In April of 2011, Councilman Richard Alarcon and Tony Cardenas submitted the proposal to name Van Nuys Blvd and Glenoaks "Marie Harris Square," due to her great contributions to the people and community of Pacoima.

(Courtesy Marie Harris Collection)

Mary Helen Ponce

Born January 24, 1938, in Pacoima, Mary Helen Ponce attended Pacoima Elementary and San Fernando High School. She is known for her book "Hoyt Street," which chronicles her life as a Latina growing up in Pacoima. This autobiography goes into detail about the Chicano culture, clothes, language, houses, and food during the fifties and sixties.

After graduating from High School, Ponce married and had four children. She later attended Cal State University, Northridge, and received two degrees, one in anthropology and one in Chicano Studies. Ponce continued her education and earned a Ph.D. from the University of New Mexico in American Studies. She is also the author of a series of short fiction novels.

She worked as an instructor of Chicano Studies at Cal State Los Angeles and was a professor in women's studies at the University of New Mexico. Mrs. Ponce was also a writer for the Los Angeles Times, and her image is on the Pacoima City Hall Mural.

Mary Helen Ponce and California State Senate Senator Richard Alarcón, who presents Ponce with a Senate Resolution to commemorate the Lifetime Commitment to Literacy Award from the Friends of the San Fernando Library in 2009.

Mary Helen Ponce image on Pacoima City Hall Mural

John Mance

John Mance purchased his home in the San Fern Manor tract on Filmore Street in 1952. He was originally from Chicago but grew up in Pasadena, California, where he met his wife, Elenore Edson. Mance entered the military directly out of high school during World War II. Upon release from service, he married Elenore in October 1948. They lived in Pasadena while waiting for their house on Filmore Street to be built. He and his wife Eleanor had two children born to them David and Richard (Rick).

Mance found employment at one of the largest employers in the Valley, Lockheed Martin, where he worked in Human Resources. He was promoted up the ladder of success to become a Lockheed executive and was the first African American to have his own plant.

While doing that, he also took an active role as a community activist by being on the first Pacoima NAACP Board of Directors as Parliamentarian in 1955. He then became President in 1958. Mance rose in that as well by becoming a member of the National NAACP Board. He received numerous honors, including the 2010 Roy Wilkins Freedom Fund Award, which recognized his civil rights contributions.

John Mance aided in the formation of the NAACP Image Awards, which is still taking place annually today. In 1965, he also founded the Pacoima Skill Center along with Carl McCraven to help the youth develop abilities to succeed in the workforce.

One of his co-workers at Lockheed, Ed Rose, who founded MEND, referred to John as a true gentleman.

"I called him Gentleman John. We both worked on an outreach plan headed by John, called the 'Student Motivation Program.' We were assigned to High Schools to help students stay in school," said Rose.

"I was assigned to Burbank High school, where we picked up 'at risk' boys and gave them a tour of the facility and showed them how we made aircraft. This helped turn their lives around while giving them the incentive to stay in school. John Mance was a good man."

After WWII, the Lockheed plant in Burbank became a major provider of well-paying jobs and opportunities for many countless Pacoima residents. John Mance advanced to become a successful Lockheed executive.

Ethel Cole Bryant

Ethel Bryant was born on August 16, 1917, in Texarkana, Texas, but moved to Omaha, Nebraska, when she was two years old. She came to Los Angeles in 1941 and was married to William Jennings Bryant, a warrant officer.

Ethel did various jobs, which led to her interest in civil rights and politics. In 1949, she worked as a coordinator for the AFL Voters League, where she met Sam Yorty. In 1952, when Yorty was in the US House of Representatives, Ethel became an aid to the Congressman. She also worked for the Democratic State Central Committee and County Central Committee and discovered politics was her passion.

The Bryant's moved to Pacoima in 1957. Their home was on Judd Street, near Filmore Elementary, where she worked to bring Filmore Park to the neighborhood. She then petitioned the city of Los Angeles to change the name of the Park (located across the street from the school) to Hubert Humphrey Memorial Park. Humphrey was vice-president to President Lyndon B. Johnson and the lead author of the Civil Rights Act of 1964.

When Mayor Sam Yorty became the first to have a racially integrated staff in 1961, it included Ethel Bryant, who was named his Executive

Secretary. Ms. Bryant went on to meet high officials such as President Lyndon Johnson, dignitaries and was a role model to young people in Pacoima.

While working for Yorty, she also endured the dark side of racism. Her home on Judd Street was firebombed in 1969, while she was pioneering civil rights activities during a racially charged mayoral election. The fire, ruled arson, caused five thousand dollars of damage. She was the only one at home at the time of the blaze. Ethel Bryant was a true Pacoima trailblazer.

Mayor's field deputy is ready to listen Mrs. Ethel Bryant 1961.

Ethel Bryant meets President Lyndon B Johnson
(Courtesy of the Phillips family Celestine, Debra, Diana, Mike, and Monica)

Mayor Sam Yorty and wife Vicky takes photo with Ethel Bryant
(Courtesy of the Phillips family Celestine, Debra, Diana, Mike, and Monica)

Juanita De Sosa

Like many wives of activists, Juanita De Sosa not only supported her husband but took active roles in the community. She was extremely involved in Pacoima and the San Fernando Valley. Juanita was San Fernando Valley NAACP secretary for 14 years and California State Conference NAACP secretary for six years.

Her role in education was very notable. She was president of the Pacoima Junior High School PTA and assistant director in the LACA Head Start program. Juanita was instrumental in getting many of her employees' four-year college degrees.

Over the past 40 years, Juanita also received a multitude of community awards. She and her husband Jose De Sosa have lived in Pacoima for over 60 years.

Edward Kussman

Edward Kussman was a community activist, who served as president of the NAACP San Fernando Valley branch in 1967 & 1968. He ran against Rev. Hillery T. Broadous in a hotly contested race that Kussman won to serve another term in 1974. He went on to complete a "facelift" of the Boys & Girls Club and conduct hypertension testing for the community. His occupation was a facility planner for the Northeast Valley Health Corporation, as well as co-founder. He was involved with the NAACP when there were many race issues in housing, employment, and law enforcement. Kussman also served as Field Deputy for State Assemblyman Jim Keyser.

As NAACP president, Kussman supported the building of the Filmore public pool and fought to obtain funding for it and many other community projects.

He moved to Pacoima in 1951 from Compton and purchased 2.5 acres of land where he built his house. Kussman spearheaded housing discrimination issues in the San Fernando Valley. He was pleased when African Americans were finally able to purchase outside of Pacoima but realized it also hurt their political power. He was also President of the Pacoima Chamber of Commerce for many years and received awards for his long-time commitment.

Ed Kussman and Los Angeles Mayor Tom Bradley in the 70's

(Courtesy of Camille Watkins)

James Smith

Born in Wichita Falls, Texas, Jim came to Los Angeles when he was eight years old. He graduated from Jefferson High School in LA and joined the United States Army in 1945. He and his wife Dora grew up in the same neighborhood, and while on furlough in 1946, they got married.

When Jim and Dora moved to Pacoima, very few had heard of it. They bought their brand-new home in 1956. The house, located in the Nora Lee Estates on Woodcock, cost them $11,860.

Jim worked for Southern Pacific Railroad as a Pullman traveling all over the western part of the United States and as far as New Orleans, Louisiana.

However, his community legacy came with his becoming President of the Pacoima Property Owners Association and working with Marie Harris. He also assisted Reverend Pledger with his dream of getting his senior citizens home, Pledgerville completed. He and Dr. William Huling (a CSUN Professor), helped write the environmental impact study needed for the city of Los Angeles for Pledgerville.

Jim spoke about the role of the Pacoima Properties Owner Association. "Veda James, Marie Harris, and different other people, we all belonged to the Pacoima Property Owner's Association.

"We had doctors, lawyers, school teachers, principals, people working in aircraft, engineers, people working various city jobs, street maintenance, and various other things. We were all upwardly mobile, and most everyone took pride in our homes. Raising children, it was melting pot of all the nationalities there. Everyone got along. People took pride in their houses and yards.

"At the time (the '60s), we had a very low crime rate in Pacoima. My wife was district attorney in Van Nuys, and every year the Green Sheet newspaper in Van Nuys would put out the crime rate for the San Fernando Valley, and Pacoima was always the lowest. Very, very low crime."

James (Jim) Smith, Crystal Jackson, Dora Smith - April 2015
(courtesy PacoimaStorie Archives)

Dr. William Huling

Known by some as Dr. Bill, this trailblazer was a true pioneer in Pacoima. He was born December 5, 1933, in Texas, but after serving in the US Airforce in the forties, he found his way to Los Angeles and, ultimately, Pacoima. There he raised his children.

Dr. Huling earned his Ph.D. at the University of Southern California in psychology and worked at Cal State University Northridge, where he counseled, mentored, and assisted Black students for over 30 years. While at CSUN, he also conducted oral interviews about Pacoima's history for his dissertation. Among the interviewees were Reverend Hillery T. Broadous and Rev. TG Pledger, which has proven invaluable for documenting that history for the Pacoima Historical Society.

In the early days, Dr. Bill lived by the baseball fields next to Hansen Dam and formed a minor league team (the Cubs) promising not to discriminate based upon race or skills. The Cubs took every kid who was turned down by any other team. They developed into an incredible group and tied for first place, then won the title outright the following year. He referred to that team as the real "Bad News Bears."

Mid Pacoima Little League Cubs; Lucas Grace, Keith Huling, Steven Proctor, Ernest Lee Matthews, David Grace, Murphy Su'a, Coach Bill Huling (Courtesy Kevin Huling)

Dr. Huling also worked on the advisory board for the San Fernando Valley Community Mental Health Center for over 20 years as well as Pledgerville and the Senior Citizens Center. He was a longtime friend of Jose De Sosa and the NAACP.

Mayor Tom Bradley & Dr Bill Huling
(Courtesy Kevin Huling collection)

Xenaro Ayala

The Ayala family first came to the San Fernando Valley at the start of the 1900s when Xenaro's maternal great grandmother arrived from Arizona. They settled in the Mexican section of the city of San Fernando, which was on the west side of the railroad tracks, unlike Pacoima, who segregated Mexicans on the east side of the tracks.

Jenaro (original spelling) began spelling his name with an "X "after being inspired by Malcolm X, who had a significant influence on him. He saw the discrimination his brown people faced as he lived on Vaughn Street.

During the forties, fifties and into the sixties Ayala saw massive segregation issues between Whites and Mexicans. For example, Pancake Haven, located on Maclay Avenue, prohibited Mexicans from eating there, and movie theaters limited their seating.

The treatment was similar to Jim Crow in the south. Ayala faced taunting at James Restaurant on San Fernando Road from racist White kids and restricted days for people of color at the public swimming pool. Mexicans could only swim on Thursdays because they cleaned the pool every Friday.

His parents also had struggles when he tried to enroll at Morningside Grammar School, and they wanted to deny them. Their persistence finally got him into the all-White school. Once he made it to high school, the challenge was overcoming discouragement from seeking higher education as some counselors encouraged labor jobs for Mexicans. This practice was common in minority schools.

Ayala graduated in 1962, and the US Army drafted him in 1965. Fortunate to not be deployed to Vietnam, upon his discharge in 1967 he enrolled in college, majoring in art, history, and spanish to receive his teaching credentials.

It was at this time he cascaded into activism. He joined MEChA (Movimiento Estudiantil Chicano de Aztlán), a student organization that promoted higher education, culture, history, and self-determination for the liberation of Chicano people. Ayala believed that political involvement and education was the avenue for change in society.

He established the San Fernando Valley Chapter of La Raza Unida, a Chicano political movement, and organized many marches in both Pacoima and San Fernando.

Ayala was a teacher for the Los Angeles Unified School District for 28 years. He taught classes at both Pacoima Junior High and San Fernando High, where he retired in 2003.

His activism has helped promote equality and political awareness to Brown people of all shades. His son Ernesto Ayala continues what he started and works with La Raza Unida and Chicano issues.

Pacoima youth 1985.
(Courtesy Ernesto Ayala collection)

Xenaro Ayala was a teacher for 28 years.
(Courtesy Xenaro Ayala collection)

Elvira Orozco

Elvira Orozco was born on January 25, 1933, in Pacoima. Her parents, Julian and Atanacia Camarillo, were both from Jalisco, Mexico. They had four children, and Elvira was the youngest. Atanacia passed away when Elvira was only three years old, so their grandmother raised her and her siblings. Elvira attended Pacoima Grammar school in an era when speaking Spanish in school resulted in harsh punishment. This treatment left an everlasting impact on Elvira. Growing up, she saw Mexicans mostly working in the agricultural fields and concluded that education could best improve her life. Thus, she graduated from San Fernando High School with honors and was class Salutatorian in 1951. She then went on to attend San Fernando Valley State College and earned her Associate Arts degree in Business Administration.

She married Angel Orozco in 1953, and they had four children Art, Julie, Madeline, and Manuel. Elvira was determined to instill education as a focus for her children. She did not speak Spanish nor teach them Spanish while raising them, to ensure their success as Americans. This custom was common for those who suffered the language discrimination of that era.

However, her focus on education demonstrated her understanding of avoiding manual labor jobs for her children.

The City of San Fernando hired Elvira in 1960 as the Deputy City Treasurer. She eventually became the City Treasurer, a position that she held for 40 years. She was very active in the community and worked closely with Father Luis Valbuena of Santa Rosa Church to create Santa Rosa Credit Union. She assisted parishioners in saving money and obtaining loans and was a member of their Board of Directors.

Elvira Orozco celebrates 85th birthday with her family.
(Courtesy Madeline Rodriguez)

Nancy Avery (1919-1992)

Nancy Avery was a lifelong civil rights activist. President John F. Kennedy appointed her United States Postmaster in 1961, becoming the first Black person in America to head a major U.S. post office. She was also the last person to be appointed by a U.S. President.

Before her appointment, Avery worked at Vaughn Elementary and was politically active with the Democratic Party. As an activist, she organized voter registration drives, served as president of the NAACP, and was a commissioner for the San Fernando Fair Housing Council. Avery was also active in the school PTA and board member for the Boys & Girls Club of the San Fernando Valley.

Nancy Avery retired from the post office in 1984 after 23 years. She passed away on January 29, 1992, at the age of 72.

William "Bill" Marsh

Bill Marsh grew up in Pacoima and was a track & field star as well as a football star for the San Fernando Tigers class of 1965. He was named the "Fastest Feet in the East" by the Valley News for winning the 100-yard dash in 9'9 in April 1965. He attended USC and had a brush with the pros before coming back home to his roots, where he became a legend.

In the early seventies, Marsh became a coach for his old alma mater San Fernando. His success would become legendary. Marsh created a dynasty coaching some of the nation's best talent, including Heisman Trophy winner Charles White and USC legend Anthony Davis. He is best known for coaching San Fernando High's dream backfield of White, Kevin Williams, Kenny Moore, and Raymond Williams. This team ranked number one in the nation in the 1975-76 season after winning back to back city championship in 1974 and 1975.

Marsh was also dean of students at San Fernando High and helped numerous students get college scholarships. He also developed Marsh Enterprises Inc., where he reconstructed buildings, including Marsh Arms, an apartment complex. He was married to his high school sweetheart Deborah Logan and had three daughters Kelli, Chris, and Kim.

Thomas Montgomery

Thomas Montgomery was a nationally known political activist who lived on Louvre Street in Pacoima. He worked as a Driver's License Examiner at the San Fernando DMV for many years. However, he was very involved in the political landscape as well as community projects.

In 1968, Montgomery and Ed Kussman won a hard-fought battle with the city of Los Angeles to get a pool built at Filmore Park (now called Humphrey Park). The ribbon-cutting ceremony was in June of 1971. He was Chairman to the Democratic County & State Central Committee for the 39th Assembly District and served as an official California delegate during the 1976 and 1980 Presidential elections.

Montgomery faced the challenges he experienced with racism head-on. Most notably was his battle with the Van Nuys Elks Club. Senator Alan Robbins sponsored him to become a member of the Elk Club in Van Nuys, but they denied him membership. Senator Robbins was furious at the blatant racism, and Montgomery requested a state civil rights investigation charging the Elks Club with racism. However, private clubs legally had the right to admit or deny any applicant. Ultimately, the court dropped all charges.

The local newspapers quoted Montgomery as saying, "Too bad the wall in Berlin can come down, but the wall of bigotry is still standing in Van Nuys."

California delegate Thomas Montgomery holds sign at 1980 Convention referring to Pacoima.

Tom Montgomery, Ronald "Pookey" Oliver, Los Angeles Lakers owner Jerry Buss, Joan Montgomery (Courtesy Ronald Oliver)

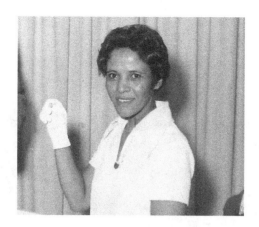

Veda Delois James

Veda James was the first woman ever to work in the LAPD Detectives Unit. Born September 8, 1918, in Los Angeles, she married Romie Craig when she was 18 years old, and they had two children, Romie Jr. (Bobby) and Alithra (Tipy). James, an African American, began working for the Los Angeles Police Department in 1950 at Newton Division. She attended the police academy with LA's future mayor, Tom Bradley.

In 1953, after joining the detective's unit, she and her second husband, George James, purchased a San Fern Manor home in Pacoima. When Foothill Division opened in 1961, she transferred.

Veda James and Chief of Detectives Thad Burney (L) – LAPD Foothill Division April 5, 1965
(Veda James Archives)

Los Angeles Police Chief Ed Davis and Veda James
(Veda James Archives)

Veda James and the ladies working at the station 1965
(Veda James Archives)

While working at Newton St. Division Veda James became LAPD's first female detective.
Veda James Archives)

Veda James retired in 1980 after 30 years with the LAPD. She received numerous awards from the department and write-ups in newspapers. After retirement, she got involved in community service and helped start the Pacoima Property Owners Association. Veda worked side by side with Marie Harris and was instrumental in the "Back to Pacoima Expo."

Foothill's Finest
The Cowboy Cop

The BIG racoon caper has Foothill Division all shook up. On a recent evening our great white hunters, AKA **Ackerman** and **Birney**, were on a quiet safari in the wilds of Tujunga. Suddenly there appeared **"Bwana" O'Neal** who ordered them to follow him. Since he is also a night watch supervisor, they hastened to do so.

Self Defense?

He led them deep into the wilderness where they faced a terrifying experienc. It seem that a vicious racoon (at least 25 pounds) had wandered under a local citizen's house, with the citizen's dog, a miniature dachshund, in hot pursuit. Fearing for the life of his favorite hunting dog, the citizen insisted that our intrepid nimrods go under the house and rescue his dog. A call to Animal Regulation Department proved futile. They don't go under a house for any reason. Faced with this situation, **Ackerman** fearlessly "volunteered" to go under the house, while Birney supplied covering fire. As those outside waited breathlessly, a shot rang out. Then another. As the outside men rushed to his assistance, Ackerman appeared, dirty and disheveled, in one hand his trusty .38 and in the other the very dead racoon. Ackerman swears that the deceased beast attacked him with a six-inch knife and he fired in self defense. His Shots Fired Report so stated. . . .

The Sunshine Ranch was the scene of a Foothill Division steak fry and liquid refreshment party. The high point of the evening was a surprise appearance of **Tex Tennesen**, of the musical group (?) the "Plucking Pigs." This group has not been heard from since the Christmas Party. Some will say that this is just as well, but they should get an "A" for effort. They sing and play loudly, if not well. The drawing for door prizes, handled by **Jim Hurley**, had everyone going around mumbling "rigged." It seemed that almost every name he drew was a motor officer. At least, all those that won the "bubbly" seemed to be motor officers. Oh well, the steaks were excellent and the party was a big success. Our thanks to the Station Fund Committee for their hard work to make it so. In the last issue I inadvertently gave **Brunzell** credit for rounding up some stray horses. He tells me that it wasn't he, but the rodeo star was actually **Gary Brewer.** Sorry about the error, Gary. To make up for it I won't tell anyone how you fell off your own horse recently.

The baseball season is upon us once again. The Foothill team started out with a blaze of glory. **Jim Grace**, pitching a one-hitter, led Foothill to a 4-0 victory over Devonshire. It's good to see Foothill back in the running again with a baseball team. It was also a surprise to see some of those old men who turned out for the team.

Veda 'Pinned'!

Veda James, the secretary to our Detective Commander, recently completed 25-years' service. She received many words of praise from notables on the Department, including her pin and a citation from the Police Commission, presented by **Dr. R. J. Carreon Jr.** of the Board of Police Commissioners.

There, a whole column without a word about the Foothill Division Troopers, who, by the time this gets into print, will have ridden in the Grand Entry at the Rodeo at the Forum. Opening night is to be a benefit for the Police Memorial Fund and they have been invited to participate, along with the Horse Detail, The Mounted Reserves, the Chief of Police and the Police Commissioners. The plan is for the Chief and Commissioners to ride in the newly refurbished horse-drawn Paddy Wagon.

Meanwhile, back at the ranch. . . .

WOLAPO News
Wanda Cronkhite

WOLAPO now has almost 200 members and with this growth it has expanded its purpose. Our members are now actively involved in community service and our yearly Scholarship as well as our social functions.

Chapter III held their "Family Fashion Fair," featuring fashions for the whole family, including Daddy. Thanks to **Paul Schlenz, John Harrington** and **John Sotello** for doing such a great job. Chapter VI's "Clothing Conspiracy" Fashion Show was a great success, too.

Dr. R. J. Carreon, president of the Board of Police Commissioners, left, presents Veda James, secretary to the Foothill Division Commander, with a citation honoring her 25-year service with the Department.

10 • THE BEAT / JUNE 1970

Veda James receives award from the LAPD Police Commission for her service
Veda James Archives)

James Robinson

James Robinson arrived in Pacoima during the 1950s and opened a real estate office next to Hillary Broadus's barbershop on Van Nuys Blvd. He became the first Black accepted in the San Fernando Association of Realtors. Robinson was also a noted pioneer of opening the door for Blacks to eventually purchase homes beyond the invisible color line that existed in the San Fernando Valley.

Robinson became the first Black president of the Pacoima Chamber of Commerce. He took pride in selling homes to Black teachers, preachers, doctors, and professionals in the early days of Pacoima.

Frank Del Olmo

Frank Del Olmo was a three-time Pulitzer Prize-winning author and publisher that became an associate editor for the Los Angeles Times where he worked for over 34 years.

He grew up in the projects in Pacoima and went on to graduate from CSU, Northridge and was one of six Latinos chosen as the outstanding graduate of the university.

In 1987, he accepted the Nieman Fellowship to study journalism at Harvard University. During his career he wrote on a wide range of topics concerning the Latino community.

He won an Emmy for his writing was inducted into the Hispanic Journalists Hall of Fame in 2002. Del Olmo was a founding member of the California Chicano News Media Foundation.

William 'Blinky' Rodriguez

William Blinky Rodriguez is perhaps the most compelling Pacoima trailblazer in modern times. He began his youth hanging out and training with Bennie "The Jet" Urquidez and excelling in the martial arts. At a very young age, he married Benny's sister Lily who was seven years older than 16-year-old Blinky. The two of them made history when they boxed as the first husband-wife in the same venue.

Blinky and Lilly had six children. In 1992 they lost their 16-year-old son, Sonny to gang violence. A rival gang member shot him. Their oldest son David served 26 years in prison for murder. These life-changing events caused the two to refocus their lives and direct them on gang violence.

In 1993 Rodriguez helped broker a peace treaty among 75 gangs in the San Fernando Valley. He has been recognized by national and international leaders for his work with "Communities in Schools" violence prevention and intervention practices. Leaders such as Nelson Mandela, Jimmy Carter, Dr. Jane Goodall and Senator Barbara Boxer have all recognized his work. In 1998 he received Medaille d' Excellence presented in Switzerland which was only presented to 14 people worldwide. He has received over 83 awards for his work in violence prevention.

Blinky Rodriguez and Benny the Jet Urquidez good friends since childhood
Courtesy Mr. and Mrs. Jet

Alex Reza

Alex Reza (C) with Stan and Vanessa Leandro at the 2015 Cesar Chávez March

Alex Reza is a retired San Fernando High school teacher and counselor, who taught US Government and Mexican-American studies. His students expressed immense respect for his devotion. Reza was an active community organizer, who fought against deportations, and championed the causes for education, healthcare, raising the minimum wage, and basic human rights. He is responsible for the annual Cesar Chávez marches down Laurel Canyon Blvd., from Mission Hills to Ritchie Valens Park.

Marilyn Sorrell was the Project Director for the Interfaith Multi-purpose Senior Center. She was involved with seniors for over 20 years serving on the Valley Task Force on Aging. She served on numerous community advisory councils, including NAACP and Pacoima Kappa Phi Sorority.

Curtis & Madell Steiner gave land usage to Parks Chapel AME Church and organized the first Cub and Boy Scouts troop # 113 in the area that accepted children of color.

Luis S. Garcia Executive Director Northeast Valley Health Corporation. Received Award from National Association of Community Health Centers in Washington DC

Louis J. Mendoza was owner of Pacoima Food Market at 13132 Van Nuys Blvd. He allowed many community health services to use the store for outreach. Mendoza was very active in Pacoima. He opened the market in 1947 and sold it in 1984.

Pauline Jenkins was an early Pacoima Historian and VP of Pacoima Business & Professional Woman's Club. She lived in the area for over 80 years and according to the Los Angeles Times, had a collection of 200,000 books. Jenkins co-wrote the book 'Pacoima 1976."

Ted Minor taught at Kennedy High School and L.A. Mission College as a Sociology Professor. He worked diligently with Jose De Sosa and others to deal with issues in the community. He also worked with the Joint Venture Community Improvement Project, an anti-poverty group that strived to get businesses and jobs in Pacoima among other community projects.

Carl McCraven was a community activist and force in Pacoima during the sixties. He worked as Vice-President of Pacoima Memorial Lutheran Hospital and was co-founder of the Pacoima Skills Center, Northeast Valley Health Corp, and President of the San Fernando Valley NAACP. He was also President of Hillview Mental Health Center where he opened a homeless transitional housing unit for people with mental disabilities.

Apostle William Broadous

Apostle William Broadous, son of Rev. Hillery and Rosa Broadous, is one of 10 offspring that originally came from Arkansas and migrated to Pacoima in the 1940s.

With his family founding Calvary Baptist Church and being very active in the community, Apostle William was equally as active. Under his guidance, he established Calvary Christen School, a children's academy, a bookstore, and a community development corporation. Also, he worked with the LAPD as a police chaplain.

Broadous led ministry trips to Africa, set up a Latino ministry, and campaigned against street violence, advocating for the community on many issues.

He was married to Rev. Gloria Broadous and together they had five children. He passed away in 2016 at the age of 71. Later that year, the city of Los Angeles named the corner of Vaughn and Dronfield, Apostle William Broadous Square, in honor of his community service.

Apostle Broadous is among many individuals who have contributed to building and improving Pacoima. This chapter only offers a sampling of trailblazers, with some mentioned earlier. However, that does not lessen anyone's status in this category. They are all still trailblazers.

27

Crack
Epidemic

Pacoima has many great people, events, and stories that show how unique and special the town is. The many highs and lows bring character and warmth to this story. However, nothing could have prepared Pacoima for the surge of drugs that flooded the town in the eighties, namely, crack cocaine. It went from a healthy upwardly mobile community to the dark side of drugs and crime, which resulted in the loss of entire generations.

During the seventies, the town of Pacoima faced the same drug issues as every other town in the valley. People in Granada Hills consumed as much marijuana, acid, and cocaine as did people in Pacoima. However, in the late seventies, a new drug mysteriously surfaced in Pacoima.

PCP (Phencyclidine), also known as "angel dust," is a mind-altering hallucinate, that can incite violent behavior. It would be rolled up like a regular marijuana joint, and the only way to know the difference was the strange smell that differed from marijuana. Some said it was elephant tranquilizer, while others said embalming fluid. The other street name for angel dust was "sherm" or "shermans." This name came from the cigarette brand used for smoking the drug, "Nat Sherman." It gained in popularity with the hard-core crowd. FDA discontinued Phencyclidine, but drug dealers learned to manufacture it synthetically. The alley behind the projects became known as 'sherm alley.' However, Angel Dust was only a precursor to the epidemic that was about to come.

During the eighties, vast amounts of cocaine began arriving in Pacoima. The influx flooded the town. Longtime resident, Pookey Oliver, who experienced that drug scene, shared his explanation.

"Bush and the Reagan administration brought it in. They flooded Watts, Pacoima, Oakland, and all the (Black) communities. I have this video that shows all these drugs coming in from overseas. Do any Blacks have that kind of push to go down to the pier and go through customs? I don't think so. Somebody had to bring it in."

As cocaine became popular, a cheaper, more addictive version of the drug began to appear, called "rock cocaine" or "crack." Patricia Hodges lived in the original Joe Louis housing tracts and described what she saw happen.

"It was really bad here in Pacoima. I knew a lot of people from school that ended up homeless. From some people I would see, you would sell pretty much your soul to get that drug...your kids — to get more of that high. They say it's a high you can never see twice. It's the best high ever. That's how good, or how bad that drug was. I heard of girls prostituting in Vegas. I heard of people losing their house and home just to get another hit."

Comedian Gilbert Esquivel grew up in the Van Nuys Apartments and experienced gang life as a teenager.

"In the five, six-year period, 1974 to 1980, those apartments went from being a regular nice place to live to a drug-infested (place) that became sherm alley. It started getting a bad reputation because of the things we saw. It was the first time we witnessed murders and robberies. The music and the people —there were a few troublemakers, but when the drugs and the sherm came into town, it was really bad— because it brought elements in from everywhere.

"From there, it started declining, and now they have two different gangs in that same area. It was never like this before. Everybody knew each other — everybody hung out. Even the dealers hung out and took care of each other. That was it. Then I got into the gang thing, and that took me in a whole different direction. I went to school to gang bang, pick up on girls, and just to go fight. That was our only purpose to go to school. I just hung out in the projects, and that became my life.

"Because in the projects on Van Nuys and Lehigh by the fire dept, that whole area, everything came to us. The girls came to us — drugs came to us, trouble came to us — we didn't have to leave. I was always in the projects — then I would dream projects. I said I gotta get out of this life."

Gilbert got out of the gang life and went on to become a successful standup comedian. He now talks to youth about staying out of gangs.

Another Pacoima resident, Jim Smith, purchased his house on Woodcock St in the early sixties. Like many others in Pacoima, he saw the dramatic change. He decided to leave in the late eighties after things began to unravel.

"Yes, I was there, and I saw that it was really bad. I saw young people devastated by getting involved in cocaine and what have you. It was very hard to see nice young people just wasting their lives away. A lot of young people want to make fast money. And it tore this community apart."

The story of Tracy Anderson is a prime example of how the crack epidemic, directly and indirectly, affected Pacoima residents. Anderson was a 6' tall 250-pound football player who graduated from Sylmar High School. He attended Glendale Junior College and received a scholarship to Fresno State, but ended up going to Cal State University Northridge. He did exceptionally well at CSUN and made Second Team Defense in December 1987.

Attending college was costly, and having a cash flow is non-existent without parents who help you, even if you have a scholarship. However, Pacoima's parents were working-class people, and finances were tight. Therefore, the crack market seemed like a viable option for fast and plentiful income. For Anderson, it was too good to pass up. So, to subsidize his collegiate life, he began selling crack.

In 1988, the market for crack was booming. For families living in the San Fernando Gardens or Van Nuys-Pierce Apartments, exposure to drugs and addicts became an everyday part of life.

Powerful drug syndicates had cornered the market and found football players to be reliable dealers. Most athletes did not indulge because they were into health and fitness, which meant they were not a threat to squander the product. However, 24-year-old Anderson was said to have a falling out with the syndicate.

According to news reports, Anderson broke from the drug organization to go on his own, and that appears to be the decision that sealed his fate.

Anderson was on Montford Street, in front of his fiancé's house, when two men carrying assault rifles approached. In the hail of gunfire, Anderson only had one escape, and that was into the house. However, in an act of heroism, he ran to other direction, drawing the fire. His fiancé Myra James, her eleven-year-old nephew Gary McCree, and his friend Caleb Craig were all in the house. The attack was carried out in broad daylight.

Former CSUN Football Standout Victim of Shooting

Tracy Anderson, the most valuable defensive player on the Cal State Northridge football team last season, was shot and killed Sunday on a residential street in Pacoima.

Caleb Craig remembers the impact of that dreadful day.

"I knew him. I was there on Montford. I lived on that street. That day when that happened, it kind of changed me in what these streets are about. How deep these streets can go...how real this sh-t is. When it went down after everything was said and done, it was a horrible scene. He was just laying out there, and I was looking at him. It was unfortunate that's the way he had to see his last days. He died with his college sweatshirt on"

Tracy Anderson and Myra James spend a weekend in Lake Arrowhead with the family in 1987. Above, Myra is holding her 5-month old cousin Lionel Grandison II.

The James family was forced to relocate after the shooting. Pictured above from right: Myra, Romie (Bobby), Joyce, and Danny

Caleb Craig (left) and Gary McCree (right) were together that day, at the house where Tracy Anderson was shot. This photo was taken months before the killing. Also shown Tony James Jr. (mid-left,) Courtney Deloney (mid-right)

"I was so focused on not dying and not getting in the way from whatever. I lived on the block. I knew him. It's unfortunate, but I never really looked at anything the same, but I'm happy that I'm still here. That day I was at Myra's house. That's where he got shot right in front of the house. To see somebody one day and see him for a split second the next and then he's gone. Life is short. You never know how you gonna go out. It was a life-changer in the point of knowing what another brother can do to you. Just like my brother got murdered.

"Crack came in and killed off the next generation of people. Gang banging and everything else started transpiring. I'm not gonna sit here and act like everything is good. It's a whole mixture of everything. It's messed up. It's too messed up."

According to newspaper reports, there were 25 other athletes caught up in that drug scene as well. There was another CSUN player named Douglas Henegan that was slain one month before Anderson. All the players were said to flee the area after these murders occurred.

Myra James' family began to receive death threats after the tragedy and the nightmare of that horrible day. It very quickly became an unlivable environment there on Montford Street, and the James family relocated out of necessity. In one fair swoop, one individual was dead, a woman's future filled with grief, a family uprooted, and children traumatized. All this was due to the savage drug epidemic that infiltrated this minority community.

By the nineties, there was an exodus of Blacks and some Mexicans to the Palmdale/Lancaster area.

General Motors was closing, Lockheed was laying off, and Price Pfister closed in 1997. With the job market dismal, crime, and drugs on the rise, Pacoima faced a rigid fork in the road. Crack addicts were giving birth to crack babies, and the legal system had incarcerated hundreds of dealers and addicts from Pacoima. That combination of loss of jobs and crack cocaine was lethal. This once exceptional middle class, upwardly mobile town, turned into a place its long-time residents no longer recognized.

28
Pacoima Pride

Despite the effects of the drug epidemic, Pacoima still exudes pride in its history and community. Through activism and education, the town has slowly turned around for the better. Pacoima pride is genuine and seen from just about anybody who calls Pacoima their hometown.

Perhaps nothing exemplifies the town's pride better than the Pacoima Mural Mile. These awesome public mural images, displayed throughout this book, represent the enduring legacy and undying spirit of the town.

The murals have gained recognition for beautifying the streets using fantastic artistry to depict Pacoima's cultural identity. These murals embody a renewed sense of pride in the town. Van Nuys Blvd, in addition to its 1911 historical origins, has risen to iconic status, thanks to the Pacoima Mural Mile.

The town's rich history inspires many of the artists, and the murals are a reflection of that. In turn, these artists inspire the community with a permanent reminder of Pacoima's legacy.

The Pacoima City Hall Mural captures individuals that have worked to make the community better and those who have achieved greatness beyond the town's borders. Although seeing the faces alone does not tell their story, it opens the door for research and acknowledgment. Moreover, it lays the foundation for new trailblazers that someday will stand worthy of being added.

That underlines the importance of acknowledging the artists whose talent and creativity have blessed the community with these amazing artistic creations. There are too many murals to include them all, but some of the artists are, Manny Velazquez, Levi Ponce, Kristy Sandoval, Manny Sandoval, Hector Ponce, Sarah Ponce, The Hood Sisters, Juan Pablo Reyes, GR818ers, Judy Baca, Serv One, Erica Friend and Ignacio Gomez.

This is the Pacoima Neighborhood Mural and was done by Ignacio Gomez with his assistants. Below it shows Pacoima children engaging in a variety of STEM (science, technology, engineering and mathematics), music, and reading.

The San Fernando Gardens Housing Projects have seen several murals throughout the years. This mural photo was taken in 2018 on Van Nuys Blvd.
(Photographer Lorenzo Grandison)

This stunning mural is located at Pacoima Charter Elementary on Norris Ave, one of the oldest schools in the San Fernando Valley. It emphasizes reading and imagination. (Lorenzo Grandison photographer)

The Tataviam were omitted from the history of Pacoima for many years. This is the first mural to give recognition to this tribe, the indigenous of Pacoima. It is a part of Pacoima Mural Mile. (Lorenzo Grandison photographer)

This mural is located on the Stylesville Barbershop building. Created by artist Kristy Sandoval, it depicts Ashanti Shakur, mother of slain rapper Tupac Shakur. (Lorenzo Grandison photographer)

Artist Levi Ponce and assistants painted this beautiful rendition displayed on Van Nuys Blvd. (Photographer Lorenzo Grandison)

Nothing captures Pacoima's excitement and pride, like the yearly Holiday Parade. In 2017, the town held its 50th annual event, which many of Pacoima's celebrated icons attended. The parade, which travels down Van Nuys Blvd, has featured kings and queens, local celebrities, and numerous political and community leaders over the years. Each year the town's residents come out by the thousands to cheer on the festivities.

The high schools were regulars at the parade. San Fernando High School marching band in 1974. (Courtesy James Tolliver III)

Actor William Marshall (Blacula) was an honorary celebrity mayor for Pacoima parade in the 70's. (Courtesy Camille Watkins)

1970's Pacoima Elementary School proudly marches down Van Nuys Blvd in front of Fire Station 98 and Crest Loan & Jewelry (Pawn Shop).
(Courtesy Camille Watkins)

This youth group called themselves Little Superstars in the late 70's. They are marching in front of the Van Nuys Chicken Shack, also known as Mom's Chicken Shack, which was the best place to get fried chicken in the 60's and 70's. (Courtesy Camille Watkins)

In the 70s, the town voted for king and queen of the parade's royal court. Parade queen Sharon Anthony enjoys the spotlight. (Courtesy Jim Smith)

80's parade marches down Glenoaks Blvd by Boys Market
(Courtesy Shauwiishi White)

1985 Sharp Elementary marches down Van Nuys Blvd in front of Trans World Bank. Councilwoman Monica Rodriguez is one of the leaders in this march.

(Courtesy Monica Rodriguez)

Bobby Chacon serves as Co-Grand Marshall for the Pacoima Holiday Parade

(Courtesy David Aguilar Photography

Jimmy Velarde waves to the crowd at the 50th annual Pacoima Holiday Parade

Rev. Arthur Broadous with muralist Manny Velazquez at the 49th annual Holiday Parade. Actor Danny Trejo can be seen, back right, on the left
(Courtesy David Aguilar photography)

Alina Grandison and Alexis Grandison march in the 50th annual Pacoima parade in 2017. (PHS archives)

Actor Danny Trejo at the 51st Pacoima parade.
(Courtesy David Aguilar photography)

El Nido Pacoima Family Source Center struts down Van Nuys Blvd in 2017 parade. This organization help low income families get on their feet.

Pacoima pride extends to current times for those who have lived there before or still reside in Pacoima. Annually the memory of Cesar Chávez is acknowledged in a march that ends at Ritchie Valens Park. These proud Pacoima people, both young and old, reflect what this town's spirit is all about.

Annual Cesar Chávez March in Pacoima. Community members walk down Laurel Canyon Boulevard celebrating his memory and accomplishments. The march ends at Ritchie Valens Park on Laurel Canyon and Paxton Street. (PacoimaStories Archives)

Cesar Chávez march to Ritchie Valens Park 2015. Pacoima youth engage every year.

Ritchie Valens Park on Laurel Canyon and Paxton Street was formerly named Paxton Park. Paxton Street was named after Charles Maclay's daughter Catherine Paxton Maclay. Councilman Richard Alarcón proposed the name changed in 1994.

Clubs and organizations in this town's history are an additional source of Pacoima pride. Leamon Vault, an African American, was President of the Continental Club at Hansen Dam Golf Course in the seventies. During that time, most people assumed minority residents did not utilize the golf course. They did not believe people of color played golf. However, that was not the case in Pacoima.

1972 Continental Golf Club (L-R) Leamon Vault II (big fro), Danny Carter, Frank Boykin, Aaron Gunner, Woodrow Augustus Sr., Will Collins, Greg Merkerson, Sander (Busty) Chapron, George Street. (Courtesy Michael Bernard Vault)

Other groups with a long history in Pacoima are the motorcycle clubs. There were stories of clubs in the fifties on Van Nuys Boulevard.

Whereas the reputations of some clubs may have been questionable, it is clear that others remained within the law.

There have been quite a few that are associated with Pacoima. The Fugitives had a place on Van Nuys Blvd near San Fernando Road. Inner

City Motorcycle Club was another well-known club along with Vagos, Pacoima 818, Invaders, and The Black Widows. Many of the clubs originated in other cities or states but had chapters in Pacoima.

The Black Widows of Pacoima advertises its group as the roughest, toughest band of rebels the country has ever known. The 1978 Clint Eastwood movie "Any Which Way but Loose" featured the club.

2017 Pacoima Christmas parade was well represented by motorcycle clubs.
(Photograph by Lorenzo Grandison)

Cruising the streets of Pacoima and showing off the shiny lowered Impala or fancy truck was and still is an enjoyable part of Pacoima. Ever since the fifties, car clubs have remained a big part of the town.

The list of clubs includes Majestics, Buganears, Original Valley Riders, The Finest New, Los Low Vergas, Primeros, Pak Town Ridaz, High Society, New Movement, Memories, United, Oldies CC, Integrity, High Class, High Society, Private Lives, Brown Sugar, New Generation and Los Vagabondos.

Majestics are one of Pacoima's most popular car clubs
(Courtesy Joshua "Jay" Young)

During the eighties, one source of Pacoima pride that topped all others was the "Back to Pacoima Expo." In 1980, Marie Harris established Back to Pacoima in conjunction with the 100th birthday of the City of Los Angeles. This expo continued annually for seven years at Hansen Dam and was undoubtedly the single largest community event that brought out pride and love for Pacoima.

Harris, sitting in her home on Welk St, first began planning the two-day festival with her daughter Rolene Naveja. Rolene, who worked for Academy of Recording Artists and the Grammy's, was able to use her experience and influence to produce the stage show. Harris would reign in businesses and the community for support. The expo name came about from the hit movie at that time, "Back to the Future." That is when the title "Back to Pacoima" was born.

Rolene described the event's growth.

"Expo grew year by year and with word of mouth came more and more, and we got a bigger, and bigger crowds. It was a two-day event, and everybody came out to Hansen Dam. They brought out their picnic baskets. We had vendors to supply food as well."

Over the years, tens of thousands of people attended the Back to Pacoima Expo, which brought in people from throughout Southern California. Sponsorship dollars funded the event as Marie, Rolene, and other dedicated community members made the expo an annual spectacle.

"Because of my affiliation with KDAY (1580-AM Los Angeles), I was able to reach back and pull my KDAY family in," said Rolene. "It was a perfect community event. They were eager to bring out the live broadcast. We were able to bring the whole community together."

Expo had a day show the first year and converted it to a night show under the stars. It brought out a host of well-known performers, including some of Pacoima's best local talent. Back to Pacoima is a source of pride that many will never forget, and still talked about in 2019.

Here are some of the uncovered photos that document this event.

Pacoima Expo in 1981
(Courtesy of Marie Harris Archives)

J.J. Johnson from 1580 KDAY does live broadcast at the Expo.
(Courtesy of Marie Harris Archives)

Marie Harris and Rolene Marie Harris work hand in hand making the Expo a success
(Courtesy of Marie Harris Archives)

Community members help with Expo planning at Hansen Dam — Marie Harris (left)
speaks to event organizers and volunteers (Courtesy of Marie Harris Archives)

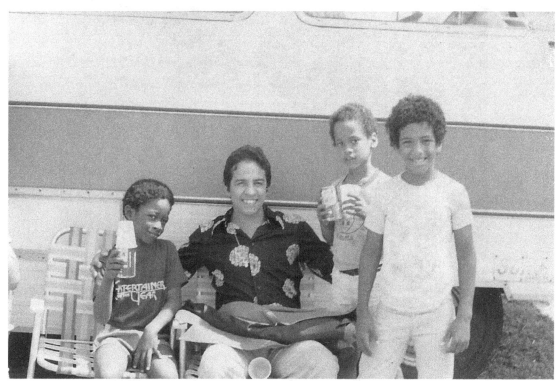

Bobby Chacon hangs out backstage at the 1982 Pacoima Expo with the grandson of Marie Harris, Che Naveja (right), and his friends. (Marie Harris Archives)

The Coleman Reunion performs at Pacoima Expo in 1986
(Courtesy Betty Coleman)

Howard Huntsberry arriving to Pacoima Expo 1981

The equestrian community was big in Pacoima. It was not uncommon to see horses going down the street next to a lowrider car.

There were stables at Hansen Dam, and two on Van Nuys Blvd, including McKivers at Dronfield Avenue. There was another stable across the street from the golf course on Glenoaks Blvd. They had clubs as well, including the Buffalo Soldiers. Many Mexicans were excellent horsemen, who often rode in the parades.

Thomas Dean with his horse at Hansen Dam in the seventies
(Courtesy Thomas Dean)

Shawn Dean, Antonio Davis, Thomas Dean and Portland Holmes ride the Hansen Dam trails by the 210. (Courtesy Thomas Dean)

These equestrians were at the 50th annual Pacoima parade in 2017. There were several that participated. (Courtesy PHS)

In 2019, Pacoima Neighborhood City Hall is a 38,000 square foot site that provides municipal outreach and creates a grand public space for the community. (Photographer Lorenzo Grandison)

Epilogue

The gleam in the eyes of people, when they talk about growing up in Pacoima, is mesmerizing. Despite the challenges and bad press, they share a love for the town, unlike anyplace in Los Angeles. While many people focus on the negative, when looking at the town's accomplishments, it is easy to understand Pacoima pride. Despite struggling with the negative reputation, true greatness is difficult to hide. It will always surface, no matter how deeply buried the stories become.

Today Pacoima is predominately Latino with a hand full of African-Americans holding on to the memories of what once was. Nevertheless, the history of Pacoima's land embellishes stories that historians have never attempted to tell. However, these stories represent a binding thread in the cultural fabric of America. Telling them is essential.

Stories such as the Tataviam tribe, whose ancestors claimed this territory in 450 AD until foreigners invaded and killed most of them off. Despite the horrific challenges, tribal members are still in Pacoima today, fighting for justice while dealing with the hand dealt their people.

The same goes for the Japanese-Americans who endured challenges both before and after World War II but still call Pacoima home. All this despite an avalanche of racism and cultural attacks that made life in America anything but a dream.

The Pacoima land is also a symbol of how Blacks built a community from scratch, as they mobilized to fight injustices at every turn by organizing and leading. Through community activism and grassroots movements, they laid the foundation for Pacoima having lawmakers at the state and national levels. Although the demographics have changed, Blacks still come back to Pacoima to relive the connection once felt to this unique historic town.

Let us not forget the Mexican families who fled their country in search of better lives but found harsh punishment for speaking their native language. They also endured being cast in the role of simple laborers who were good with their hands but ill-equipped to strive for higher goals. Despite these obstacles, Mexican-Americans have produced educated, talented individuals who fought the challenges of gangs and financial hardships. Some have become highly influential people making a positive change in our nation.

With doctors, Medal of Honor awardees, Purple Heart recipients, Tuskegee Airman, Grammy and Emmy winners, directors, producers, actors, musicians, comedians, business people, Heisman Trophy winners, NFL, MLB, and NBA All-stars, world champion boxers, kickboxers, congressional representatives, Secretary of State (CA), muralists and book authors, Pacoima's trail of excellence has far exceeded the town's seven-square mile boundary.

With numerous cultures and a modern world full of complexities, many stories remain uncovered. However, those that have are nothing short of amazing. Piecing these stories together came from breadcrumbs left in small bitesize portions, and many with no internet references. However, Pacoima pride has infused itself into the fabric of history for the world to see. No longer will the narrative of this town be driven by those who do not know, show, or care about the story of Pacoima. The entrance to this world is now open, and there is little doubt that Pacoima's story is one of America's most significant accomplishments. The truth is that America is a Pacoima story, and Pacoinga Village was here long before this nation began.

Nowhere in America has there been an evolution like that of Pacoima. From Tataviam land to New Spain; to Mexico and finally America, this land has seen change unlike any other. However, it does not stop there. As America began its push towards modernity, Pacoima found itself in the middle of a social evolution that was reshaping our nation. The town became infused with people of every race and culture. Over its 132-year American history, the majority population has evolved from Indian to White, then Black, and lastly Latino.

Now labeled as a town of poverty, in reality, Pacoima is rich. Rich in authentic American culture. Americans have ancestry from all over the globe. However, minorities are forced to distinguish themselves with a hyphen in front of the land they were born. Whether it is African-American, Japanese-American, Mexican-American, or Native-American, the bottom line is that Pacoima produces real Americans. Moreover, the town's history is genuine and authentic. When one drops the label, the common denominator becomes Pacoima is America.

There are thousands of story's surrounding "Pacoinga Village," and they go to the heart of what many Americans have endured. Although we are all separated by the ethnic history of our ancestors, the truth is there is no monopoly. We are all humans, and eliminating the racial divide should come instinctively. Judging a person or group by individual character instead of race must be commonplace. Pacoima shows that in many ways by its uniquely diverse legacy. It is time to drop the labels and hatred, and all become one.

Pacoima Historical Society

The Pacoima Historical Society is a 501 (c)3 non-profit organization dedicated to preserving the history of Pacoima. Launched in 2016, PHS has quickly become an essential source of information about the town's historical past and prideful community.

"Everything actually began in 2015, when our president, Crystal Jackson, began researching Pacoima's history for a slideshow she was doing for social media," said Lon Grandison, an executive board member for the Pacoima Historical Society.

Grandison, president of BAIT-CAL Media Group, is a veteran of numerous television shows, films, and documentaries.

"The response was so overwhelming that Crystal asked what I thought about producing a documentary film on the town. I really wasn't sure, but I asked my dad, who grew up in Pacoima during the fifties, his thoughts about it. He said, 'If you guys don't do it, it will never happen, and people need to remember the history of Pacoima. It's very special'.

"So, we decided to tackle the project, and our research began. We knew the town had experienced a massive migration explosion in the fifties, and those who knew that story were aging. It was time to talk to them. That was when PacoimaStories "Land of Dreams" began production."

Film's producers (from left), Lance Grandison, Crystal Jackson, Lon Grandison. PacoimaStories: Land of Dreams was nominated for "Best Feature Documentary" at the 2018 Pan-African Film Festival

"As we were completing the film, it occurred to us that the videos, photographs, and oral stories we had collected while making this documentary needed to be preserved. We also realized how much material and how many photos didn't make the final cut — and not just that, we knew how much more there was to uncover still. That's when we decided to start Pacoima Historical Society."

The organization officially launched in January 2016. Because of the town's diverse history, they decided to elect a board of directors reflecting that diversity. Crystal Jackson was unanimously elected to be president, Suzanne Llamas of Vaughn Next Learning Center as secretary, and Tonice Gilmore-Thomas of K-Swiss as treasurer.

The executive board was Rudy Ortega Jr. of the Fernandeño-Tataviam Band of Indians, Lon Grandison of BAIT-CAL Media, Nancy Takayama of the SFV Japanese American Community Center, Stan Leandro of Vaughn International Studies Academy, Jimmy Velarde of CBS Broadcasting and Rolene Marie Harris Naveja of Primrose Productions were all onboard.

Pacoima History Day June 2017 - PHS board members and organizers (l-r) Suzanne Llamas, Crystal Jackson, Alma Nava, Rolene Naveja, Nancy Takayama, Chanelle Grandison, Tonice Gilmore-Thomas, Lon Grandison, Stan Leandro.

In February 2016, PHS hosted its first event, which was the premiere screening of PacoimaStories: Land of Dreams. Held at Vaughn G3 Theater on Herrick Avenue, some of Pacoima's most notable alumni were in attendance including actor Danny Trejo, and US Congressman Tony Cárdenas.

"It was quite an honor to have such high-profile people at our premiere screening in Pacoima," said Grandison. "The turnout was amazing, and Tony Cárdenas gave an extremely passionate and emotional speech about growing up in Pacoima and what the town has meant to him. There weren't many dry eyes in the house."

In 2017, with the support of Councilwoman Monica Rodriguez, Pacoima Historical Society hosted their inaugural Pacoima History Day celebration. In past years, this event has honored the town's pioneering heroes of business, education, community activism and politics. California Secretary of State Alex Padilla graciously attended Pacoima History Day in 2018 to accept his award for Excellence in Public Service.

The California State Assembly has officially recognized PHS for "Excellence in Community Service." State Assembly member Luz Rivas issued the organization a certificate of recognition for their work.

"Preserving Pacoima's history is something we're all proud of," says Grandison. "In the future we want to produce more films and books telling the many amazing stories we have uncovered. This town's history really is special. In fact, two of our main goals are to have Pacoima declared an official "historic town" and establish a museum to showcase the media and artifacts we're collecting.

"As with most non-profit companies our biggest challenge is resources. We hope this book encourages readers to lend their support to the Pacoima Historical Society. We are trying to catalogue and archive all this history before it gets away from us and that would be a tragedy. History doesn't get more American than the Pacoima experience. We have to make sure the world knows that."

Max Martinez, Lily Moreno, Carolina Mendoza and Danny Trejo at premiere screening of PacomaStories "Land of Dreams" Feb 27, 2016.

Rep. Tony Cárdenas (D) Panorama City, speaks to a packed house at the premiere screening of PacomaStories "Land of Dreams" at Vaughn G3 Theater on Feb 27, 2016.

California Secretary of State Alex Padilla with PHS board members at Pacoima History Day 2018 - (l-r) Jimmy Velarde, Suzanne Llamas, Stan Leandro Crystal Jackson, Alex Padilla, Alma Nava, and Lon Grandison

Community award recipients 2017 Pacoima History Day. L-R Ed Rose (MEND), Deacon David Johnson, Dr. Yvonne Chan, Crystal Jackson PHS, Salvatore Del Gaudio (DelGaudio's Market), Carolina Mendoza (Pioneer Paula Hernandez) Councilwoman Monica Rodriguez, Pamela Broadous (Broadous family)

Pacoima Historical Society engages with the community to help children and young adults understand the value of their own American history.

PHS remains active in the community, working with multiple Pacoima-based organizations. It also partners with local libraries and other historical societies in Los Angeles to help others share Pacoima's history. PHS hosts one of the town's largest social media platforms on Facebook, reaching thousands of people.

Pacoima Historical Society is a non-profit organization supported entirely through public grants and private donors. Donations can be made directly through the PHS website at PacoimaHistoricalSociety.org and are tax-deductible.

It takes a village to tell a history. These family members are there through thick and thin. PacoimaStories "Land of Dreams" first screening was a huge success. L-R Calvin Thomas, Yvonne Hayes, Tonice Gilmore-Thomas, Samir Muqaddin, Tara Jackson, Crystal Jackson, Wesley Jackson, (front) Alina Grandison, Alexis Grandison, Shanice Harrison (holding Carter Harrison), Lance Grandison Sr., Corbin Jackson, Chanelle Grandison, Lorenzo Grandison, Lon Grandison, Maria Brown, Lionel Grandison II.

Bibliography

AIR Worldwide. Verisk.com: 10 Historic Earthquakes in the US. What would they cost today? January 6, 2017: https://www.verisk.com/insurance/visualize/top-10-historical-earthquakes-in-the-us-what-would-they-cost-today/ 10/16/2019

allmusic.com: Rose Royce Biography: https://www.allmusic.com/artist/rose-royce-mn0000343215/biography 10/15/2019

AmericanAirMuseum.com: Michael Alba: http://www.americanairmuseum.com/person/158873 10/16/2019

americanfootballfilms.com "Gridiron Gang-American Football Film" 8/6/2012 https://americanfootballfilms.com/gridiron-gang-american-football-film/ 10/15/2019

Andrae Edward Crouch Early Years https://en.wikipedia.org/wiki/Andra%C3%A9_Crouch 10/22/2018

AndraeCrouch.com: A Living Gospel Legend https://andraecrouch.com/ 10/14/2019

Anthony, Earl: "The Time of the Furnaces" 1971 New York The Dial Press 49-63

anthonydavishof.com: Anthony Davis Biography; http://www.anthonydavishof.com/bio.html 10/15/2019

AnyFlip.com: Pastor Chatman Memorial: http://anyflip.com/usbt/lnhm/basic 10/16/2019

Atlas Obscura: "Beale's Cut Gouged in the mountains to make stage coach access easier through the Fremont Pass" : https://www.atlasobscura.com/places/beales-cut 8/8/2019

baseballreference.com ; Garret Anderson; https://www.baseball-reference.com/players/a/anderga01.shtml

Biography.com: Rodney King (965-2012) April 2, 2004: biography.com: https://www.biography.com/crime-figure/rodney-king 10/16/2019

Bluenote.com: Al McKibbon Biography; http://www.bluenote.com/artist/al-mckibbon/ 10/15/2019

Broadous, Hillery T: Silver Threads Chronicles of Ministry: Calvary Baptist Church of Pacoima 1955-1980: unpublished

Cantor-Navas, Judy: Ritchie Valens La Bamba Inducted into National Recording Registry of the Library of Congress: Billboard: https://www.billboard.com/articles/columns/latin/8503463/ritchie-valens-la-bamba-inducted-national-recording-registry 3.21.2019

cardenas.house.gov: Congressman Tony Cardenas Representing the 29th District of California: Biography: https://cardenas.house.gov/about-tony/biography 7/18/2019

Chalquist, Craig PHD: Deep California: 2008 Bloomington Indiana Universe 262

Chatsworth Historical Society

Cheevers, Jack & Abramhamson, Alan: Los Angeles Times; "Earthquake: The Long Road Back: Hospitals Strained To The Limit by Injured : Medical Care: Doctors Treat Quake Victims in Parking Lots. Details of some disaster-related deaths released." Jan 19, 1994 https://www.latimes.com/archives/la-xpm-1994-01-19-me-13343-story.html 10/16/2019

Chou, Elizabeth: Daily News "Leroy Chase, leader of Pacoima youth center, fought to keep doors open in a community with a stigma" Dec 14, 2018 https://www.dailynews.com/2018/12/14/leroy-chase-leader-of-pacoima-youth-center-fought-to-keep-doors-open-in-a-community-with-a-stigma/ 10/15/2019

City of Los Angeles Archives & Records: Historical Records: https://clerk.lacity.org/city-archives-and-records-center: 7/7/2019

Claremont School of Theology. History: https://cst.edu/about 10/16/2019

Cristero War: https://www.cs.mcgill.ca/~rwest/wikispeedia/wpcd/wp/c/Cristero_War.htm 2007 09/8/2018

Daily Kos The Great California Genocide: https://www.dailykos.com/stories/2008/8/14/567667/-8/14/2008

Daily Sundial: "Student-administration tension leads to change" Sept 29, 2005

Davis, Anthony and Rosenberg, Jeremy. "Kick-Off: Concussion" 2014 US Lulu Publishing Services 69

DeGuzman, Jean-Paul Race, "Resisting Camelot Race and Resistance to the San Fernando Valley Secession Movement" 2016 Regents of the University of California: California History, Vol. 93, Number 3, pp. 28–51

DeGuzman, Jean-Paul: "Finding Buddha in the Barrio: Reflections of Unanticipated Archival Research" 2016 UCLA Historical Journal 27 (1)

DeGuzman, Jean-Paul: "The San Fernando Valley's Multiethnic Past: Unexpected Communities of Color in American Suburb" 6/23/2011 UCLA BlackPast.org

discogs.com: The Alkaholiks: https://www.discogs.com/artist/14759-Tha-Alkaholiks 10/15/2019

Doctor, Christopher et al. "Mexican American Baseball in the San Fernando Valley" 2015 Charleston, South Carolina Arcadia Publishing 30 34

Dominguez, Fernando, Los Angeles Times: " Where are They Now: Buddy Bradford: They put on a professional block party: Baseball: Five pals from the same Pacoima neighborhood signed contracts, and two of them made it to the majors" July 2, 1994 https://www.latimes.com/archives/la-xpm-1994-07-02-sp-11160-story.html 10/15/2019

Dorman, Stephen: "The story of a championships team fall and rise" Aug 17, 2005 http://www.malibutimes.com/life_and_arts/article_f775f409-304c-5f2a-adb4-fb33afc331da.html 10/15/2019

East Kern Genealogical Society: Death Homer A. Hansen Homer : Mojave Desert News California City, Kern, CA Published: 01 Dec 1960: https://www.ancestry.com/boards/localities.northam.usa.states.california.counties.kern/8642/mb.ashx?pnt=1 10/13/2019

Editor & Publisher: "Frank Del Olmo of LA Times dead at 55" Feb 20, 2004: http://www.editorandpublisher.com/people/frank-del-olmo-of-la-times-dead-at-55/ 10/13/2019

Edy, Jill A; Brittanica.com: Watts Riots of 1965: https://www.britannica.com/event/Watts-Riots-of-1965 10/15/2019

Encyclopedia Britannica: Tom Bradley American Politician; Sept 25, 2019: https://www.britannica.com/biography/Tom-Bradley 10/15/2019

Explore APA Heritage: Chinese Heritage sites of America; San Fernando Tunnel https://exploreapaheritage.com/index.php/sites/san-fernando-tunnel/ 2019

Factcardscalifa.org: Social Studies Fact cards California Indians Tataviam http://factcards.califa.org/cai/tataviam.html 10/15/2019

Fernandeño Tataviam Band of Mission Indians: "Pacoinga Village" unpublished 2015

Fritish, Jane ; New York Times; "Tom Bradley, Mayor in era of Los Angeles Growth Dies" Sept 30, 1998; https://www.nytimes.com/1998/09/30/us/tom-bradley-mayor-in-era-of-los-angeles-growth-dies.html 10/15/2019

georgelopez.com: George Lopez Bio; https://georgelopez.com/bio 10/15/2019

Gil, Carlos B: "We became Mexican American" 2012 United States Xlibris Corporation 23, 119, 238

Gite, Lloyd; mochamanstyle.com; "Producer/Director Leslie Small uses film to change the narrative on Black men" Feb 3, 2017 ; https://mochamanstyle.com/2017/02/producerdirector-leslie-small-uses-film-to-change-the-narrative-on-black-men/ 10/15/2019

glamourgirlsofthesilverscreen.com; Darlene Thompkins; http://www.glamourgirlsofthesilverscreen.com/show/516/Darlene+Tompkins/index.html 10.15/2019

Glover Ben: Foxsports.com "The Superbowl Winner who Rocked Rugby" Aug 25, 2015: foxsports.com.au/more-sports/the-super-bowl-winner-who-rocked-rugby-league-after-walking-the-reverse-path-to-jarryd-hayne/news-story/4393e3bb9fce8ddb6241a4e07e3c8eb8 10/13/2019

Grossman, Marlene: "Pacoima Beautiful history" unpublished 2019

Harris, Elander Victor career https://en.wikipedia.org/wiki/Vic_Harris_(outfielder) 2019

Haugabook, Ayala-Feder: Compton Ca (1867-?) https://www.blackpast.org/african-american-history/compton-california-1867/ 10/13/2019

Hensen, Steve Los Angeles Times: "The Jet: Born to Brawl, Benny Urquidez Lived Through a Death Match to Become One of the Greatest Unknown Fighters in America" AUG. 17, 1985 https://www.latimes.com/archives/la-xpm-1985-08-17-sp-2240-story.html 9/19/2019

History of Watts city of Los Angeles: Watts Neighborhood Council

History.com: "Brown vs. Board of Education" Oct 27, 2009: https://www.history.com/topics/black-history/brown-v-board-of-education-of-topeka 10/16/2019

Hodges, Hugh Thomas: Charles Maclay "Portrait of a California Pioneer 1821-1890" USC thesis Aug 67

hollywoodshow.com "Skinny Minnie Gwen Miller" http://hollywoodshow.com/starDetail.php?id=1499 2019.

Holmes II, Emory: Mother Rosa Broadous Oral history Interview Cultural Affairs Dept City of Los Angeles, Northeast valley oral history project: June 7, 2002 CSUN

Hudnut, Kenneth W & Behr, Jeffrey A: Seismological Society of America "Continuous GPS Monitoring Structural Deformation at Pacoima Dam, California" July/August 1998: *(vol. 69, No. 4; pp. 299-308)* of *Seismological Research Letters*: https://pasadena.wr.usgs.gov/office/hudnut/SRL/ 10/13/2019

Huling William: CSUN Northeast Valley oral history digital-library csun.   TG Pledger/ Hillery T Broadous pdf 1977

IMDB Eddie Dean biography: https://www.imdb.com/name/nm0212761/ 10/13/2019

IMDB.com: Cheech_Marin Biography; https://www.imdb.com/name/nm0001507/bio

IMDB.com: Gary Matthews biography ; https://www.imdb.com/name/nm2884783/bio?ref_=nm_ov_bio_sm 10/15/2019

imdb.com; Poncie Ponce; https://www.imdb.com/name/nm0690291/bio: 10/15/2019

IMDB; Kurt Russell Biography: https://www.imdb.com/name/nm0000621/bio

Jarryd Hayne A Long Shot Worth Taking 9/19/2019

Johnson, Chip: Los Angeles Times "Helping the American Dream Come True for African Americans: Housing: James Robinson defied racism as a realtor and an agent for the neighborhood change" April 14, 1995

Johnson, Mark: "Basketball Slave Andy Johnson Harlem Globetrotter" 2010 Mantua NJ, Junior Cam
Publishing 1-8

Jones, Monique; shadowandact.com ; "Kelley Kali's award winning short film 'Lalo's House' to screen at Canes Short Film Showcase Co-Sponsored by Viola Davis" April 19, 2019 ; https://shadowandact.com/kelly-kali-lalo-house-cannes 10/15/2019

Keep the Wisdom: Interview with Mary Helen Ponce : June 8, 2009: http://keepthewisdom.blogspot.com/2009/07/interview-with-mary-helen-ponce.html 10/13/2019

Kowalick, Vince , Los Angeles Times "Moore: Giving It All Back: Fallen Football hero Helps Wayward Youths" Aug 29, 1992 https://www.latimes.com/archives/la-xpm-1992-08-29-sp-5506-story.html 10/15/2019

Lane, Mark. Diary Part 1 Untitled- Alternative considerations of Jonestown & People's Temple jonestown.sdsu.edu : https://jonestown.sdsu.edu/wp-content/uploads/2018/02/08-06-lane-diary.pdf 28

lee.house.gov; Barbara Lee Congresswoman for the 13th district of California; Biography : https://lee.house.gov/about/biography 06/12/2018

Library.ccsa.org: "California Charter Schools Yvonne Chan Celebrating 20 years." March 2014: http://library.ccsa.org/services/professional-development/20th-annual-california-charter-schools-conference-highlights.html 10/16/2019

Littleton, Darryl "D Militant" humormillmag.com ; 'On This Day in Comedy ...1962 Comedian Gilbert Esquivel was born" June 20, 2016 ; http://humormillmag.com/day-comedy-1962-comedian-gilbert-esquivel-born/ 10/15/2019

Los Angeles Almanac; Los Angeles City Mayors Past to Present; http://www.laalmanac.com/government/gl11.php 10/15/2019

Los Angeles County deed book 3824 pg 41-42

Los Angeles Daily News: " LAPD's Foothill Station celebrates 50 years of service": 8/9/2011 https://www.dailynews.com/2011/10/09/lapds-foothill-station-celebrates-50-years-of-service/ 2/15/2018

Los Angeles Daily News: Prep Football Notebook San Fernando to honor 75 "Sept 29, 2010 : https://www.dailynews.com/2010/09/29/prep-football-notebook-san-fernando-to-honor-1975-champs/ 10/13/2019

Los Angeles Herald "San Fernando Valley and City" July 17, 1874
Los Angeles Herald "Editor Herald" July 19, 1974
Los Angeles Herald "Was it Insured" Sept 16, 1889
Los Angeles Herald "A Story of the Terrible Wrongs that have been put upon Rogerio Rocha" Feb. 2, 1896
Los Angeles Herald "Rocha's Grant Questioned- Contention that Any title he may have had has been extinguished" Feb 3, 1896
Los Angeles Herald "Wrongs of Rogerio Rocha" March 1, 1896
Los Angeles Herald "Sale of Pacoima Lots" Sept 6, 1905

Los Angeles Housing & Community Investment Dept: William "Blinky" Rodriguez : https://hcidla.lacity.org/william-blinky-rodriguez 10/13/2019

Los Angeles Public Library: A Brief Watts Branch Library History-https://www.lapl.org/branches/watts/history 10/15/2019

Los Angeles Times "Big Land Deal" May 17, 1887
Los Angeles Times: "New Skills Center Dedication Today": 11/17/1995

Los Angeles Times: "Crash Claims Kevin Williams" Feb 3, 1996: https://www.latimes.com/archives/la-xpm-1996-02-03-sp-31937-story.html: 10/13/2019

Los Angeles Times: "World's Largest Earth-filled Structure" Aug. 18, 1940

Los Angeles Times: L.A. Police Battering Ram: Feb 20, 1985: https://www.latimes.com/archives/la-xpm-1985-02-20-me-354-story.html 10/13/2019

Los Angeles Times: The New Battering Ram: Feb 13, 1985: https://www.latimes.com/archives/la-xpm-1985-02-13-me-4639-story.html 10/13/2019

Lynch, John; Los Angeles Times; "WHERE ARE THEY NOW?: ANTHONY DAVIS : A.D.'s Past Always Present : Notre Dame Nemesis Treasures Long Run as USC, Valley Legend July 14, 1990 ; https://www.latimes.com/archives/la-xpm-1990-07-14-sp-271-story.html 10/15/2019

Madley, Benjamin. "An American Genocide": 2016 New Haven & London Yale University Press 18-355

Maida, Carl A. "Pathways through Crises": 2008 Lantham, MD Altamira Press 187-199

Martin, Douglas: New York Times: "Frank Del Olmo , 55 Los Angeles Journalist" Feb 20, 2004: https://www.nytimes.com/2004/02/20/us/frank-del-olmo-55-los-angeles-journalist.html 10/13/2019

Martinez, Diana: The San Fernando Valley Sun "Boys &Girls Club President Leroy Chase Dies" Nov 28, 2018 http://www.sanfernandosun.com/news/article_4b614ffa-f394-11e8-b0e0-bb7e4094af82.html 8/18/2018

maryimmaculateparish.org: History of Mary Immaculate ; https://maryimmaculateparish.org/about/mary-immaculate-history/ 10/15/2019

Maupin, Ann & Jenkins, Pauline: "Pacoima in 1976" A bicentennial project of the Pacoima Branch Library of the City of Los Angeles

Mendheim, Beverly. Ritchie Valens "The First Latino Rocker" 1987 Tempe Arizona Bilingual Press/Editorial Bilingile 27-38

Metro Digital Resources Librarian: Primary Resources: "40 Years Ago Today: San Fernando Earthquake Topples Freeways & Prompts Seismic Retrofitting Plan; Feb 9, 2011 http://metroprimaryresources.info/40-years-ago-today-san-fernando-earthquake-topples-freeways-prompts-seismic-retrofitting-plan/773/ 10/16/2019

michaeloneillmusic.net/ 10/15/2019

Mohan, Geoffrey: Los Angeles Times, "Black History Month /Valley Retrospectives Perspectives on the past and future": Feb 22, 1994 https://www.latimes.com/archives/la-xpm-1994-02-22-me-25833-story.html 10/13/2019

Murch, Donna: The Journal of American History:" Crack in Los Angeles: Crisis, Militarization, and Black Response to the Late 20th Century War on Drugs" by June 1, 2015: *Journal of American History*, Volume 102, Issue 1, June 2015, Pages 162–173

Music Hall of Fame: Inductee Biography for Andy Devine http://www.azmusichalloffame.org/andy-devine/ 2019

NELSON, VALERIE J: LOS ANGELES TIMES, "Lilly Rodriguez, 59; martial arts champion helped open up kickboxing for women" Jan 21, 2007 https://www.latimes.com/archives/la-xpm-2007-jan-21-me-rodriguez21-story.html 9/19/2019

Nelson, Valerie J: Los Angeles Times "Lilly Rodriguez, 59, Early Female Kickboxer" January 22, 2007: https://www.nysun.com/obituaries/lilly-rodriguez-59-early-female-kickboxer/47100/ 9/19/2019

Newyorktimes.com: "Chacon's wife in Suicide; Wanted him to Quit Ring" March 16, 1982 : https://www.nytimes.com/1982/03/16/sports/chacon-s-wife-in-suicide-wanted-him-to-quit-ring.html

NFL.com: Frank Cassara: http://www.nfl.com/player/frankcassara/2511258/profile 10/14/2018

Northeast Valley Health Corp: nhchc.org : About us : https://nevhc.org/about-us/ 10/16/2019

npr.org: "Kenya Barris on black-ish and what kids lose when they grow up with more" May 18, 2016; https://www.npr.org/2016/05/18/478414550/kenya-barris-on-black-ish-and-what-kids-lose-when-they-grow-up-with-more 10/15/2019

nytimes.com/2018/08/14/opinion/charter-schools-desegregation-los-angeles.html

oocities.org : Los Angeles Police Department Chokehold Deaths 1975-1982: http://www.oocities.org/mraley.geo/choke.html 10/13/2019

Paine, Jake: hiphopdx.com; "King T says Dr. Dre & Xzibit Motivated him to rap again, recalls years at aftermath" Mar 21, 2013: https://hiphopdx.com/interviews/id.2065/title.king-t-says-dr-dre-xzibit-motivated-him-to-rap-again-recalls-years-at-aftermath 10/15/2019

pbs.org: Film Bio Kenya Barris; Jan. 10, 2017 : https://www.pbs.org/wnet/the-talk/2017/01/10/film-bio-kenya-barris/ 10/15/2019

Pledgerville.org/ History of Pledgersville Senior Citizens Inc : http://pledgerville.org/html/About%20Us.html 10/8/2017

Proszenko, Adrian: Sydney Morning Herald "Former NFL player Manfred Moore backs San Francisco 49ers recruit Jarryd Hayne to replicate his try-touchdown double." https://www.smh.com.au/sport/nrl/former-nfl-player-manfred-moore-backs-san-francisco-49ers-recruit-jarryd-hayne-to-replicate-his-trytouchdown-double-20150912-gjkzaa.html

Pugmire, Lance: LATimes.com "Bobby Chacon former two-division boxing champion dies" 9.7.2016: https://www.latimes.com/sports/boxing/la-sp-sn-boxing-bobby-chacon-obituary-dead-20160907-snap-story.html 10/14/2019

Rainy, James: Los Angeles Times: " Final Suit over LAPD's Use of Chokehold Settled " Sept 29, 1993: https://www.latimes.com/archives/la-xpm-1993-09-29-me-40159-story.html 10/13/2019

Reich, Kenneth; Los Angeles Times: "71 Valley Quake A Brush with Catastrophe" Feb 4, 1996 https://www.latimes.com/archives/la-xpm-1996-02-04-mn-32287-story.html 10/15/2019

Ripley, Vernette Snyder: Historical Society of Southern California: "The San Fernando Newhall Pass" June 1948: https://scvhistory.com/scvhistory/ripley13.htm 10/13/2019

Rogers, J. David Ph.D., PE., P.G., C.E.G., C.HG: California Colloquium on Water Lectures: " Dams and Disasters: A brief overview of dam building triumphs and tragedies in California's past" November 3, 2002: 76, 135-139

San Fernando Valley Historical Society

San Fernando Valley Hongwanji Buddhist Temple; sfvhbt.org about us: https://www.sfvhbt.org/ 10/2/19

San Fernando Valley JACL: Major Supporters The Oda- Sakaguchi Family : https://sfvjacl.weebly.com/major-supporters.html 10/13/2019

Sanfernandohs.com: History: https://www.sanfernandohs.com/apps/pages/index.jsp?uREC_ID=366570&type=d 7/13/2019

Santa Clarita Historical society

Schultz, Tom: Los Angeles Times: "Anti-Gang Leader to get Award in Geneva" Aug16, 1998: https://www.latimes.com/archives/la-xpm-1998-aug-03-me-9692-story.html 10/13/2019

scvhistory.com : Moe DiSesso: https://scvhistory.com/scvhistory/lw2747.htm 10/13/2019

Sheeler, Ryan. Ritchie Valens His Guitars and Music 2019 Anaheim Hills, Ca Centerstream Publishing 6-12

Shermanpianoman.com: Bili Redd Thedford vocalist: Shermanpianoman.com/bili-redd-thedford-vocalist/ 11/3/2018

Simon, Richard & Thackrey, Ted Jr: Los Angeles Times: "Councilman Finn stricken, dies at age 68" Aug 13, 1986: https://www.latimes.com/archives/la-xpm-1986-08-13-mn-17679-story.html 10/13/2019

Somerville, Sean: The Baltimore Sun "B&D: Moving jobs to Mexico 200 slots in Calif. Cut earlier this year." Nov. 23, 1996 : https://www.baltimoresun.com/news/bs-xpm-1996-11-23-1996328077-story.html 10/16/2019

Sonksen, Mike: L.A. Taco: 'The Mural Mile-The History of Pacoima told through the tapestry of street art" April 7, 2019: https://www.lataco.com/mural-mile-pacoima-history/ 10/16/2019

sos.ca.gov: Alex Padilla California Secretary of state Biography: https://www.sos.ca.gov/administration/about-alex-padilla/ 10/15/2019

Stewart, Jocelyn: Los Angeles Times: "1997 NAACP President achieved LAPD reforms " Aug 4, 1997: https://www.latimes.com/archives/la-xpm-1997-aug-04-me-19320-story.html 10/13/2019

Sydney Morning Herald smh.com When an American Bled for Newtown Manfred Moore: https://www.smh.com.au/sport/nrl/when-an-american-bled-for-newtown-20070824-gdqxt6.html 10/22/2018

Survey L.A: Historic Resources Survey Report Arleta-Pacoima Community Plan Area by Architectural Resources Group Inc March 20, 2014

Terry, Do: New York Times; "Sam Yorty-maverick mayor of Los Angeles dies at 88" June 6, 1998 ; https://www.nytimes.com/1998/06/06/us/sam-yorty-maverick-mayor-of-los-angeles-dies-at-88.html 10/15/2019

The glory Multimedia Network: Bio: http://theglorymultimedianetworks.com/bio/ 10/16/2019

The Jonestown Institute San Diego state university; Alternative Considerations of Jonestown & People's Temple "Who died" https://jonestown.sdsu.edu/?page_id=33 9/4/2019

theglorymultimedianetworks.com; The Greater Community Church History; http://theglorymultimedianetworks.com/the-greater-community-church-pacoima-ca-top-banner/ 10/15/2019

thesportsdrop.com/college-football-legends-who-failed-in-the-nfl/17/ 10/15/2019

thoughtco.com "Biography of Jim Jones, Leader of the Peoples Temple Cult" https://www.thoughtco.com/jim-jones-and-the-peoples-temple-1779897 9/4/2019

United Press, Corona Daily Independent "White House Looks into Plane Crash; CAA to Set Up Special Test Areas" Feb 3, 1957

Urban Archives Center: Cal State University Northridge: "Dr. Mary Oda Oral History Interview": April 23 & 30, 1982: 2004 University Library

Urquidez, Sensei Benny: The Jet: 2014 USA Benny Urquidez 1952 11, 37, 39

Valley News: "Skills Center Given Credit for Job Gains" Nov. 2, 1967

Water and Power Associates : Early Views of the San Fernando Valley: https://waterandpower.org/museum/Early_Views_of_the_San_Fernando_Valley_6_of_10.html 2019

Wikipedia free encyclopedia: Kurt_Russell: wiki.org: https://en.wikipedia.org/wiki/Kurt_Russell 2/8/2019

Wikipedia free encyclopedia: Old Yeller : https://en.wikipedia.org/wiki/Old_Yeller 10/13/2019

Wikipedia free encyclopedia: Tommy_Kirk: https://en.wikipedia.org/wiki/Tommy_Kirk 10/13/2019

Wikipedia The Free Encyclopedia: George Clayton Johnson: https://en.wikipedia.org/wiki/George_Clayton_Johnson 10/13/2019

Wikipedia.com: The_McCrarys; https://en.wikipedia.org/wiki/The_McCrarys 10/28/2018

Wilson, Terry USAdojo.com; "Lilly Urquidez and Blinky Rodriguez Champions In And Out Of The Ring" November 1, 2012 https://www.usadojo.com/lilly-and-blinky-rodriguez-champions-in-and-out-of-the-ring/ 9/19/2019

Worldatlas.com "What is the Cristero War? https://www.worldatlas.com/articles/what-was-the-cristero-war.html 10/15/2019

Wright, Lynn: "A Victorian in the Valley"   unpublished 2018

Wright, Phil: Valley News: "Site of Veteran Hospital Disaster Marked by 50 ft Pile of Rubble" Feb 9, 1971

Wynn, Ron: Artist Biography Greg Phillinganes; https://www.allmusic.com/artist/greg-phillinganes-mn0000157063/biography 10/15/2019

ORAL INTERVIEWS

Biggs, Charles (2017 June 6) Interview by Crystal Jackson (no recording) PHS archives
Broadous, Abdula (2019 March 17) Interview by Crystal Jackson (no recording) PHS archives
Broadous, Pamela (2017 August 19) Interview by Crystal Jackson (video) PHS archives
Broadous, Rev Arthur (2018 June 3) Interview by Crystal Jackson (video) PHS archives

Campbell, Dwayne (2018 Aug 6) Interview by Crystal Jackson (no recording) PHS archives

Cardenas, Tony Congressman (2015 May 4) Interview by Crystal Jackson (video) Pacoimastories

Carter, Nell (2019 April 25) Interview by Crystal Jackson (no recording) PHS archives

Chan, Dr Yvonne (2015April 28) Interview by Crystal Jackson (video) Pacoimastories

Craig, Caleb J (2019 June 5) Interview by Crystal Jackson (video) Pacoimastories

Davis, Anthony (2015 Sept 12) Interview by Crystal Jackson (video) Pacoimastories

De Sosa, Jose (2018 June 3) Interview by Crystal Jackson (video) PHS archives

DeGuzman, Jean-Paul (2018 June 3) Interview by Crystal Jackson (video) PHS archives

Diaz Irene (2015 June 6) Interview by Crystal Jackson (video) Pacoimastories

Emory Sharon (2019 Sept 20) Interview by Crystal Jackson (no recording) PHS archives

Esquivel, Gilbert (2015 June 28) Interview by Crystal Jackson (video) Pacoimastories

Faucett, Gregory (2015 March 28) Interview by Crystal Jackson (video) Pacoimastories

Galindo, Carmen (2015 sept 10) Interview by Crystal Jackson (video) Pacoimastories

Hernandez Paula Lupe (2015 Sept 10) Interview by Crystal Jackson (video) Pacoimastories

Hodges, Jaqueline (2018) Interview by Crystal Jackson (no recording) PHS archives

Hodges, Patricia (2015 June 7) Interview by Crystal Jackson (video) Pacoimastories

Hodges, Printes (2015 April 12) Interview by Crystal Jackson (video) Pacoimastories

Huntsberry, Howard (2015 April 5) Interview by Lon Grandison (video) Pacoimastories

Jackson, Arvel (2015 April 12) Interview by Crystal Jackson (video) Pacoimastories

James, Myra (2015 June 5) Interview by Crystal Jackson (video) Pacoimastories

Johnson, David Deacon (2017 August 19) Interview by Crystal Jackson (video) PHS archives

Leandro, Stan (2015 March 29) Interview by Crystal Jackson (video) Pacoimastories

Lee, Barbara Congresswoman (2019 March 8) Interview by Crystal Jackson (audio) PHS archives

Louda, Tipy James (2019 June 17) Interview by Crystal Jackson (video) Pacoimastories

Love, Ron (2015 April 25) Interview by Crystal Jackson (video) Pacoimastories

Lozano, Daniel (2015 September 10) Interview by Crystal Jackson (video) Pacoimastories

Matthews, Ernest Lee (2018 November 11) Interview by Crystal Jackson (no recording) PHS archives

McCree, Jackie (2019 Oct 11) Interview by Crystal Jackson (no recording) PHS archives

Mendoza, Carolina (2015 Sept 10) Interview by Crystal Jackson (video) Pacoimastories

Moore, Malcolm (2018 Dec. 26) Interview by Crystal Jackson (no recording) PHS archives

Muqaddin, Samir (Frenchy Grandison) (2015 June 7) Interview by Crystal Jackson (video) Pacoimastories

Neal, Mary (2015 March 29) Interview by Crystal Jackson (video) Pacoimastories

Naveja, Rolene (2015 Mar 29) Interview by Crystal Jackson (video) Pacoimastories

Oliver, Ronald "Pooky" (2015 April 26) Interview by Crystal Jackson (video) Pacoimastories

Ortega, Rudy Jr (2015 April 24) Interview by Crystal Jackson (video) Pacoimastories

Richter, Colleen (2019 Feb 21) Interview by Crystal Jackson (no recording) PHS archives

Robinson, James J-Ro (2019 Oct 10) Interview by Crystal Jackson (no recording) PHS archives

Rodriguez, Madeline (2018 Oct 6) Interview by Crystal Jackson (no recording) PHS archives

Rodriguez, Sal (2019 Jan 16) Interview by Crystal Jackson (audio) PHS archives

Rose, Ed (2017August 19) Interview by Crystal Jackson (video) PHS archives

Rosenberg, Jack (2015 Nov 9) Interview by Lon Grandison (video) Pacoimastories

Rosenberg, Sarah (2015 Nov 9) Interview by Lon Grandison (video) Pacoimastories

Smart, Juanell Dec 20, 2018 Interview by Crystal Jackson (no recording) PHS archives

Smith Jim (2015 April 26) Interview by Crystal Jackson (video) Pacoimastories

Takayama, Nancy (2015 June 5) Interview by Crystal Jackson (video) Pacoimastories

Takayama, Patricia (2015 June 5) Interview by Crystal Jackson (video) Pacoimastories
Thedford, Bili "Redd" (2019 Feb 21) Interview by Crystal Jackson (no recording) PHS archives
Thomas, Robert (2015 June 7) Interview by Crystal Jackson (video) Pacoimastories
Tolliver, James III (2018) Interview by Crystal Jackson (no recording) PHS archives
Urquidez Bennie "The Jet" (2018 Dec 8) Interview by Crystal Jackson (no recording) PHS archives
Williams, Vanessa (Brown) 2015 June 7) Interview by Crystal Jackson (video) Pacoimastories

PHS--- Pacoima Historical Society archives
Pacoimastories "Land of Dreams" documentary produced by Crystal Jackson Productions/BAIT-Cal Worldwide 2016

Index

M